MW01222519

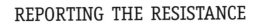
REPORTING THE RESISTANCE

# REPORTING THE RESISTANCE

Alexander Begg and
Joseph Hargrave on the
Red River Resistance

Edited and annotated with an introduction
by J.M. Bumsted

UNIVERSITY OF MANITOBA PRESS

University of Manitoba Press
Winnipeg, Manitoba  R3T 2N2 Canada
Printed in Canada on acid-free paper by Friesens.

Cover Design: Doowah Design Inc.
Text Design: Sharon Caseburg
Map: Weldon Hiebert

National Library of Canada Cataloguing in Publication Data

Begg, Alexander, 1839-1897
   Reporting the resistance : Alexander Begg and Joseph Hargrave on the Red River Resistance / edited and annotated with an introduction by J.M. Bumsted.

Letters originally written in 1869 and 1870, by Alexander Begg to the
   Toronto Globe and Joseph Hargrave to the Montreal Herald.
Includes bibliographical references.
ISBN 0-88755-675-2

   1. Red River Rebellion, 1869-1870—Sources. 2. Begg, Alexander, 1839-1897—Correspondence. 3. Hargrave, Joseph James 1841-1894—Correspondence. I. Bumsted, J. M., 1938- II. Hargrave, Joseph James, 1841-1894. III. Title.

FC3214.B43 2003          971.05'1          C2003-906542-1

A full bibliography is available on the University of Manitoba Press Web site at www.umanitoba.ca/uofmpress.

The University of Manitoba Press gratefully acknowledges the financial support for its publication program provided by the Government of Canada through the Book Publishing Industry Program (BPIDP); the Canada Council for the Arts; the Manitoba Arts Council; and the Manitoba Department of Culture, Heritage and Tourism.

*To my son Michael, who helped with the research*

# CONTENTS

# Maps and Illustrations

# PREFACE

Preparing historical documents for publication is no easy matter, even if the material involved has been printed in a contemporary newspaper, as was the case for these letters. The transcriptions were made from microfilm versions prepared forty years ago by the Canadian Library Association. These microfilms are not perfect sources. Occasionally the microfilm would miss part of the page, or reproduce either a fold or a hole in the original. Moreover, because of their age, the microfilms have faded and have in some places become virtually illegible. Since the newspapers involved are almost 150 years old and printed on less than high quality paper, it has proved impossible to consult original versions to check the transcriptions. Thus in a few cases there are illegibilities, noted with square brackets in the text.

The material provided several other problems as well. One difficulty occurred in the Begg series, where the numbers employed by the newspaper to refer to the letters as originally printed did not always agree with the actual number of the letter in the sequence as reprinted. This was particularly noticeable toward the end of the series, where there appears to be a letter missing, both from the numbered sequence and in terms of the sense of the narrative. As for the Hargrave series, there was a problem with the pen names attached to the letters. A number of Red River correspondents, including J.J. Hargrave, signed themselves "Red River" and had their letters printed in the eastern newspapers. To make matters worse, the Montreal *Herald* occasionally lumped together several different letters signed "Red River," although not all of the text had come from Hargrave. This edition has tried to sort out the Hargrave letters from the other "Red River" correspondence that appears not to be by Hargrave.

If accurate transcriptions, numbering the letters, and the nomenclature of authors of newspaper correspondence in 1869-70 proved a problem, so too in a different sense did the way of presenting annotations. Both Begg and Hargrave refer to people and events that seemed to require additional clarification or elaboration. That additional information has been treated in three ways. Where the information provides a brief definition or is directly referring to the text in a way immediately useful to the reader, it has been set as a footnote and appears at the bottom of the page. Where the information directs the reader to additional printed resources not so immediately essential, it has been incorporated into endnotes at the end of the book. Information that elaborates on Begg's and Hargrave's accounts is provided in the Editor's Notes at the end of each letter. In addition, to prevent excessive annotation, a biographical appendix of major participants has been included at the end of the volume. A full bibliography is available on the University of Manitoba Press Web site at www.umanitoba.ca/uofmpress.

As is the case with all scholarship, the editor is indebted to a variety of institutions, particularly archives and libraries, and a number of individuals, especially archivists and librarians, for assistance in the preparation of this volume. Regarding archives, he would like particularly to thank the chief archivists and archives staffs at the Public Archives of Manitoba, the Hudson's Bay Archives, the National Archives of Canada, and the University of Manitoba Archives. As for libraries, he would like to thank the chief librarians and library staffs at the Dafoe Library of the University of Manitoba, the Rare Books division of the University of Manitoba, the National Library of Canada, and the St. John's College Library. In addition, the editor would like to acknowledge a special debt of gratitude to the University of Manitoba Library system in general. Its decentralized nature, which made it necessary for constant trudges back and forth across the campus in all sorts of weather, helped contribute substantially to his fitness programme. The editor would also like to thank David Carr, Patricia Sanders, and the other members of the staff at the University of Manitoba Press for coffee, conversation, and especially professional expertise in producing this volume. To his family the editor acknowledges a special debt of gratitude for assistance only other authors and editors can properly understand. Siân and Michael helped with the research, and everybody sustained the editor's spirit when he got down in the dumps.

REPORTING THE RESISTANCE

# INTRODUCTION

As the Red River Settlement approached its formal transfer from the Hudson's Bay Company to Canada in 1869, it appeared to the outside world to be a small, isolated, frontier community teetering precariously on the edge between civilization and savagery. This was the view presented by Alexander Ross in his book *The Red River Settlement*, which had been published only a scant dozen years earlier.[1] Certainly this was the view of the settlement held by the Canadians, who intended to take it over and run it as a colony in tutelage to civilization. In some ways the perception was accurate. Physically, the settlement certainly was isolated—although it was rapidly becoming less so—and it was still on the frontier edge of free land. Travelling to Red River either required a lengthy summer journey by water from Lake Superior, or a lengthy overland sojourn of over 350 kilometres from the end of the railroad in Minnesota. Canadian politicians like Joseph Howe and Charles Tupper in 1869 demonstrated that the settlement could be reached in about a month even in the middle of winter, but it was no easy journey. Demographically, Red River was not numerically large. It contained about 13,000 people, including a few hundred Aboriginals and a large population of mixed bloods, both French-speaking and English-speaking. If one excluded the mixed bloods, there were probably little more than a thousand people of European origin residing on the banks of the Red and Assiniboine rivers.

Appearances were, in some senses, deceiving. A vast gulf separated the Red River described by Alexander Ross in the early 1850s and the Red River of 1869. The external community had made an enormous impact on the settlement, beginning in the late 1850s.[2] Red River's inhabitants, especially the Métis, were rapidly becoming linked to the capitalistic society of the United States through the medium of the Red River cart trade, on which so many of them worked.[3] Spiritually and intellectually, Red River's élite had long since become an integral part of the outside world.[4] It would have been no idle boosterism to maintain that, for its size and situation, Red River harboured one of Canada's most lively and best-educated intellectual communities. As early as 1860, the settlement had three choral societies.[5] The Institute of Rupert's Land had been organized in 1862 to provide a forum for scientific and humanistic discussion within the community. There was a subscription library of 2500 volumes.[6] Most of the leading fiction and non-fiction books of the Victorian era were readily available either in the library or at the bookstore operated by the printers of the local newspaper, *The Nor'-Wester*. Regular perusal of that newspaper ought to have suggested the difficulty of visualizing the place as utterly barbaric.[7] Many residents were highly critical of the newspaper. It certainly was highly partisan, hostile to the Hudson's Bay Company and blatantly enthusiastic about Canadian annexation. And it was the only newspaper in town, at least until late in 1869. But in its pages one could find much attention paid to the cultural amenities, ranging from imperial political philosophy to racial theory to the history of the settlement itself.

For a supposedly isolated and barbaric place, Red River had an astoundingly self-conscious historical vision of itself. By 1869 the settlement had already produced three indigenous historians in the persons of Alexander Ross, Donald Gunn, and an anonymous writer (probably a clergyman) whose work, like Gunn's, was first published in the pages of the *Nor'-Wester*.[8] The settlement also had two younger historians—Alexander Begg and Joseph James Hargrave—waiting in the wings to offer on-the-spot accounts of the major upheaval about to occur. Also in residence was a Canadian poet in the person of Charles Mair, who may have been a recent immigrant to Red River, but had already published *Dreamland and Other Poems*, a well-regarded book of verse. In addition, Mair was also a regular correspondent to Ontario newspapers. Other bright young men were present as well. The leaders of the two mixed-blood communities, Louis Riel and James Ross, were both well educated, articulate, and bilingual. Riel had recently returned from Quebec, ready to write to that province's newspapers in defence of every slight to his people. James Ross, fresh from years as a Toronto journalist, had only recently returned to his homeland to begin a new newspaper.

Thus the insurgency against Canada that developed so suddenly and unexpectedly in the autumn of 1869 could be chronicled by a highly literate and historically self-conscious group of residents. For a backcountry revolt, the Red River Rebellion was always remarkably erudite, as its chronicles and chroniclers attest. For an event occurring hundreds of miles from "civilization," moreover, the rebellion was remarkably well covered in the big-city newspapers of Canada, the United States, and Great Britain. Between November 1869 and March 1870, the Toronto *Globe* printed at least one Red River story almost every day, and from December 1869 to February 1870, an editorial on Red River appeared on the *Globe's* editorial page virtually daily. The Canadian newspapers, especially the Canadian dailies, occasionally sent their own correspondents to attempt to cover the story in Red River, although the *Globe's* reporter was thrown out of the settlement by Louis Riel soon after his arrival and reported little fresh insight beyond the comparison of Riel to a failed Napoleon. The newspapers also reprinted anything off the American wires that they could find, although the Yankees published mainly exaggerated second-hand information filtered through Pembina. Under normal circumstances, the Canadian papers would have also copied extensively from the pages of the *Nor'-Wester*, as they had been doing for years. But the Métis led by Louis Riel had been in conflict with the *Nor'-Wester* for some time, and in early December of 1869 Riel actually closed down both this newspaper and a potential rival (*The Pioneer*, to be printed on a new press brought to the settlement in the autumn of 1869).[9] The *Globe* turned to the *New Nation*, a newspaper edited by Major Henry Robinson, as soon as it made its appearance early in 1870.

Nevertheless, there clearly were problems in the media coverage. One was caused by the isolation of the settlement, from which news could not be sent to Canada in much less than two weeks, even by employing the telegraph from St. Paul. Another was caused by the difficulty of obtaining accurate first-hand coverage with some larger sensitivity to the community and the issues. The bulk of what eastern Canadian readers learned about the events of the rebellion came in the form of news stories from American sources distant from Red River and highly partisan letters from private correspondents within it.[10] Occasionally private correspondence to friends and family about events in Red River was also printed, especially in the pages of the non-metropolitan newspapers. Sometimes excerpts from single letters found their way into the larger dailies, which copied from one another and from the provincial papers. Among francophone newspapers, *Le Nouveau Monde*, the *Courrier de Saint-Hyacinthe*, and

*L'Evenment* carried occasional letters from Red River, although no French paper appears to have had a regular series by a single author over the winter of 1869-70.[11] Some information also came in the form of interviews with persons returned to Canada from Red River, such as the former prisoner Stewart Mulkins, who offered his assessments of the personalities of the Métis leaders in the *Globe* in late January of 1870.[12] However, there was another source of information. Letters were also written expressly by Red River correspondents to a handful of leading newspapers to inform their readers. This correspondence made some effort to be responsible and to provide authentic first-hand information about the course of events. Despite a seeming wealth of information from Red River, not all groups in the settlement had their views equally represented. There was little material emanating from the Métis, for example, and none whatsoever from either the anglophone mixed-blood community or the Aboriginal residents. The supporters of the Canadian Party were better represented, however.

Most of the best-informed correspondence that filled the pages of the eastern press and told Canadians of events in the west in 1869-70 came from the pens of a handful of writers resident in Red River, who supplied regular letters to the newspapers. These letters were usually published under pseudonyms or without any authorial attributions, although at least some of the authors' names were known in the settlement. The two major writers were Joseph James Hargrave, who supplied copy to the *Montreal Herald*, and Alexander Begg, who wrote to the Toronto *Globe*. These two series of letters are reprinted in their entirety here. Remarkably little overlap and repetition occurs between the two series. Hargrave's letters are written mainly before the end of December, and Begg's mainly afterwards. These young men were very close together in age. Begg was thirty and Hargrave was twenty-nine. Both men had been in the settlement for some years, but were not exactly old-timers, although they were well informed about the history and present state of Red River. Both were outsiders who represented particular local interests that had been upset by the transfer of Red River to Canada, and so they did not necessarily represent majority opinion in the settlement. Hargrave was employed by the Hudson's Bay Company, and Begg was a Winnipeg merchant. Both men were well placed to know what was going on in the settlement, and they shared a suspicion of Canada.

The letters from Begg and Hargrave offered a first-hand running narrative of events—Beggs at one point wrote, "I have endeavoured to keep you posted with events in their proper relation as they have occurred"—over the fall and winter of 1869-70 that was closer to the scene than anything else available in eastern Canada, and contained much fascinating material presented nowhere else—such as Hargrave's description of the firehall meeting of late October or Begg's account of the meeting with the Sioux on New Year's Eve. But the real strength of both sets of letters resides in their background information—the sketching of the history of the settlement and the descriptions of its institutions and resident population, neither of which could really be gotten anywhere else. Begg wrote other accounts of these events in his journal and in his subsequent history of the rebellion, *The Creation of Manitoba*, but the descriptive material in the letters is both more concentrated and more extensive than in his other efforts. Other writers from the settlement were reprinted in the eastern newspapers, but none offered as lengthy and sustained a correspondence, and none of their other correspondents made any effort to provide detailed background information on the settlement and its population. Very little of the Hargrave-Begg correspondence to the newspapers has survived as manuscript text, so it is very difficult to tell what editorial changes might have been made to the original versions. In a few cases, it would appear that the eastern editors added subheads that may not have existed in the originals. Besides a large amount of correspondence from the settlement, other letters from the settlement over the autumn and winter of 1869-70 survive in manuscript form, but were not published in a contemporary newspaper and thus were not "public knowledge" in eastern Canada.[13] Since there was neither an official nor semiofficial source of information in Red River that could be drawn upon by the contemporary media, Begg and Hargrave—with their wealth of background detail and all their limitations—were easily the best sources available. The reporting of events in remote regions seldom reflects either majority opinion or a full spectrum of views.

The two major newspapers in anglophone Canada that followed most closely the Red River story were the *Montreal Herald and Daily Commercial Gazette* and the Toronto *Globe*. These two newspapers had quite different editorial policies and reasons for interest in Red River. The *Herald* was no friend of the Macdonald government and was quite happy to report on its imperial deficiencies. A newspaper with long-standing connections to the western fur trade, the *Herald* had also been critical of William McDougall (the newly appointed governor of the territory) for years. It carried at least two sets of letters from Red River, one much more extensive than the other, which were often difficult to distinguish from one another. George Brown's *Globe* had a historic interest in westward expansion that went back nearly two decades.[14] Unlike the *Herald*, which was happy with local correspondents, the *Globe* had actually sent its own reporter to try to cover the story. He failed. Detained by Louis Riel upon his arrival, he never actually got to remain in Red River. The dispatches he filed were not very insightful. Because the eastern newspapers circulated widely in Red River, in their pages local residents eventually got to read about the events with which they were living on a daily basis. The time between the dates of composition and the dates of publication varied between three weeks and a month, suggesting how long it took to get correspondence from Red River to Canada, even employing the American postal system and railways. Return travel took at least another month. But after the suppression of the *Nor'-Wester* by Riel and apart from a handful of issues in the early months of 1870 of the *New Nation*, a newspaper blatantly controlled by the provisional government, the eastern newspapers were the major printed source for events in Red River, even for its own population.

As the correspondence herein reprinted makes perfectly clear, the two major reporters in Red River gathered their information under difficult conditions. Formal press releases from the various parties did not exist, and providing authoritative accounts was no easy matter. A number of "listening posts" existed in the settlement, mostly in the village of Winnipeg. The camp of the Métis at Scratching River was one early source of information. After the Métis captured Upper Fort Garry, it became a centre of news. The guard room at the fort, as described by Robert Cunningham, appears to have been another good source. According to Cunningham, "The room was a low roofed apartment about twelve feet square with a red hot stove in the centre, and with about twenty men seated on tables, chairs, and the floor, smoking assiduously their Indian pipes."[15] The bar at Emmerling's Hotel, frequented by most travellers and especially by American visitors, was a good place to pick up news. So too was the post office in the store of Alexander Begg and A.G.B.

Bannatyne. One correspondent in the St. Paul *Press* detailed a discussion on the rights of the settlement carried out in mid-November by a number of leading anglophones "at Bannatyne & Begg's store."

The correspondents relied to some extent on gossip and rumour, using various terminology to express their evaluation of their sources.[16] That terminology was doubtless not entirely consistent among the writers. But both Begg and Hargrave talked about "well-founded" or "reliable" sources: "reports," which seem to have been information that could be attributed to someone; "reports we can hear" or "it is reported," which were probably less well attributed; and "rumour," which was completely unattributed and often wildly incorrect. Anyone familiar with Red River knew of the prevalence of rumour and gossip in the settlement. Two subjects of rumour were particularly prevalent. One was Aboriginal movement on the plains, reports of which had circulated in exaggerated fashion in the settlement since its earliest days—often originating in the United States—and continued to do so in this period. The other was more specific: the rumours circulated about the military organization of the Canadians in early December 1869. None of the correspondents writing from Red River suggested the origins of either of these sets of rumours, although "Justitia" noted that "False rumours have done a great deal of harm in exciting the people and keeping up the present difficulties."[17] There is a clear sense from the letters that much rumour was deliberately started and often had either partisan or malicious intent.

### THE HISTORIOGRAPHY OF THE RED RIVER OPPOSITION TO CANADA

For such a relatively minor series of events in a relatively isolated corner of North America, the happenings in Red River over the autumn, winter, and spring of 1869-70 have always attracted a surprising amount of attention from historians. As a result, a considerable body of literature has accumulated over the years recounting, documenting, and explaining what happened in Red River. That literature is exceedingly complex in its resonances. There are two major interpretive schools, both having their origins in the contemporary debate.[18] One school has always seen the resistance, insurgency, uprising, or rebellion—and there is no agreement on how to characterize the Red River movement of these months—as an

illegitimate and unnecessary lot of trouble imposed on the government of
Canada in its efforts to administer the new territory acquired from the
Hudson's Bay Company. This was, of course, the Canadian line at the
time. The Canadians officially refused to allow any break in the political
continuity of Red River, or to acknowledge the legitimacy of the resistance to their attempted takeover of the settlement. Most writers in this
tradition would insist that the insurgents—the francophone Métis—never
had the full support of any of the other elements of the population in the
settlement, and thus could not possibly be a legitimate government.

This Ottawa-centred tradition was not only the common one
employed at the time, but remained the dominant one until at least the
1890s. Most of this literature was naturally quite hostile to Louis Riel, a
man who had murdered Thomas Scott and had ultimately fled the country.[19] Insofar as it dealt with events inside the settlement itself, it tended
to make heroes out of the "Canadian Party," the handful of men in Red
River—John Schultz, Charles Mair, Charles Boulton, George Young,
John O'Donnell, and Thomas Scott—who supported Canadians' imperial
aspirations on the ground. Over the years, men from this party contributed a series of memoirs to the cause.[20] One of the consequences of
their writing was that Thomas Scott was transformed from a victim into a
Canadian leader. The outer limits of the partisanship of this approach
were probably tested by Donald Creighton in the second volume of his
biography of Sir John A. Macdonald.[21] In the chapter titled "The West in
Jeopardy," Creighton not only demonized Louis Riel, but developed
events in such a way as to justify the dispatch of the military expedition led
by Colonel Wolseley and the use of force. What is most important about
the view from Ottawa is not really its overall sympathy with the government of Sir John A. Macdonald, however, for that sympathy was never
essential to the perspective, which had its focus on nation-building, well
conducted or not. Contemporary papers and letters published by the government itself or by members of the government provided a paper trail of
blundering, and the published report of the 1873 parliamentary enquiry
established by the government of Alexander Mackenzie even demonstrated
that the Macdonald government had been—at the very least—duplicitous
in its dealings with the delegates from Red River over the negotiations for
the Manitoba Act.[22] L.H. Thomas's modern study of the political

development of the Northwest Territories is extremely critical of the behaviour of the Canadian government in 1869-70, for example, but still concentrates on the imperial problems of nationhood rather than on the local internal developments within the settlement.[23]

The competing school has seen the movement in Red River as an appropriate and justifiable local response to imperial blundering, usually associating it with the national aspirations of the Métis people of Red River and Louis Riel, and often viewing Red River as a colonial victim of Canada, treated badly because of both racial and especially religious hostility. For the most part this interpretation has its origins in the writings of Catholic clerics like George Dugas, who published *Monseigneur Provencher et Les missions de la Rivière Rouge* (1889), and Father A.G. Morice, who produced *Histoire de l'Eglise Catholique dans l'ouest Canadian* (1912) and *A Critical History of the Red River Rebellion* (1935). This literature recognized the leadership contribution of Louis Riel, but was hardly swept away in hero-worship of him. These were, after all, Catholic clerics. What was absolutely clear in these works, however, was that the only mixed bloods who mattered in Red River were the francophone Catholic ones led by Riel, however flawed he was as a leader.

The critical year for Riel rehabilitation was doubtless 1936, the year in which A.H. Trémaudan published *Histoire de la nation métisse* and George Stanley published *Louis Riel; The Birth of Western Canada: A History of the Riel Rebellions*.[24] Trémaudan had worked with members of the Métis community, including those in the Riel family, who were unhappy with the treatment in the standard clerical works. Stanley came at the subject via a careful and detailed scholarly study of the documentary record, in both languages. Neither work changed public opinion on Riel in the short run. Most copies of Stanley's book, indeed, were destroyed in a London air raid during World War II. But gradually the emphasis on Riel as the constructive Métis leader began to gain ground, assisted by the publication of Marcel Giraud's massive *Le Métis Canadian* in 1945 and Joseph Kinsey Howard's passionate *Strange Empire: The Story of Louis Riel* in 1952. Most of these works, hearkening back to Alexander Ross's 1856 history of Red River, emphasized that Riel and his people were caught halfway between "savagery" and "civilization," suggesting that the Red River reaction was a cultural rather than a political response. Stanley sharpened his interpretation along these lines in a full-fledged biography of Riel published in 1960, and other interpreters weighed in over the years. One of the most satisfying Riels, of course, was one attempting to stem the tide of WASP progress in the name of other, older, values.

While these two conflicting interpretations are fairly clearly demarcated in the literature, describing them does not tell us very much about the historiographical subtleties, nor about the essence of Red River. Basically grouping interpretations in this way sacrifices understanding of the local dynamic in favour of the importation of issues from the national historiography of Canada, thus seeing Red River as another episode in the struggle between anglo Protestantism and French-Canadian Catholicism (or Franco-Canadian Aboriginal Catholicism) for control, in this case, of western Canada. Within these two general lines of interpretation it is hard to make much sense out of the execution of Thomas Scott or the whole question of the divisions of the mixed-blood community in Red River in 1869.

A whole new dimension on the Red River troubles was opened up by W.L. Morton in 1956 with the publication of his edition of *Alexander Begg's Red River Journal and Other Papers Relative to the Red River Resistance of 1869-70.*[25] Morton (1908-1981) was a native Manitoban who had long been critical of the national school of Canadian historical writing exemplified by such works as Donald Creighton's biography of Sir John A. Macdonald. In Begg's journal he had the basis for a quite different parallel story. Begg was a Red River merchant who obviously had a keen sense of the historical moment, for he had kept a detailed daily account of the occurrences in the settlement from November 1869 to the arrival of the Wolseley expedition in August of 1870. Begg had written a number of letters to eastern newspapers describing events in Red River in this period, and he had used this manuscript journal as the base of a history of the events of 1869-70 entitled *The Creation of Manitoba*, which he had published in 1871 and which had sunk like a stone in the contemporary debate over Manitoba, leaving virtually no historiographical trace. To Begg's contemporary diary entries, Morton added substantial annotations and an introduction of nearly 150 pages. The whole package made quite plain that much had happened internally in the settlement over the months between the beginning of objection to the Canadian takeover and the proclamation of the province of Manitoba.

Begg's central theme—and thus by implication Morton's—revolved around the efforts over this period to find local unity, particularly between the francophone Métis and the anglophone mixed bloods of Red River, while preventing the Canadians (both Ottawa and the local Canadian Party) from wresting control of the agenda in favour of Canadian annexation. In this struggle Louis Riel played an important but not totally dominant part. Morton thus placed the local conflict, particularly that between the francophone and anglophone mixed bloods, as well as between the mixed bloods and the Canadian newcomers, at the centre of the story. This provided a fresh way of understanding 1869-70, one which contextualized both the execution of Thomas Scott and the various conventions of mixed bloods held in the settlement. On the other hand, Morton did not attempt to counter the picture of Riel emerging from the work of Stanley, Giraud, and Howard. Indeed, in the opening pages of his "Introduction" he asserted that it was in the sense "of nationhood of the *métis* that an understanding of the Resistance of 1869 is to be found."[26] But in his "Preface," Morton also acknowledged a debt to Monsieur L'Abbé Pierre Picton of St. Boniface, who had revealed to Morton "that web of blood relationship which not only held the *métis* together, but bound the two halves of the Red River Settlement with ties that were not to be disregarded."[27] Morton subsequently published most of the major documents of the negotiations conducted between the delegates of Red River and the Canadian government in the spring of 1870.[28] These documents strongly suggested that the provisional government had been badly outmanoeuvred by a duplicitous Canadian government, particularly on the issue of an amnesty for deeds committed in the course of the resistance.

Since the publication of Begg's journal and Stanley's biography, much of the historical debate and the best historical writing about both Red River and 1869-70 has revolved around the question of the nature of the mixed bloods in the settlement. Although he understood the complexities of the mixed bloods in Red River, W.L. Morton tended to identify the "métis" with the buffalo hunt, with an "Indian concept of trade," and with "a nationalism that was French in its demand for equality with the English and *métis* in its sense of local corporate identity."[29] Alexander Begg and Joseph Hargrave would probably have accepted this characterization. As with Giraud's and Stanley's *métis*, as well as Begg's and Hargrave's,

Morton's *métis*—Catholic and francophone—were uneasily poised on the
bridge between savagery and civilization; he frequently used negative
words to describe what he saw as their volatile temperament. Morton did
not see Red River solely in terms of the *métis*, of course, but they were, in
his view, the key to the settlement and its development up to the arrival of
the Canadians in substantial numbers. He acknowledged the existence of
the English-speaking "halfbreeds" (the term he employed in most of his
work for them), but except in his introduction to the Begg journal, did not
take them very seriously. George Stanley's biography of Louis Riel, published in 1963, made the case for seeing 1869-70 more plainly in terms of
Riel and the Métis.

Not surprisingly, the scholarly neglect of the anglophone mixed bloods
soon produced its own corrective. The new approach did not, for the most
part, focus on 1869-70, but dealt with the ethnic mix within the settlement. John Foster wrote an MA thesis entitled "The Anglican Clergy in
Red River Settlement, 1820-26" at the University of Alberta in 1966, and
completed his PhD thesis in 1972 at the same institution on "The Country-born in the Red River Settlement, 1820-1850." "Country-born" was
the term Foster introduced into the scholarly literature to refer to the
anglophone mixed bloods, most of whom were communicants of the
Anglican Church in the settlement. Foster's work introduced a new com-
plexity into the mixed-blood element in Red River, one based on race and
religion. Frits Pannekoek further emphasized the importance of religion,
and especially the role of the Anglican church, in Red River in his 1978
doctoral thesis "The Churches and the Social Structure in the Red River
Area 1818-70."[30] Pannekoek did concentrate specifically on what he
called "the Riel Resistance." His thesis did not appear as a book until a
revised version was published in 1991 as *A Snug Little Flock: The Social
Origins of the Riel Resistance 1869-70*, but its outlines were clear from journal articles published over the years. According to Pannekoek, the anglophone mixed bloods had, in the last years of the settlement, developed
their own identity, quite distinctive from that of the francophone Métis.
In terms of 1869-70, the question became, how do the two communities of
mixed bloods ever expect to be able to work together? In the later 1970s,
Jennifer S.H. Brown began publishing journal articles that anticipated her
book *Strangers in Blood: Fur Trade Company Families in Indian Country*.[31]

Brown's work not only distinguished two "linguistic solitudes," but explained their historical origins in the marriage patterns of the two fur-trading companies. The francophone mixed bloods had their beginnings in marriages between Native women and traders of the North West Company, while the anglophones came from marriages of Hudson's Bay Company traders. Moreover, along with her colleague Sylvia Van Kirk, Brown not only introduced gender and family relations into the mixed-blood picture, but also a far more ambivalent and edgy notion of the racial tensions in Red River society.[32] The new view of Red River emerging from the scholarship of the 1960s, 1970s, and 1980s—much of it done at the University of Alberta—was of a settlement composed of two sharply separated mixed-blood communities, one francophone and Catholic, one anglophone and Protestant, prone to disagreement.

The question of the nature of mixed-blood society in Red River was reopened in 1986 by Brian Gallagher in an important unpublished MA thesis, somewhat misleadingly entitled "The Whig Interpretation of the History of Red River."[33] Gallagher insisted that most historians of Red River, beginning with Morton and Stanley, and continuing through John Foster, Frits Pannekoek, and Sylvia Van Kirk, had misleadingly exaggerated racial and religious differences among the mixed bloods. He argued that Foster had ignored the common Cree heritage of most mixed bloods in Red River and created in the "country-born" a term not often employed by contemporaries. Both Foster and Pannekoek had magnified religious strife in the settlement to a considerable extent, Gallagher claimed, and Pannekoek had taken matters one step further by erroneously recasting the Protestant mixed bloods as the loyalist supporters of Canada in 1869-70. Gallagher was equally critical of the work of Sylvia Van Kirk, insisting that her work was built on the assumptions of Foster and Pannekoek. Later Red River was not divided by marriage patterns in which mixed-blood women were excluded.

In 1995, I published *The Red River Rebellion of 1869-70*. I saw that book very much in the tradition of W.L. Morton, documenting a surprising amount of cooperation between the mixed-blood communities and the achievement of unity within the settlement in the spring of 1870 as delegates were sent to negotiate with Canada. Gerhard Ens expanded his views in his book *Homeland to Hinterland: The Changing Worlds of the Red*

*River Métis in the Nineteenth Century*, published in 1996, making clear the extent of his disagreements with Giraud and Morton.[34] Instead of being victims of progress, many Métis did their best to adapt to it and share in it. The mixed bloods were not dispersed after 1870, for they had been moving westward since 1840. The buffalo-skin trade was preferred to subsistence agriculture not because the Métis were primitive hunters, but because it was more profitable. The decline of the buffalo meant that the Métis may have made a bad choice, but buffalo hunting was not in and of itself a sign of their "savage" heritage. Instead of monolithic mixed-blood groups, Ens saw a continuum across the linguistic/religious divide, particularly in terms of responses to economic opportunity. Not all francophones supported Riel; some Métis were able to cooperate with their anglophone cousins in a variety of ways, including an insistence on their rights as heirs of the Aboriginals to land claims in the region.

This edition of letters to eastern newspapers over the winter of 1869-70 is very much in the tradition of Alexander Begg and W.L. Morton, especially in its concentration on the internal events in the settlement. Begg is, after all, one of its two chief contributors. Morton clearly knew of these sorts of letters and even reprinted a few of them in his edition of the Begg journal, but he appeared unaware of the extent of the Begg correspondence, or of the existence of the full Hargrave material. It is not often that we have two such detailed eyewitness accounts of a series of events. Not only are the eyewitnesses on the spot, but they are both men with an historical bent and a substantial later reputation as historians. Their analysis was made available to readers in eastern Canada on a regular basis. Nobody would claim that Begg and Hargrave spoke for anything more than a small segment of the European population of the settlement; both represented different parts of the long-time resident community, and shared a hostility to the Canadian newcomers. But this edition provides further descriptive evidence of the complexities of life in Red River at the time and of the problems of achieving unity among the mixed-blood inhabitants. It offers for the first time the narrative and analysis of J.J. Hargrave, so curiously missing from his book on Red River.

THE "RED RIVER" LETTERS OF JOSEPH JAMES HARGRAVE

Early descriptive letters from Red River by Charles Mair commissioned by eastern newspapers to provide background for the Canadian assumption of authority in the region were quickly succeeded in September 1869 by a correspondence in the *Montreal Herald* labelled "Red River Settlement, British North America." The anonymous author of this series of fifteen letters written between 18 September 1869 and 29 January 1870[35] was Joseph James Hargrave, the private secretary of Governor William McTavish of the Hudson's Bay Company. The oldest son of Chief Trader James Hargrave and Letitia Mactavish Hargrave, young "Beppo," as he was called, grew up among the Scottish fur-trade aristocracy in the settlement before being sent to Scotland to be educated.[36] He returned to Red River in 1861 to enter HBC employment. It is not clear whether Hargrave had already drafted the manuscript which would be published as *Red River* (1871) at the time he began his *Herald* correspondence, but it would appear likely. The volume published in 1871 dealt with the history of the decade of the 1860s, and Hargrave's declared intention to provide an appendix to this work covering the rebellion of 1869-70—presumably to be based on his *Herald* letters—suggests that he saw the material he had produced as part of a single whole.[37] It also seems likely that Hargrave, like his fellow correspondent Alexander Begg, kept a detailed diary or journal at the time of the rebellion to serve as the basis of his account. If so, it unfortunately has not survived.

Hargrave's reputation as a historian has always been an uneasy one. A few scholars have recognized his work, but almost nobody takes it very seriously, perhaps because of its microcosmic approach and its seemingly gossipy nature. The only contemporary review of *Red River*, in the *Canadian Monthly and National Review*, complained: "Events which happen out of the ordinary dull and monotonous routine of life in such a place, no matter how trivial in themselves, or how unimportant to the outside world, have acquired in the mind of the author, solely by reason of their rarity, an historic dignity."[38] Hargrave certainly had a fine eye for the detail of scandal, and was obviously often much entranced by the shenanigans in the small community he had chosen to chronicle. He also intuitively sensed that gossip and scandal flourished best at the public and private margins of society, and were thus symptomatic of the underlying tensions.[39] Far from being a myopic local historian, Hargrave is thus one of the unacknowledged forerunners of modern Canadian social history.

Underneath the amusing surface of *Red River*, Hargrave did have some definite theses about what had been going on in Red River. These were carried over (or anticipated) in his letters to the *Herald* in 1869-70. In the letter, for example, dated 13 November 1869 and published on 4 December, Hargrave insisted:

> Regarding the advisability of removing the responsibility of government from the Company it can hardly be a matter of doubt that the time has fully arrived for such a step. The action of the Government here for some years past has been grossly misrepresented to the Canadian public through interested agencies, the nature of some of which I may have occasion hereafter to explain. It has certainly been an administration ruled by expediency, inasmuch as men accused and found guilty of criminal offences have been permitted to remain at large after having been rescued from prison by the illegal violence of their adherents—but the spirit of government has been pure, and its administration more lenient. It wanted, however, the element of strength to be found only in a material force to uphold the law.

For Hargrave, it was the breakdown of the system of justice and the failure to be able to maintain order, thoroughly documented by him in *Red River*, that had led to the rebellion. Many historians of early Manitoba have adopted this viewpoint without acknowledging its source. The HBC needed to be replaced with a more formal government, either British or Canadian, but not Métis, insisted Hargrave. In his 1869-70 correspondence, however, Hargrave was neither a slavish supporter of the HBC nor a particular friend of the Canadian Party.

Beyond the political analysis of Red River lay Hargrave's understanding of the microcosm's dynamic, something not likely to be appreciated by contemporary historians in Ontario or by their national history successors. Others in Red River saw the prevalence of local scandal as little more than evidence of the backwardness of the settlement. William Ross wrote his brother James in 1856, for example: "You know the fact that Red River is half a century behind the age—no stirring events to give life and vigour to our debilitated life. . . . Just for the reasons above given and because we in Red River live for ourselves and care for no one else—nothing but the little tattle of scandal in every one's mouth—of this we have plenty."[40] But for Hargrave, rumour and scandal were what the place was all about, as he continually demonstrated in all his writing, including his rebellion correspondence. His book *Red River* would have been immeasurably strengthened by the inclusion of Hargrave's epistular accounts of the origins of the uprising of 1869-70, which emphasized the gossip and scandal surrounding the events.

Hargrave began his correspondence to the *Herald* with a letter dated 18 September 1869.[41] This letter was plainly intended as the introduction to a correspondence describing Red River beyond the "general features of the country and its people," which the author insisted were "pretty widely known." The ambition appears little different from that of Charles Mair, although Hargrave perhaps gave his readers more credit for knowledge of the region than did the Canadian poet. As the chapters in his subsequent book demonstrated, Hargrave's strength was in providing insider detail. Gradually, however, the stirring events within the settlement began to overtake the author's background detail. At the end of the letter dated 22 October, Hargrave dropped his description to take up a brief narrative of the events literally swirling all around him. The letter dated 30 October 1869 also began as description and ended as narrative. By the letter of 6 November, Hargrave had fully shifted his attention to the disturbances. He lived in bachelor's quarters in Upper Fort Garry, as one of his subsequent letters made clear. Particularly after the occupation of the fort by Riel's Métis in early November, Hargrave was literally right in the middle of the action. His detailed account of Riel's seizure of the land records and accounts of the settlement in November offered examples of what was undoubtedly first-hand intelligence. Hargrave was also clearly present at the meeting held at the Winnipeg Fire Engine House on 26 November at which Louis Riel spoke. The report of the subsequent discussion demonstrated Hargrave's eye for telling detail, as did his revelation that when, after the meeting, he had ridiculed the notion that those in attendance had been armed, he was answered by each of three friends who pulled out a revolver from under his coat.

One major problem with Hargrave's correspondence is distinguishing it from other letters—by "Nor'West," by "Nor-Wester," by "Riviere

Rouge"—also published in the *Herald*. These other letters are also by residents in the settlement, probably mainly Canadians. They are often not particularly insightful, and, more to the point, they often are not part of an ongoing series, although there were several letters from "Norwester" to the Montreal newspaper. Hargrave did not sign his earlier letters, and occasionally the *Herald* would run the letters of more than one correspondent together, as it did on 7 January 1870. Hargrave himself eventually recognized the problem, and in his letter published 29 January 1870 wrote, "I beg to conclude by saying that, as I see the fact of my having adopted no specific signature to my letters seems likely to end in committing me, through mistake, to the opinions of fellow correspondents, from which in reality I might dissent, I shall adopt for distinction's sake in any future communications to your Journal the signature RED RIVER." Unfortunately, Hargrave was nearly at the end of his correspondence when he took this step.

Joseph James Hargrave's overall perspective was that of a Hudson's Bay Company official, which led him to a continual ambivalence towards the uprising in Red River. Hargrave was no particular friend of the Métis led by Louis Riel, but he fully acknowledged that Canadian policy toward the settlement had been badly misguided from the beginning. Not only had the Canadians failed to communicate with the local officials of the Hudson's Bay Company, but "successively arriving officials seemed altogether unaccredited to those of the old order of things, and attached themselves to a party, which, while professing itself peculiarly representative of Canada, had always openly gloried in throwing difficulties in the way of the old administration. This party, what influence soever it may have in Canada, never possessed any in Red River."[42] Hargrave saw the subsequent issuance by Governor McDougall of a premature proclamation of the Canadian takeover and the actions of Colonel John Dennis attempting to stir up opposition to the insurgents in the settlement as further evidence of Canadian irresponsibility. In a letter dated 22 January 1870, Hargrave attempted to correct some of the misstatements he had read in the Canadian newspapers. He insisted that Colonel Dennis had not behaved with lack of courage; instead, "having once commenced hostilities, he persevered with determination and rashness which covered him with failure and obloquy." He also maintained that were Canada to withdraw from Rupert's Land, its inhabitants would not "be consigned to the state of political serfdom, from which they have so lately been emancipated." The recent events denied such a result, Hargrave wrote, for "No such thing as political subjection has ever been known in Rupert's Land."[43] He did not think that the Hudson's Bay Company wanted to continue in control of the settlement, and at this point insisted that events appeared to be drifting toward ultimate American annexation, a conclusion that would "prove fatal to the great project of confederation of British American Provinces."

In private correspondence, Hargrave could be far less sympathetic to the Métis cause than he was in the letters he wrote for publication. In one private letter to William McMurray, penned on 10 December 1869, he insisted that the interruptions of the insurrection would seriously damage the fur trade and would eventually have to be met with a military occupation. He added, "It is said Fenianism and Yankee conspiracy have much to do with the present state of the colony."[44]

Hargrave's Red River letters ended abruptly with one dated 29 January 1870.[45] In this epistle he advocated a "Canadian Pacific Railway" and blamed the present "troubles" on "the shameful neglect of the Colonial Office." He left the parties in Red River in the midst of constructing a bill of rights, writing "at present there appears to be no obstacle in the way of an ultimate solution of the difficulty." He warned that the real question was how much plunder would be taken from the HBC storehouses. The sudden termination of his correspondence means that the Canadian public was deprived of Hargrave's accounts of the stirring events of February and early March 1870, including the arrest of the "Portage Boys" and the subsequent execution of Thomas Scott. There is no evidence to suggest that Hargrave became any more disenchanted with the behaviour of the provisional government, however. He indicated in a letter of 8 February 1870 to Sir Curtis Lampson that his original intention had been a series of descriptive articles. Nor does the surviving evidence suggest the eastern readers would have learned very much from further correspondence from Hargrave. In one private letter to William McMurray at Fort Chipewyan dated 14 March 1870 (after the Portage "invasion" and the execution of Thomas Scott), Hargrave described the events of the preceding few months in a balanced and distant voice without making any judgement on them whatsoever. Hargrave was mainly concerned that the Métis would seize provisions and furs of the HBC in the spring. He noted the seizure of prisoners, but added that "it is thought probably many of these will soon be released." He dealt with the Scott execution by reference to a "fyle of the issue of the *New Nation* newspaper," forwarded to his correspondent by John McTavish.[46] We are equally ignorant of why Hargrave published *Red River* in 1871 without including the material on the rebellion, or why he published nothing more after that book. It is possible that the lukewarm reception to *Red River*—according to Isaac Cowie, Hargrave lost £600 by its publication—discouraged him from further activity.[47] The surviving Hargrave Papers contain a brief thirty-one-page fragment of a history of the fur trade, headed in another hand "Story begun by Joseph Hargrave 1878," but its sketchy and incomplete nature suggests that Hargrave had lost whatever incentives had earlier motivated his writing. He may have been another one-book author, of which Canada has had many.

Present at the raising of the British flag at Upper Fort Garry by Colonel Wolseley's troops in August of 1870, Joseph Hargrave was one of those who raised his voice in the singing of "God Save the Queen." After the dust had settled from the "restoration," and certainly after the appearance of his book on Red River in 1871, Hargrave settled into a comfortable niche in the HBC. He was not rapidly promoted, however, serving for a total of fifteen years as a clerk before being appointed a temporary cashier in 1877 and in 1878 a chief trader in the Red River District. He was transferred to Edmonton in 1884, retiring there in 1889. His later correspondence frequently offered the usual complaints of the petty bureaucrat who had reached a plateau, including low wages. In 1878 Hargrave was appointed secretary of an association founded to improve working conditions in the company, and he helped negotiate improvements with Donald A. Smith. Not surprisingly, in the Winnipeg boom of the 1880s he was an active investor, probably losing heavily when the bubble burst. In any case, he retired only after receiving an inheritance, which enabled him to live comfortably. In its obituary, the *Manitoba Free Press* commented on a paralysis in later years "which eventually disabled him completely and hastened his death."[48] If this motor disease was one of the hereditary ones which become progressively more severe, it may help account for the cessation of his historical activities. In any event, he removed to Montreal in 1890 and joined kinfolk in Edinburgh in 1893, residing at 7 Atholl Crescent. He died unmarried.

Joseph James Hargrave deserves to be better known as an historian than is presently the case. He was not among the early historians of Red River who saw the settlement as "moribund."[49] He saw a far more complex dynamic, in which the story weaved rather than unfolded. He was certainly a "participant historian" in the nineteenth-century sense of the term.[50] Hargrave's reputation (or rather, lack of it) has certainly been influenced by his microcosmic regional approach, but also by the fact that his historical writing on the Red River rebellion has never been properly recognized or made available to the public. A revision of the rebellion letters, added to his 1871 book on Red River, would certainly have given that book a sense of direction and purpose it appeared to lack when it was first published. Not even those historians—like W.L. Morton—who knew that Hargrave had written a series of letters for the *Montreal Herald* have appreciated how extensive that correspondence really was.

## THE "JUSTITIA" LETTERS OF ALEXANDER BEGG

The other principal Red River correspondent for the eastern newspapers was Alexander Begg. Like both Mair and Hargrave, Begg was a relative newcomer to Red River. He had been born in Quebec City in 1839, his parents having immigrated there from Scotland. After local education at St. John's, Quebec, Begg went off to school at Aberdeen before entering the world of commerce. In 1867 he came to Red River as agent for several firms based in Hamilton, Ontario, and a year later he became a partner of Alexander Bannatyne, who operated a general store (and the local post office) in the centre of the village of Winnipeg. Begg's connection with the post office meant that he, like Joseph James Hargrave, had a particularly useful vantage point from which to learn about the ongoing events of 1869-70. While much of Hargrave's information came from his residential position at Upper Fort Garry, much of Begg's intelligence came from the local post office, where residents doubtless chatted as they picked up and posted their mail. There was no mail delivery in Red River in 1869-70. Those wanting their mail had to pick it up at Begg's store. In the stirring days of the insurgency, fact, rumour, and speculation alike circulated at the post office wicket.

While we may suspect that Joseph James Hargrave probably kept a regular diary or journal, we know that Alexander Begg did. It was edited and published by W.L. Morton in 1956. As well as making detailed entries in his journal, Begg also wrote—between 10 November 1869 and 26 February 1870—a series of lengthy letters under the *nom de plume* of "Justitia," which were sent off and published in the Toronto *Globe*. W.L. Morton knew of "Justitia" and even reprinted several of his letters, and he suspected that "Justitia" was indeed Alexander Begg.[51] Indeed, the proof of this identification itself was in the pages of the Morton edition, for a verbatim version of the first "Justitia" letter served as the "Preface" to Begg's manuscript journal. In some ways the *Globe* was a curious choice of outlet for Begg to have made. It was a strong booster of Canadian expansionism, a phenomenon about which Begg harboured deep suspicions. But Joseph James Hargrave and others were already publishing in the *Montreal Herald*, and Begg doubtless preferred not to bury his reports among many others. Moreover, from Begg's perspective, his letters could provide a useful corrective to the *Globe's* usual editorial policy on Red River and the West. Even more curious than Begg's choice of the *Globe* is that newspaper's willingness to publish his correspondence. From his first letter, dated 10 November 1869, Begg set out to be revisionistic. He intended to lecture Canada and Canadians about Red River and their mistakes about it. By the time he picked up his pen in November of 1869, it was clear to Alexander Begg and every other thoughtful person in Red River that the Métis would resist the annexation of Red River by Canada.

Joseph James Hargrave had already sent eight letters to the *Montreal Herald* by the time Begg wrote his first "Justitia" one, but Hargrave had not set out to write about the resistance and only gradually discovered that his account of it was assuming so much space in his correspondence. Begg clearly intended to focus on the insurgency. He began his first letter by emphasizing, "That which has been foretold for some time past in the settlement has taken place." A long gestation period of discontent had eventually produced open resistance by the "French half-breeds." Begg proceeded to excoriate the Canadian government, the Canadian party in the settlement, and the *Nor'-Wester* newspaper on which the *Globe* had often relied for information about Red River, for their collective failure to take the people of Red River, especially its mixed-blood population, sufficiently seriously. Rhetorically Begg asked, "Would it not have been wiser policy for them [the Canadians] to have sent authorized Agents to this country as soon as the transfer of territory was agreed upon, for the purpose of feeling the pulse of the settlers, find out their ideas on the change proposed, and opening out, as far as possible, the views of the Canadian Government towards them?" With these sentiments most of the population of the settlement, with the possible exception of the more extreme members of the Canadian Party, would probably have concurred. It is likely that even the editorial people at the *Globe* would have admitted privately, at least with hindsight, that Canada had not approached Red River very sensibly.

From the outset, "Justitia" made clear that he was no particular friend of Canada. What was less apparent in the opening letter was the extent of his sympathies for the Métis people of the settlement. In his first epistle, Begg did not much distinguish the parties or classes of Red River. He had identified the resistance as coming from the French-speaking Métis, but most of his discussion revolved around the many errors of Canada, some of which had involved working within the settlement with what Begg (joining Hargrave) insisted was a totally discredited Canadian Party. Begg's readers could have been forgiven for thinking after reading his first letter that the opposition to Canada, whoever was leading it, was pretty general in the settlement. In some senses, this doubtless was Begg's belief. He could not know, at the outset, how totally the events of the next few months would come to divide Red River. Begg's general attitude, at least until March of 1870, was that all those who did not support Riel and his colleagues were part of the problem. The small but active Canadian opposition was only the most objectionable of the local obstructionist forces. The English-speaking residents, mostly mixed bloods, who sat on their hands, were also obstacles. As for the Americans, Begg suspected their motives but had to admit that they generally backed the insurgency.

Like Hargrave, Alexander Begg relied heavily on local "rumours" for his analysis of events. Hargrave's rumours originated mainly in Upper Fort Garry, the headquarters of the Métis and the Hudson's Bay Company; they tended to reflect mainly accurate intelligence. From his vantage point at the post office, Begg had access to a much wider range of gossip and speculation, which he reported in both his journal and his correspondence (but especially the former) without much discrimination. At what point the Canadians came to suspect that Begg was "Justitia" is not clear—some certainly had made the connection by the time of the Wolseley "invasion"—but Begg had always made far less effort than Hargrave to be fair to those with whom he did not agree. Begg cordially detested both John Schultz, the ostensible leader of the Canadian Party, and James Ross, the leading English-speaking mixed blood in the settlement. He also had considerable admiration for Louis Riel. These prejudices certainly helped colour his narrative.

Alexander Begg has left us three different versions of events in 1869-70. He doubtless began with entries in his journal, then wrote up the journal entries for his "Justitia" letters, and, finally, employed both sources to compose his 1871 history, *The Creation of Manitoba*. There is substantial overlap between the three versions, but they are by no means identical. Take, for example, the account of the raising of the new provisional government's flag on 10 December 1869. In his journal, Begg recorded:

> The French to-day hoisted the Provisional Government flag as below [the sketch was left blank] and fired off a volley of small arms and salutes from the cannon at Fort Garry—the guard at Dr. Schultz's house returned the salute. After several vollies had been fired at the Fort and the band of St. Boniface under the leadership of Father Dugast had played several tunes there—a party with the band proceeded to the town and serenaded Genl. Malmoras the American Consul. Three cheers were given for the Provisional Government—three for the leaders and three for the band—followed by three groans for Mulligan—late chief of police now a prisoner at Fort Garry. Mr. Riel addressed the French at Fort Garry and in the course of his speech hoped his men were all loyal to the Queen.[52]

"Justitia" reported this event as follows:

> The Friday last, the 10th inst., the French went through the ceremony of hoisting the flag of their Provisional Government. About four o'clock in the afternoon, a number of armed men assembled in the Court yard of Fort Garry, and were addressed by Mr. Riel, who called upon them to support the new flag until their rights, as free born subjects of Queen Victoria, were respected. The idea of this movement is simply another step

towards the grand scheme of a Provisional Government—and emblem, as it were, of its actual existence. After Mr. Riel's address, the flag (the design of which is the *fleur de lis* and shamrock combined) was hoisted, and a salute fired by the men in the Fort, at the same time the brass bands from St. Boniface, struck up some lively tunes; again and again the salutes were fired, until at last they thought they had wasted powder enough. The bands accompanied by a guard then proceeded to the town and serenaded its citizens. The shamrock on the flag looks significant; but on inquiry I find that it is merely a compliment to Mr. O'Donoghue, an Irishman, who has greatly assisted Mr. Riel in the present undertaking. This, at all events, is the only version of the matter I have heard. I sincerely hope there is no deeper meaning to the emblem. I am sure there is not as far as the general body of the French are concerned.[53]

Begg's 1871 book records:

On the 10th December, the French provisional flag was hoisted for the first time at Fort Garry, amidst the shouts of the men assembled to witness it. The flag consisted of a white ground, on which was worked a representation of the *fleur de lis* and *shamrock* combined, the latter being in honour, it was said, of W.B. O'Donohue, a young man who, having thrown off the soutane, left the college of St. Boniface, where he had been studying for the priesthood, and joined the insurgents. He was an Irishman by birth, having lived, however, for some time in the city of New York, and was suspected of possessing strong Fenian proclivities. He afterwards became a leading spirit in the insurrection, and we will often have occasion to speak of him in connection with some of the most important actions of the insurgents. As the flag was hoisted on the pole, a volley was fired in its honor, and the band from the College of St. Boniface being present played several tunes, the French in the meantime cheering lustily; after which Riel made a speech to the crowd.[54]

The shamrock is not mentioned in the journal entry; it is explained away by "Justitia" for his Canadian readers; and it is treated with more suspicion in 1871 through an expanded description of W.B. O'Donoghue.[55]

Of the three versions of the flag-hoisting, the "Justitia" one offers the most background description and detail. This is generally true of Begg's three accounts. "Justitia's" letter of 2 December, which describes the anatomy of the settlement in some detail, has no counterpart in either the journal or the history. The letter of 17 December 1869 contained thumb-nail descriptions and character sketches of the Métis leaders: Louis Riel, John Bruce, W.B. O'Donoghue, and Father Ritchot, which appear nowhere else in Begg's writing. Of Riel, "Justitia" wrote, "His utterance is rapid and energetic, and his remarks at times are very sarcastic. . . . Riel by his energy and perseverance, has, you may say, conducted the whole of this movement; and, if he does not now overstep the mark, he will doubt-less bring his people out safely yet." Begg presented the Métis leaders not as rebels or troublemakers, but as individuals concerned with the Métis community. The letter of 11 January 1870 opens with a wonderful description of a Métis wedding celebration that establishes Begg's creden-tials as a social commentator, like Hargrave with a sense of humour. The tongue-in-cheek mode is carried forward in this letter with a description of a meeting with the Sioux at the end of December 1869 in which the Aboriginals are all given a charge with a galvanic battery. The "Justitia" correspondence demonstrates that Begg was a far more compelling writer than he appeared in either *The Creation of Manitoba* or his novel *Dot-it-Down*.

Unfortunately, Begg stopped writing his letters to the *Globe* on 26 Feb-ruary 1870—or at least, no more were published after this one. Since Begg's next letter would have probably dealt with the Scott execution, one suspects the *Globe* would have printed it whatever was its interpretation of that event. We must therefore presume that Begg simply stopped writing. It is certainly tempting in his case to associate the Scott death with the cessation of the correspondence. There is no doubt that Begg's journal—and his 1871 history—became far less sympathetic to the provisional government of Louis Riel after 4 March 1870 and the death of Thomas Scott. In his history, Begg wrote that "Riel, who professed to be working for the good of his country, had in one day brought a curse upon it—a dreadful blot on the name of his countrymen, and a lasting disgrace upon himself."[56] His journal makes clear Begg's utter shock at the execution of Scott. Since Begg's correspondence had consistently attempted to defend the uprising to eastern Canada, he may well have dropped his pen at the point when he felt his support could no longer be sustained. Certainly in his subsequent history, Scott's death takes place on page 300 of a 400-page book, and there is in the remaining pages no more support for Riel or the Métis. Begg obviously had nothing useful to say about the negotiations over the admission of Red River into Confederation or about the Wolseley Expedition, beyond its arrival at the end of August. These events occurred beyond his purview. His journal and his later history both suggested that Riel's provisional government did a reasonably good job of administering the settlement over the spring and summer of 1870, although he had ceased to present this perspective to the eastern newspapers.

Like the careers of his fellow correspondents Mair, Hargrave, and even Louis Riel, that of Alexander Begg after 1870 was distinctly anti-climactic.[57] Along with other Riel supporters, he was distinctly unpopular with the Canadians who "occupied" Manitoba in the autumn of 1870. He found it expedient to be absent from the settlement during much of this time. According to one local newspaper, opinion was divided "as to wether [sic] he should be tarred and feathered ... or whether he should be ridden on a rail" for the "Justitia" letters, "which have earned him the title of Renegade Canadian."[58] Begg weathered the storm, and became increasingly involved in writing, both historical and fictional. He was the author of what was arguably the province's first novel, a thinly disguised satire of the pre-rebellion period published in the same year (1871) as his history of the rebellion, *The Creation of Manitoba*. He was appointed Queen's Printer in 1877. Two years later, in 1879, with journalist Walter Nursey, he published *Ten Years in Winnipeg*. He wrote at least one more novel, which was not well received. Begg also composed a highly nostalgic volume of reminiscences in 1884 entitled *Seventeen Years in the Canadian North-West*, in which he commented that the pre-rebellion Red River Settlement was one offering as close an approach "to perfect freedom" as he had ever seen or known.[59] From 1884 to 1888 Begg served as Immigration Agent for the Canadian Pacific Railway in London. He then moved to British Columbia, where he resumed his writing, producing his *History of the North-West* (three volumes) in 1894 and becoming confused with another Alexander Begg who also wrote western history. Despite substantial subsequent literary and historical output, Begg never achieved the same level of mastery of his prose and his material that had characterized his hastily written "Justitia" letters in 1869-70.

With the cessation of correspondence by both Hargrave and Begg, eastern Canadian newspapers and their readers no longer had access to coherent and continuous eyewitness accounts of the course of the insurgency. Nor did they have access after early March to the *New Nation*, which Louis Riel closed down. Although the rebellion ought to have, for all practical purposes, ended with the passage of the Bill of Rights by the Convention of Forty and its transmission to Donald A. Smith to be given to the Canadian government as soon as possible, it did not. The event that both prolonged it and complicated it, of course, was the trial and execution of Thomas Scott in early March. Not long after that event, the provisional government sent its delegates east to negotiate with Canada, and the spotlight shifted from Winnipeg to Ottawa, and then to the military expedition led by Garnet Wolseley that headed back to Red River.

In any event, affairs in Red River after late March no longer received very much sympathetic and knowledgeable treatment in the eastern media. After the capture of the "Portage boys," recounted in detail in his last letter by "Justitia," eastern newspapers' accounts of the rebellion tended to lack both authority and focus. Reliance on the "wire"—telegraphic accounts from St. Paul recounting the information reaching Minnesota from Red River—was joined to solitary letters on particular points and then to the reprinting of the tales of the returning Canadians, which began appearing in Canada in early April. Not only the death of Thomas Scott but the relative absence of reliable alternative information enabled the Canada Firsters to capture control of the media in Ontario.[60] An internal perspective on events in Red River was almost totally lost in eastern Canada, with unfortunate results for Riel and his people. Virtually no opposition to the Wolseley Expedition was voiced in eastern Canada, and the rebel leaders ended up fleeing from the military in August 1870.

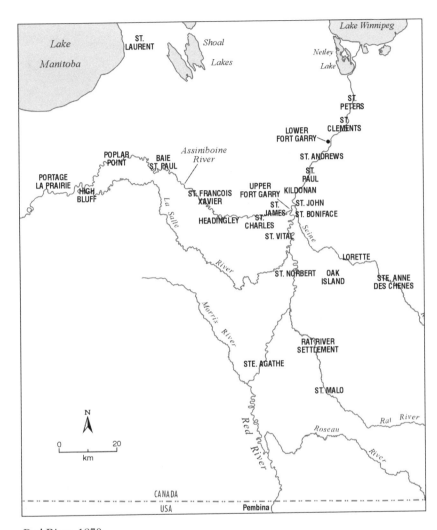

Red River, 1870

Joseph James Hargrave (Public Archives of Manitoba)

Alexander Begg (National Archives of Canada)

# J.J. HARGRAVE

18 SEPTEMBER 1869

[This is the first letter from Red River written by Joseph James Hargrave. There is obviously no sense of urgency about it. Hargrave plans to give a fairly leisurely description of the settlement Canada will soon be taking over. Printed in the *Montreal Herald and Daily Commercial Gazette*, 11 October 1869.]

Red River Settlement, B.N. America,
18 September 1869

The public interest so generally evinced of late years in everything connected with this Colony, has called forth so many communications on the subject in the various Canadian journals that the general features of the country and its people are pretty widely known. However, as a first step in writing a series of letters on the country, I think it well to repeat some of the leading characteristics of the present population. These may be described as the French half-breed, the English half-breed, the Indian, and white people.* The French half-breeds depend almost entirely on the chase for the means of livelihood; they number over five thousand souls in the settlement and its neighbourhood and are all of the Roman Catholic religion. While the buffalo were within easy reach of this place, they contrived, by a well arranged system of hunting, to maintain themselves on the produce of their hunts. Of late, however, chiefly I believe on account of the settlement in course of formation in the Missouri, the herds of buffalos have so far fled to the westward as to be beyond the reach of Red River hunters. During the present season, it is true, the prospects of the latter in this respect, have improved, but the steady march of civilization contains in it the seeds of the extinction of this source of supply in the cultivation of those prairies over which the buffalo have hitherto wandered.

The term "half-breed" as applied to the English speaking portion of the mixed population, is very apt to convey a false impression to a stranger.[1]

---

* This division of the population by "races" was not terribly useful once the rebellion had begun.

The number of those to whom the expression in its literal signification can be applied is comparatively small, but the local custom prevails of speaking of every one, how remotely soever of Indian descent, as a half-breed. This section of the population is quite competent to hold its own in presence of any amount of immigration.

The Indian population is comparatively small. A part of the colony termed the "Indian settlement" is situated on the banks of the Red River, about twenty miles from its mouth, at Lake Winnipeg.[2] It has been formed entirely by the missionary agents of the English Church Missionary Society who, since about the year 1830, have devoted a large proportion of their exertions to further its interests. The Indians are of the Saulteaux tribe. Each family, on quitting the wigwam for the log-house, encloses a small portion of ground in the immediate vicinity of their cabin which they bring under cultivation. Agriculture was first taught to these people by the Rev. William Cochran, who founded the Indian settlement, and who, after forty years of missionary work, died in 1865. For a number of years before his death Mr. Cochran had occupied the position of Archdeacon of Assiniboia. His course in inducing the Indians to settle was an arduous and uphill one, and the permanence of the result of his labors is yet doubtful, as the mode in which the Salteaux farm is primitive, and they cannot get rid of the inherent desire to hunt or roam the country as *voyageurs*.

Since the middle of the last decade a gradually increasing influx of Canadian and American settlers has been going on. Such along with the survivors and descendants of the original Scotch settlers first established in the country by Lord Selkirk in the early part of the present century, constituted the "white" population. Previous to 1850 or 1855 the accessions to the population derived from outside, had consisted entirely of Orcadian and Scotch retiring officers and servants in the service of the Hudson's Bay Company.[3]

The above is a very general survey of the distinctive races of the people now resident in the colony, of which the total population may be estimated at from eleven to twelve thousand souls.

Hitherto the Fur Trade has been the motive spring of all Red River industry. The vast quantities of food required by the Company to provision their posts situated in the interior have created a market in the colony. Grain and Flour are purchased from the farmers and pemmican and dried Buffalo meat from the French half-breed hunters. Vast numbers of tripmen are employed to man the boats and drive the carts by which the freight transport is conducted on the rivers and plains between Red River, York Factory, Portage La Loche, the Saskatchewan and St. Paul.[4] During the summer season the whole male population is in the main occupied on journeys hundreds of miles in length.

Previous to 1857 communication with the outside world was irregular and rare. Once a year the Company's ship to the Bay brought letters and supplies to York Factory, while a winter packet overland to Canada and a trip of the Canoes from Montreal in spring for many years offered the only available facilities for regular transport. Gradually the Postal operations of the United States were extended westwards, and some public spirited settlers organized a monthly mail service betwen Fort Garry and the nearest Post Office, which were still several hundreds of miles apart. Subsequently the American Government established a Post Office at Pembina, on the United States' frontier about 65 miles from Fort Garry, to which a monthly mail was carried. In course of a few years the monthly delivery became a fortnightly, a weekly, and latterly a bi-weekly one. The Local Government here at present send a Courier twice a week to Pembina.

About 1859, a great attempt was made by the Canadian Government, to establish a mail route between Red River and Lake Superior, over the line of communication now in course of being opened up.[5] This system, which continued in operation for at least more than one year, gave rise to extreme annoyance on account of the irregularity of the delivery of mail matter which seldom arrived before it had been several weeks overdue. In vain did correspondents expressly direct that letters should be forwarded through the States, by which route the mails arrived as regularly as the others did the reverse. No attention was paid to such inscriptions, and ridiculous to the unconcerned were the expressions of perplexity evinced by expectant correspondents here, as the non-arrival of anxiously lo[o]ked for letters by successively incoming mails pointed with increasing certainty to the conclusion that the objects of their solicitude were on the way from Fort William.

The gratitude of the Red River public is due to the authorities of the United States Post Office for their liberality in this respect. It is true that some irregularities occasionally occur very much, I believe, on account of the name Red River being applicable to more places than one. The process of sub-letting contracts has also been, I believe, to blame for accidental instances of deficiency in point of punctuality of delivery in consequence of the unhappy horse of the sub-contractor breaking down somewhere between Georgetown and Pembina. Red River correspondence has also sometimes evinced an eccentric tendency to find its way to "San Francisco." But the service has been on the whole so reliably conducted that the public have every reason to be grateful. I may mention that having been for several years in the habit of subscribing to an English weekly newspaper, and for part of the time to a daily one, I am not aware that in one single instance has a number failed in reaching me in good order and time. Until a "through" mail bag from St. Paul to Pembina had been secured to the settlement by the influence of Senator Ramsay, however, this regularity of delivery was not so great, the attractions of "Punch" and the illustrated "London News" being too great for the official virtue of postmasters at all the isolated stations on the way at each of which the bags were opened and examined.

The freight route through the States began to be regularly used about 1859.[6] Previous to that time the annual shipment by York Factory was the sole reliance of the colony, the inhabitants of which were entirely dependent on the Hudson's Bay Company. A variety of causes led to the opening up of the St. Paul route, among which one of the most pressing was the inability of the Company, and others to supply the growing requirements of the Colony for freight over the rugged and toilsome route between York Factory and Red River. The direct line from Canada by the Canoe route was even more difficult than by York Factory. An impression has gone abroad that the route from Fort William is less difficult than by the Bay, and the argument used bi [in] its support is that it is the old route used by the "North West Company of Montreal" in its freighting operations.* Practical experience has however taught the reverse, and if the testimony of the "North West" officials itself is of any value, it corroborates this view, as these people maintained it as a grievance that the Hudson's Bay Company prevented them shipping by the Bay. Practically this question must soon be set at rest by the reports and operations of responsible Canadian engineers.

Since its commencement the public patronage afforded to the route through the states has steadily increased from year to year. The outbreak

---

* This suggests how ridiculous was the notion entertained in Canada that the military expedition led by Garnet Wolseley had done anything spectacular when it employed this route in 1870.

of the Sioux in 1862 gave a temporary check to traffic in that direction, but the outbreak having been once quelled measures were taken by the formation of a line of military posts to secure peace along the frontier on a basis more secure than had ever been the case before.[7] The immediate prospect of a railroad between St. Paul and Breckenridge now seems before us, and promises to bring us within easy reach of civilized parts.

The direct route between Red River and Lake Superior is also in progress. The party at work, under Mr. Snow, at this end of the line, is small at present, in consequence of the difficulty of engaging labourers during the harvest season. This cause of delay will, however, disappear after the lapse of a few weeks.

The present harvest promises to be finer than any that has been seen here for a great many years.[8] The ground is said to have been much improved by lying in a fallow state for a year. The season has also been favourable. I regret, however, to have to state that about four weeks ago the settlement was again visited by grasshoppers. The crops were too far advanced before their arrival to be in any great danger from them; they have, however, deposited their eggs in the ground, and doubtless much damage, if not entire destruction, to next year's crops will be the result.

Profound quiet reigns in the settlement at present. Among the topics of the hour, is the expected advent of the Hon. Joseph Howe, whose presence on a visit to the country is daily expected.

We were lately favoured for the first time by the presence of a Consul appointed by the United States Government to reside in our midst.[9] Mr. Malmros, the gentleman so nominated, has taken up his quarters in the village of Winnipeg.

Colonel Dennis with a large and able staff of assistants has been for some weeks at work on his contemplated Land survey. Commencing at a point on the United States frontier west from Pembina the Colonel will run his principal line due northward in such a position as to be clear of the lots previously surveyed, which extend back to a distance of two miles from the main river.

A residence has been secured for Lieutenant-Governor Macdougall, whose arrival is expected within a couple of months. The house is at a place called "Silver-heights" at Sturgeon Creek, about six miles from Fort Garry, on the great highway to the Western plains. It is certainly the most eligible residence in the country.

EDITOR'S NOTE

[Hargrave's letter shows he holds the opinion that the Métis are almost solely hunters. Another assessment of the Métis was made by "Nor'West" in a letter to the *Montreal Herald* printed 22 November 1869:

Your correspondent on his arrival at St. Paul heard rumours of a rising among the half-breeds. Knowing as he did that considerable dissatisfaction was felt by this class of the community at the mode in which the purchase of the Territory was effected, and having previously heard from many of them their strongly expressed disapprobation of the change of government[,] your correspondent was not surprised at their rumours, and when he reached Pembina was prepared for the news that the half-breed population were up in arms to resist by force the entrance of the new Governor. During the summer they have been grumbling that their views were not ascertained before the transfer, and this discontent was increased when they read in the Canadian papers that a form of government had been devised for them without their sanction. They claimed that as natives of the country they should have been consulted not only as to the transfer of the country, but as to the mode in which it should be governed. Whatever the ultimate population of the Country may be they claim to be at present the only parties to be governed, and they demand the Briton's right of self government. Almost every man above twenty years of age is a freeholder, and would be entitled to a vote under the Canadian franchise. Most of them have received a common education, and nearly all of them have made frequent journeys as freighters with their own cattle to St. Paul's and St. Cloud in the state of Minnesota. They have there seen the rapid improvement of the country, and have not been slow to note the good points in the prevalent mode of Government. For some years past they have abandoned the buffalo hunt and every family cultivates more or less the soil. They contrast their position with that of the pure Indian and appreciate their own high standing in the scale of civilization. Their frequent visits to the United States have given them at least no dislike to democratic institutions while it has engendered that spirit of independence which is sure to be acquired by any inferior race when placed under that form of Government.

For the classic historical view of the Métis, see Marcel Giraud, *The Métis in the Canadian West*, 2 vol. (Edmonton: University of Alberta Press, 1986). For a more recent revision, more consonent with "Nor'West," consult Gerhard Ens, *Homeland to Hinterland: The Changing Worlds of the Red River Métis in the Nineteenth Century* (Toronto: University of Toronto Press 1996).]

# J.J. HARGRAVE

25 SEPTEMBER 1869

[In this letter J.J. Hargrave offers his eastern readers the conventional wisdom of Red River on agriculture and its problems, partly as a counter to any notions abroad that the West was ideal agricultural country. Printed in the *Montreal Herald and Daily Commercial Gazette*, 21 October 1869.]

Red River Settlement, B.N. America,
September 25, 1869

Chief among the inducements held out to intending immigrants by those who of late years have employed their talents and their pens in giving publicity to the natural resources of this country, is the capacity of the land for agriculture.

A vast zone extending westward has been represented as the wheat field of the New World. At Red River the prairie is entirely free from timber, except in narrow belts winding along the margins of streams. The ground consists of good earth for a depth of from four to seven feet, beneath which for a depth of perhaps forty feet exists a white watery mud. This state of matters prevails throughout the whole Red River Valley. It is very unfavourable for building purposes, on account of the difficulty to which it gives rise in securing a foundation for a stone structure.

In such a country what difficulties exist are certainly not those incident to laborious clearing and tillage. So far as preparation is concerned, breaking up with the plough is sufficient. The fertility of the soil is also great, and the number of returns averaged throughout the Colony in a good season is very considerable indeed. The present season is in many respects of almost unprecedented success.* Details it is yet too early to give, the crops not being yet gathered in, nor even cut down, on account of the backwardness of the season. I shall, however, report on them in due course.

It must also be borne in mind that the farming practised hitherto in this

---

* The reference is to the famine of 1868.

place has been on the rudest scale. The Hudson's Bay Company certainly have farmed "experimentally" and practically.[1] The "experimental" farms ended disastrously through other agencies than the natural defects of soil and climate. Where practised men have directed the farms, they have turned out tolerably well. At present the Company have two large farms; one at Lower Fort Garry, on the bank of the Red River, twenty miles south [north] from its confluence with the Assiniboine; the other on the bank of the latter river, about twenty-five miles west from Fort Garry, on the highway to the plains. The latter is, this year, a magnificent success.

The French half-breeds are a parcel of hunters, who have no taste for farming.[*] Their rude and somewhat careless efforts do not deserve to be named as a serious agricultural experiment. The original Scotch settlers were a band of peasants brought by Lord Selkirk from a remote corner of the North of Scotland. They were a persevering pig-headed party of Presbyterians, who practised what little they knew, and bequeathed it all as a heritage to their successors.[†] They will probably welcome the Scotch Canadian when he comes to settle beside them, as they have a weakness in favour of old country ties. The stranger might do far worse than reciprocate their good feelings and good offices.

All these people have, generally speaking, raised enough of farm produce for their own consumption. Sometimes, undoubtedly, it has been found necessary to import grain for the use of the Colony.[‡] Formerly the grand complaint was that no market existed for superfluous produce. This was a necessity under the circumstances. Yet, although the years when land lies fallow, are limited to those when such a calamity as a flood or a visit of a host of locusts befalls the place, although the system of rotation of crops is unpractised, manure is unused, and still the ground brings forth its returns.

The now [non] use of manure is a feature of the place. The clearings of the stables heaped in unsightly mounds at the top of the rivers' banks, crop prominently before the eyes of wayfarer[s]. In Spring, when the

---

[*] Hargrave here enunciates the standard settlement stereotype of the Métis.

[†] This is one of the few harsh comments ever made about the Scots settlers in Red River.

[‡] The last time was as recently as 1868. Hargrave is being disingenuous here.

snows melt, and in rainy weather, the river serves for the purpose of a common sewer, receiving the water filtered through these heaps, with which its course is lined. The state of impurity to which its waters have attained before their arrival at the lower reaches, renders them unpleasant drinking for those living near their channels.

The obstacles to successful agriculture at Red River then consist chiefly in the periodical floods, which inundated the country and render it for weeks a mere extension of Lake Winnipeg; in early frosts which during the Summer months often interfere with the progress towards maturity of the crops; in droughts which during the burning heat of Summer days, cause vegetation to wither, and most serious scourge of all, in the destructive visitations of the locust armies.[2]

The last flood occurred in 1861.[3] The country was then as usual devastated over a vast extent of Plain. The flat nature of the prairie offered no impediment to the waters, which rising above the level of the river banks, spread far and wide, leaving a few hillocks here and there of a higher level than the rest of the ground visible. The people had to sail between each others' houses in canoes, and the ground floors of the dwellings were deserted. Much property was destroyed, fencing swept away, and landmarks obliterated. Seed time having elapsed before the waters fell, the harvest of 1861 was a failure, and much distress fell upon the poorest classes during the following winter and spring, when they were indebted for their seed wheat to a public grant in their favour voted by the Governor and Council of Assiniboia.

Previous to 1861 floods have occurred in 1826 and 1852.[4] The former was the most disastrous of them all. Houses were swept away to Lake Winnipeg, and articles of furniture of all kinds jostled each other as they floated down the stream. The colony was yet in its infancy, and the calamity fell more heavily on that account. In 1852 the people were richer, though the actual value destroyed was greater than on the previous occasion, amounting on a moderate calculation to £25,000 sterling, it was less felt.

The most feasible explanation of the cause of these calamities is as follows. A wet season saturates the level country and fills swamps, lakes and streams. A series of heavy snow storms prevail throughout the winter. A late spring suddenly unseals the main rivers at their sources in the south. Burning sun clears away the snow in all directions and warm winds from the south press the waters down upon the still solid ice of Lake Winnipeg, which obstructs their flow.* The result of such a combination of causes is inevitable. Since 1861 the seasons have been dry and the channels of the rivers have proved adequate to carry away what spring floods have existed.

The peculiarly soft nature of the ground consisting for a great depth of earth must render a rude drainage on the plains easily attainable. A deep furrow run down towards the river becomes in a few years a ravine capable of carrying off a great quantity of water. The Red River and the Assiniboine have both increased greatly in sectional area within the last fifty years according to the unanimous testimony of the old inhabitants. It is therefore to be hoped that when improved by the operations of a large agricultural population, and by the works which will doubtless be brought to bear on it of an engineering character, the country will be freed from the evils which the over flowing of its rivers has hitherto at intervals entailed upon it.†

Summer frosts have often as already mentioned exercised a tendency for evil in the crops. Throughout the warmest summer weather it is one of the most remarkable features of the Red River climate that the nights are always cool. This coolness frequently falls to downright frost in June and August, occasionally this also happens in July. Cold North winds lower the temperature. Sleet and hail storms have been known to level and destroy large fields of nearly ripened grain. Perhaps an amelioration of climate in this respect, also may attend the persevering labours of man on a large scale.

Dry seasons frequently exercised a silent but heavily felt influence for ill on the prospects of the farmer. The burning earth gapes for water, fires fly across the country, devouring herbage, which disappears like tinder, and the streams fall down to their lowest level or altogether dry up. For such seasons travelling tells severely, and cattle die in great numbers on the Plains.[5]

Before the grasshopper nevertheless the united power for mischief of all the other scourges "hales its ineffectual fires."[6] Having done what mischief they can do, a generation deposits their eggs in the earth and fly

---

* The theory that flooding in Red River was caused by ice plugs was common in the nineteenth century.

† This is a different version of the common theme of the nineteenth century that settlement would end flooding.

away. Next Spring the young ones come to life and clear the fields of every growing blade. Then bodies collect in heaps round every wall, and threaten, by the noxious effluvia with which they fill the air, to breed a pestilence. Succeeding swarms appear from year to year clearing all before them. Since the year 1864 the Settlement has not been suffered to enjoy one season's entire immunity from their depredations. Generally speaking the mischief done has been only partial, but as is well known in Canada, the loss of crops in 1868 was complete. Within the last few weeks swarms have again arrived from the West, and have laid their eggs, which are now in the ground. The magnificent crops of the current season, which the insects came on the ground too late seriously to damage, will, it is hoped, largely assist the inhabitants to tide over a season of scarcity. The range of country over which the eggs are buried, also does not include the whole. Settlements in the Northern portion of the Colony, comprehending the populous agricultural parishes of St. Andrews and St. Peter's, fortunately having escaped. The farmers therefore on the lower reaches of the Red River will lay down a crop next year with good hopes that it will be suffered to come to maturity.

Previous to 1864 the settlement had twice since its formation been exposed to the devastation of Locusts. These events occurred in 1818 and 1857. It is to be hoped that the approaching Spring will be the last occasion on which they may be seen at least for a great many years.

Meanwhile it is necessary that the leaders in any large scheme of immigration should know the present prospect in the Country. Any parties coming here next Spring, except in so far as their immediate necessities may be concerned will not suffer from the presence of the grasshoppers, as they will not of course lay down a crop until the Spring of 1871. It must however be remembered that no security exists for the withdrawal of the grasshoppers even then, and, as it is, their immediate wants will have to be supplied with imported grain which will be sold at a high price.

Newcomers have been dropping in all Summer, and travelling over the face of the Country with the object of fixing in eligible spots on which to "take claims." Throughout the entire neighbourhood of Winnipeg the prairie is cut up with pickets intended to serve as evidence of possession having been taken within the boundaries which they mark. Whether or not such steps will be recognised as worth anything by the directors of the new order of things, I cannot tell; but large portions of the Country have been so "located" by enterprising local speculators who are said to harbour somewhat romantic ideas as to the value of this State.

Regarding current events there are none of importance to chronicle. Colonel Dennis, who some weeks ago went to a point on the international frontier west from Pembina had determined the position of his Meridian Line thence, to within a few miles of the Supplement, which he will probably reach in some few days. The operation on which he has been engaged, is most important on account of the fundamental relation which it will bear to all his subsequent proceedings. It is therefore fortunate that he has been able satisfactorily to complete it at this early date.

Intelligence has reached us of the departure from St. Paul, of the Hon. Joseph Howe, and his immediate arrival here is consequently expected.[7] Unless he has had better weather on the plains than we have had here, he has probably had but a disagreeable trip, for about a week past a good deal of rain has fallen round. All the roads are very muddy.

# J.J. HARGRAVE

2 OCTOBER 1869

[J.J. Hargrave was the private secretary to William Mactavish, the governor of Assiniboia and head of the HBC in Red River. He was thus well placed to know how the company's transportation system had been developed and how it worked. This account is probably the best brief and all-encompassing description extant of transportation to and from the settlement at the end of the colonial period. Printed in the *Montreal Herald and Daily Commercial Gazette*, 28 October 1869.]

Red River Settlement, B.N.A.

The isolation of Rupert's Land with respect to Canada renders a system of through communication between the latter place and Red River a subject of primary importance.

Ever since the commencement of trading operations in the Indian Country the Hudson's Bay Company has been in the habit of sending ships annually to one of their great coast depots, Churchill, York and Moose Factories. The North West Company of Montreal and the other Canadian Fur Companies adopted the route by Fort William and Winnipeg River. On commencing the system of establishing Inland Posts for the purpose of opposing their Canadian rivals, the Hudson's Bay people continue to import by the Bay and to supply their outposts by navigating the streams between Hudson's Bay and Lake Winnipeg. On the coalition between the rival companies taking effect in 1821, the Lake Superior route was practically abandoned as a freight route, and the whole supplies for the country were imported by the Bay.

After a lapse of about forty years the requirements of the Indian trade and the necessities of the Red River Settlement had so far outstripped any thing which could be supplied by the boating facilities at their command on the York route that the Company took advantage of the advance of the American settlements in Minnesota to import large quantities of goods through the United States, and encouraged the Settlers to do likewise by refusing to ship property belonging to any one not in their service from London to York.[1]

The result has been the formation of a well travelled route between St. Paul and Fort Garry, over which quantities of goods, steadily increasing from year to year, are imported, while a considerable number of Furs, more especially of Robes for the Canadian and the American markets, are exported by the same road.* The old canoe route has for several years been abandoned even as a means for introducing and taking out servants of the Company engaged in Canada, and the heaviest packets.

The immediate agents in opening up the Saint Paul route, were an American firm, Messrs. J. Coad, H.C. Bedson, Company, who were largely engaged in contracts for the Postal Department of the United States Government. These gentlemen recommended that the means of communication between St. Paul and Fort Garry should be of a two fold character— transport by season and to standard. The freight was to be carried overland, from St. Paul at the head of Mississippi to navigation to a point at the head of that of the Red River of the North, where a battle station was constructed, and named Georgetown, whence a steamboat should transport the goods down stream to Fort Garry, centre of the Red River Settlement.[2] This arrangement was, for several seasons, successfully carried out. A series of dry summers, however, subsequently interfered with the running of the land, which of late years has been able to make but a very limited number of trips above a spot called Frog Point, between which and Georgetown occur the Goose Rapids, which, after the Spring floods have subsided, become very shallow. Frog Point may, therefore, be regarded at present as the virtual head of Red River navigation. A light steamer might ply between it and Fort Garry throughout the season.

With reference to that portion of the route between St. Paul and Georgetown, or Frog Point,—a railroad has for some years past been in working order as far as St. Cloud, a village about eighty miles west from St. Paul, and St. Cloud is, therefore, considered by the freighters as the limit of prairie travel. Between it and the Settlement a train of freight can travel both ways in about six weeks.

The present mode of passenger conveyance over the present route is therefore as follows. Between St. Paul and St. Cloud railroad is in working order. Between St. Cloud and the United States frontier military station of

---

* Hargrave's reference is to the cart route between Red River and St. Paul.

Fort Abercrombie, a coach runs three times a week carrying the Mails and Passengers. The distance between St. Cloud and Fort Abercrombie is about 169 miles and is performed in three days, the stage stopping in the interval at Sauk Centre and Pomme de Terre where wayside houses exist, the accommodation at which cannot I believe be truly extolled. All along the route, at intervals varying from fifteen to twenty-five miles, stations are erected in connection with the line of coaches and horses are changed. Settlements are gradually and rapidly extending well and a considerable population lives along the track.

The Red River of the North is the boundary between the State of Minnesota and the Territory of Dakotah. Fort Abercrombie being built on the western bank of the stream, is therefore in Dakotah. It was a prominent point in the operations of the American troops during this Sioux campaign of 1862 and 1863. Situated on the elevated bank of the river the vast prairie stretch away west from it as far as the horizon. A considerable number of settlers are already located on the eastern or Minnesota side.

Between Fort Abercrombie and Fort Garry, when the steamboat is running, it is necessary only to procure a passage in a waggon or cart as far as Georgetown or Troy Point, which is a considerable distance further down stream, and the journey thence can be undertaken in the steamboat. But when the latter is not running, horses, mules or oxen with carts and servants must be procured at Fort Abercrombie and individual parties must make their own arrangements for reaching the settlement. The distance overland between Forts Abercrombie and Garry is about 250 or 300 miles. In consequence of the intricate sinuosities of the stream the distance by water is very much greater indeed. The mail runs between the two places in six days running time. Two of these days are occupied in traversing the seventy miles over which the line runs through British Territory between Pembina and Fort Garry.

The above is a description of the Mail and Passenger mode of travel by which the whole distance between St. Paul and Fort Garry may be accomplished in ten days running time.[*] I shall now attempt a description of the Freight traffic between the two places.

Two thousand Red River Carts, of which perhaps fifteen hundred make a

---

[*] This estimate is quite optimistic—it took Hargrave himself considerably longer in 1861 to make this journey.

second trip, are employed on this road. They now go only as far as St. Cloud to which point goods are brought to meet them by rail. The track is a mere line formed by the passing vehicles. On that portion of it traversed by the stage coaches between St. Cloud and Abercrombie the worst parts of the road are "corduroyed" or improved by having a roadway of faggots placed transversely across them. The jolting over these parts is tremendous. Between Fort Abercrombie and Fort Garry no attempt has been made to improve the ground, which in wet seasons, is so bad as to compel vehicles to keep far out on the prairie from the river where the ground is on a higher level. This system compels the traveller to carry his own wood and water over long traverses of country. It is practised however only in very wet springs. The ordinary track is provided with rude bridges across the more difficult streams and creeks, tributaries of the Red River which it crosses. Between Fort Abercrombie and Georgetown the track runs along the east bank of the Red River. At the latter place there is a Ferry boat, which takes the traffic across the stream and the route thence forward to Fort Garry runs along the western bank.

The Red River and its tributaries are skirted with a belting of wood, but on the prairie there are no trees. Nothing is to be seen save a sea of plains stretching away to the remote horizon. The whole country is luxuriantly covered with grass, and over a great part of it, the scenery is so fine as to have obtained for it the name of "Park Region." This is in Minnesota. The Landscape in Dakotah is less picturesque.

The Red River cart is a vehicle peculiar to the country and well adapted to meet the exigencies of a journey over the Plains. It is entirely formed of wood without any iron about it. Should any part of it give way it can be at once repaired with a piece of wood from the nearest grove. A hatchet, an auger, a knife and a handsaw are the tools necessary for its formation and repair. With these, so far as breakages are concerned the driver is independent of the accidents of the road. The most difficult part of the structure to make are the wheels which are composed of wooden segments. The cart, apart from these is a mere light box balanced on the axle. It is drawn by a horse or an ox, the former generally in the case of a party travelling "light," the latter in the transport of heavy freights. The load is about eight hundred pounds in weight, and is drawn by only one animal. Twenty or twenty-five miles per day is considered a fair journey for heavy ox carts.

These vehicles generally travel in large brigades, and are managed by three men to each party of ten carts. The duties of the drivers comprehend harnessing and unharnessing the animals, hoppling them, and seeing them properly fed and watered. Considerable dexterity is also occasionally required to guide them through the miry swamps, and unbridged water courses on the way. The night camp is a feature of Prairie travel, with its blazing circles of fires, its rows of carts arranged so as to serve the purposes of tents, and its groups of oxen and horses grazing round the site. Each ox is provided with a bell attached to its neck, the tinkling of which proclaims its whereabouts, and prevents losses from straying or wandering among the thickets and bushes.

The foregoing is a description of the distinctive vehicle of heavy traffic used in the Settlement. The Americans use waggons drawn by mules or oxen, which can be purchased by incomers at St. Paul. The cart can of course only be obtained here.

The question of future freight and passenger traffic between this country and Canada being an important one, and containing much of a suggestive nature in its details, I shall recur to it on a future occasion.

Of current events there is but little to relate. Colonel Dennis has laid down his "Meridian Line," so far as the Settlement, and is carrying it north I believe as far as Shoal Lake. Having finished that operation he will run a line westward from Fort Garry to a place called Portage La Prairie, about sixty miles up the Assiniboine, the soil round which is particularly favourable for agricultural Townships and lots will there be laid off.

Immigrants still drop in, a few at a time. Reports of a well founded character speaks of the advent of another newspaper to be named the "Red River Pioneer" to be conducted by Mr. William Caldwell, who for a number of years conducted the "Nor'-Wester." For various reasons this paper is welcomed as likely to be useful.

Reports have just reached the Settlement of an unfortunate occurrence among the people employed in making the Fort Garry section of the Red River and Thunder Bay road. A number of the labourers employed on the works, it appears, demanded payment from Mr. Snow, the Superintendent, on account of time during which that gentleman considered they had been "off work." On his refusal they are said to have attacked him, and after having undergone very expert treatment, carried so far as blows, he acceded to their demands under protest. He came to headquarters, and demanded assistance from the authorities, who have sent constables to the spot to apprehend the offenders. They are said to be twenty in number, chiefly deserters from the American army, some of them very reckless characters.* We have as yet, of course, only the one side of the story, but it is said Mr. Snow's life was threatened, pistols being pointed at him, measures taken after tying him to have him thrown into a stream. The result of the investigation I shall record in my next. Meanwhile you will please remember it has not yet taken place, and the above is merely the version currently believed.

EDITOR'S NOTE

[The *Nor'-Wester's* large printing press (a Hoe-Washington Super-Royal Model Press) was lost in a fire in 1865, and was replaced by a far inferior press. More detail on the newspaper is provided in Charles Mair's letter to the Montreal *Gazette* of 11 August 1869, printed in the newspaper on 11 October:

> The peculiar institution of the village is, of course, the *Nor'-Wester* newspaper, which was started eleven years ago by Messrs. Buckingham and Coldwell. Subsequently Mr. James Ross, afterwards of the Toronto *Globe* staff, was associated in the management, but in a year or two he, together with Mr. Buckingham, sold out to Mr. Coldwell and Doctor Schultz, who ran the paper conjointly until the following year, when the office was burned to the ground. At this juncture the future of the lively little sheet appeared ominously dark and doubtful. Nothing was left to the owners but the wreck of their press and a mass of fused type which, having done duty in hebdomodally goring the Hudson's Bay Company, were at length sold to the plain hunters to shoot buffalo.
>
> The Doctor, however, a man of great vigor and energy, determined to restore the concern once more to life and usefulness. He bought out Mr. Caldwell's rights, refurnished the office and issued the paper on his own account, and in the Canadian interest, until it became the property of the present owner, W.R.

---

* The men working on road construction were not American deserters but Canadians.

Bown, in July, 1868. A great deal of credit attached itself to every one connected with this paper, from first to last, but more especially of late years when, attacking the policy which kept this great country from Canada, excluded settlement, by invisible but powerful restrictions, it laid itself open to, and incurred, the wrath and malice and persecution of the Hudson's Bay Company and their supporters. By its persistent and keen attacks upon the grand monopoly, and by its honest and trustworthy descriptions of the country itself, it fairly opened the eyes of the outer world, and formed, in fine, the entering wedge which released the hold of an association which would have secluded this country from the world to the end of time. All the printing materials had to be transported on carts for 500 miles; the labour required to produce the printed sheet was difficult to obtain and costly; the circulation in the settlement itself very limited, and the advertising patronage nothing.

Yet all this expense and difficulty was encountered by its managers without hope or promise of reward, and week after week the little journal issued with almost constant regularity, advertising to all Canada what she had in this country, at a weekly and considerable loss to its thoroughly Canadian and Canada loving proprietors.

A paper which can be so stout of spirit as this deserves success and a long lease of life. The *Nor'-Wester* will probably have both. It has earned the thanks and good will of every true Canadian, and it is to be hoped that hereafter it will take its stand as the paper of the people, and as the exponent of the national life and sentiment in the North West.]

# J.J. HARGRAVE

## 9 OCTOBER 1869

[This letter from J.J. Hargrave, mainly dealing with future transportation needs of Red River, demonstrates the extent to which the settlement was familiar with both the arguments and the details involved in Canadian westward expansion. Printed in the *Montreal Herald and Daily Commercial Gazette*, 2 November 1869.]

Red River Settlement,
British North America,
9th Oct., 1869

The ultimate aim and object of the promoters of a Canadian Pacific Railway, I understand to be the construction of a through system of Rail communication between Halifax and New Westminster.

That portion of the scheme, extending from the former place to Montreal, has been provided for by the machinery of the Intercolonial and Grand Trunk Railways. Between Montreal and the Pacific coast the work has still to be carried out, and the line, I presume, may generally be expected to run up the Ottawa Valley by Nipissing along the northern shore of Lakes Huron and Superior, over the height of land to Red River, Edmonton, the Yellow Head Pass, and the sea coast. The distance is great, the work most arduous, and the time necessary for its accomplishment probably extremely long. If the Lower provinces of the Dominion are really in earnest about sending a large portion of their people to settle in those newly acquired lands, means must be devised to bridge over the rugged wilderness which intervenes between them at no distant day.

The route through the States offers an easy channel of communication for goods and passengers. So far as St. Cloud traffic is carried on by steam and rail, and on the 1st July next it is confidently believed that the railroad will have been finished as far as a point on the Red River of the North. Breckenridge is the one at present spoken of, but I am led to understand there is a possibility that Frog Point, a spot about fifty miles further down the river, may be preferred as the point of intersection. The advantage of the latter would be that, whereas Breckenridge is practically at a great distance from Fort Garry; Frog Point being immediately at the head of Red River navigation, is virtually in its vicinity. Between the latter place and Fort Garry a steamboat might run all Summer, even during seasons of very low water; the system of communication would therefore be complete, and the Pacific Railroad would at once reap the benefit of the large and important traffic through this place. Whereas between Frog Point and Breckenridge a gap would exist, rendering transhipment necessary, and probably in a great measure nullifying the benefits offered by a Railroad. There is also the possibility that, though adhering to their original scheme of carrying their main branch across the river at Breckenridge, the Directors of the Pacific Railroad may run a branch from that place as far as the frontier post of Pembina. This might be performed at comparatively small expense, there being no material difficulties whatever to be surmounted on the way.

The route by steam to the head of Lake Superior and thence through the State of Minnesota to the Red River, has been mentioned, and I believe already tried as a good and short one to be used by Canadians coming west. As yet it is a rough and untravelled way, and is open to the objection that passing as some of it does through portions of Minnesota, of magnificent agricultural capabilities, it might be the means of tacitly, but eloquently dissuading immigrants more sensitive to ease than feelings of Nationality from coming any further. It must not be forgotten that vast quantities of unsettled land intervene between the British Settlements and the American frontier of civilized life.

The Canadian Government not yet having published any sketch of its intentions with regard to the detailed mode in which it will conduct and promote immigration, it is impossible for any one not in its confidence to foresee how it is to grapple with what appears a most perplexing problem. The certain means by which the feat could be accomplished would be the immediate construction of a railroad between Lake Superior and Red River. The physical difficulties in the way of such an enterprise require an expenditure of much time and of a sum of money roughly estimated at twenty millions of dollars. This sacrifice accepted, the most serious part of the difficulty would I presume disappear.

An amount of freight which may be roughly estimated at between 1,500 and 1,800 tons is annually conveyed in carts between Red River Settlement and St. Cloud, the cost of transport being 16s. per hundred pounds and the distance perhaps five hundred miles. Of this amount the vast bulk is imported and consists of all kinds of manufactured English, American and Canadian merchandise. There are as yet only a few parties who export on any scale, and the articles exported are Robes and Furs. Generally speaking therefore the carts make their out going trip light, and depend for profits on the return tour.

The bulk of the freight carts visit St. Paul early in Spring and late in Autumn. The Spring "brigades" leave the Settlement as early as the snow has disappeared from the Prairies and the grass has grown long enough to be of service as feeding for the cattle. The Fall "brigade" starts so as to arrive on its return immediately before the closing in of winter. Between these dates all the imports have to be made. It will therefore be seen that the opening up of a route which would remain open all the year round would exercise a most serious influence on the whole system of importation, and by decreasing the time during which stock must be on hand, would tend to lower the price of goods.

With regard to the portion of the road west from Red River it is yet comparatively little travelled. Loaded carts take 35 days to make the trip between Fort Garry and Carlton in the course of which journey they cross 3 rivers, viz.; the Little Saskatchewan, the Assiniboine and the South Branch of the Saskatchewan.[1] Between Carlton and Fort Pitt 8 days are occupied. The North branch of the Saskatchewan is crossed in a boat at the same place, and the road continues on the same side all the way to Fort Pitt. The road is good, but there are two, and sometimes three small streams to be crossed on this stretch of the way. At Fort Pitt the river is crossed on a boat, and the road runs along the south bank to Edmonton. This stage occupies ten days and two small rivers have to be crossed. The track generally runs over good grounds.

Between Edmonton and Jaspers House the road is very rough and occupies 19 days. Thence to Tete Jaune Cache includes the pass across the Rocky Mountains which may be got over in 9 days. From the Cache to the Pacific, there is not I believe any existing means of communication, and parties must rely on their our [own] resources to cut out a track for themselves.[2]

The entire road between Red River and the Mountains is a mere cart track, used by the hunters and the freighters in the Company's service. The ground is [?] ever so level that it is only at rivers and creeks that any difficulty is experienced.

The most serious obstacles to be encountered in the regions through which the overland route will run, will, I expect arise from the hostility of the Indians, the scarcity of fuel and the ravages of Prairie fires. The Saskatchewan valley is crowded with tribes of Blackfeet, whose habits are so warlike that the utmost caution is necessary in their dealings with them even on the part of the Company's traders. These Indians would most certainly give trouble in the event of their lands being invaded; and under any circumstances, liberal subsidies will be necessary.

Fuel and Lumber exist only on the banks of streams. Long stretches of prairie along which the track will run, are quite destitute of it. Water is also very scarce in many places. Prairie fires make great ravages but these will cease as the country gets settled up.

It is reported here that the first operations preparatory to opening up the country will consist in erecting a telegraph, the portion of which between St. Paul and Red River will be completed at an early day.[3] I presume the object of this is that the work may be carried across the continent. The line necessary for the purpose has for some years past been lying here, at York Factory and at Victoria V[ancouver] I[sland]—A mere telegraph will be at the mercy of the Indians and will run considerable risk of damage from fires. Of course it is to be presumed that the portion of the work between St. Cloud and this will suffer only from the latter evil, the Sioux having been pretty generally subdued in Minnesota.

The remedy against both evils towards the West is, I believe, the carrying of a railroad as soon as possible. It will protect the telegraph, and convey fuel from places where it is plentiful to those where it is required. The engineering difficulties as far as the mountains are very small. The portion of the way between Canada and this place is as already stated, very rugged; but in the mean time it is confidently expected that the railroad through Minnesota will reach this place in a very few years. The direct Lake Superior Line need not necessarily be completed before the western portion is commenced. The most serious difficulty experienced in the construction of the St. Paul and St. Cloud portion of the route was I understand the transport of the <u>iron</u> up the Mississippi before the connection by rail had been made between the former city and Lacrosse.

Of passing events there is as usual but little of importance to communicate. The reports of a disturbance among the men employed under Mr. Snow on the Canada road have been confirmed. The parties accused were apprehended without any trouble, and after a preliminary examination before the local Justices, were committed for trial at the November Quarter Sessions. They have been admitted to bail. Meanwhile the works will suffer to a certain extent from delay.

A more serious matter for residents in the village of Winnipeg is a tendency which has been of late making itself felt on the part of certain individuals unknown to fire raising. Some weeks ago a fire broke out in a very unaccountable way which ended in the complete destruction of a house in process of erection in the village. Again within a few days past an outhouse connected with the Company's store in the village took fire and was burned down. During the past week on one evening two deliberate attempts were made at fire raising, the combustibles being found on the respective localities.

The result of the first of the above fires was the formation of a fire brigade, the Company providing the engine from Fort Garry. They are indebted to the exertions of the Fire Company for preventing the conflagration spreading from the outhouse to their store.

The result of the two latest attempts has been the formation of a vigilance Committee, several members of which watch nightly in the village. The inhabitants indeed have a very serious stake in this matter. The houses are all of wood, and so closely built together that were a fire once to get headway nothing could stop it. Indeed the escapes which have been already made seem providential. A very light increase in the force of the wind in some cases, or in its direction in others would have proved destructive to the majority of houses in the place.

It may interest some of your readers to know that the Hon. Mr. Howe has just arrived this morning in the Settlement.

# J.J. HARGRAVE

## 16 OCTOBER 1869

[This letter, written by J.J. Hargrave in mid-October of 1869, gives evidence of the slowness with which even those on the spot understood the developing crisis in the settlement. As Hargrave suggests, information about Canada's plans for Red River was only just reaching the region, and, as of this writing, Hargrave obviously had not yet understood the extent to which the several developments he describes were related to one another. Printed in the *Montreal Herald and Daily Commercial Gazette*, 4 November 1869.]

Red River Settlement,
British North America,
16 Oct., 1869

Newspaper and other reports have reached us lately in considerable numbers relative to the Council to be appointed temporarily to assist Mr. Macdougall until his Government here shall have settled into permanent form. The prevalent idea appears to be that this Board shall consist of delegates to be sent from each of the older provinces of the Dominion, and possibly one or two individuals of local reputation.[*]

A glance at the history and composition of the body which has hitherto been known as the Council of Assinboin may not be uninteresting in connection with this subject. Previous to 1835 the personal influence of the richer people in the colony was the principal means by which order was maintained among the small and scattered community, while the unimportant and rare instances in which disputes waxed so high as to require the adjudication of an independent authority for their settlement, were met by an informal judgment obtained from the resident Governor.

Early in 1835 however the frequent recurrence of serious offences by which the rights of property had been invaded, necessitated the institution of some recognised means for the maintenance of public order. The

---

[*] Hargrave obviously did not expect much local involvement.

Hudson's Bay Company accordingly issued the necessary authority, and on 12th February of the above year the first meeting of the new body was held under the presidency of Sir George Simpson, the Governor of Rupert's Land.[1]

The board consisted of members nominated and appointed by the Company, which issued a Commission to each in virtue of which he became a Councillor. The system of popular representation has never existed at Red River. The rule followed by the Company in their nomination of parties to seats at the Council Board appears to have been, to select the principal men of influence connected with each of the leading sections of the colony—French half-breed, Scotch and Episcopalian. The Bishops of Rupert's Land and St. Boniface have always been members of Council and some of the more influential clergymen have also held Commissions.

The number of members has never been fixed but has generally ranged from twelve to twenty. The chairman or President is the local "Governor of Assiniboin" who however is superseded by the Governor of Rupert's Land when present. For some years past these two offices have been filled by the same individual.

The legal adviser of the Council is the Recorder of Rupert's Land. This official is Chairman of the Court of Quarter Sessions which sits in February, May, August, and November, and has jurisdiction in cases from any quarter in Rupert's Land. On the Bench he is accompanied by any Justices of the Peace who may choose to attend. These latter are always members of Council, and receive their nomination and commission as Justices from the Hudson's Bay Company. They have always been a hardworking and deserving body of public functionaries, and have fulfilled difficult duties in a most creditable way.

The jurisdiction of the Council of Assiniboin is confined within a district extending in a circle of fifty miles radius round Fort Garry as a centre. Beyond this limit the commissions of its members do not extend, and the only magistrates are the officers in the Hudson's Bay Company's fur trade, who meet annually at the Council of Rupert's Land, the President of which is the Governor of that territory, who is, in virtue of his office, the representative of the Board of the Company in London.[*]

---

[*] The settlement at Portage la Prairie was outside the boundaries of the courts of Red River.

Although this latter Council is superior to that of Assiniboin, the instances have been very rare in which it has exercised any control over the affairs more immediately pertaining to the latter, which has, ever since its constitution, been left to exercise an independent authority within the limited sphere of its jurisdiction.

It has its stated session, and is convened, whenever anything of public importance calls for its interference by the Governor of Assiniboin, who, through the Clerk of Council, notifies each of its members of his intention to hold a meeting. Its members receive no compensation for their services, and the position of councillor is merely honorary. The President and Recorder, as a matter of course, are paid officials, but are not so on account of holding seats at this Board.

The subjects on which it has hitherto been called to legislate are generally speaking of but a trivial character relating to the internal management of the colony. It has met the moderate demands of a pecuniary nature made by the public service on its resources, by a Customs duty of four per cent ad valorum levied on imports. This is the only tax, except those connected with liquor selling, which has ever been imposed on the inhabitants of the colony.

The Council sits with closed doors, and the public is not admitted to hear its deliberations. These circumstances, along with the fact that the four per cent duty [is] levied, has given rise to a good deal of misunderstanding. It has been represented to the public by certain parties, that the secret nature of the deliberations favours the "Star Chamber" while "taxation without representation" is essentially un-English. These statements have always been received at their true value in the colony itself; but it is to be feared that to outsiders, they have conveyed a very incorrect impression of the truth.

The principal part of the amount raised by the Customs tax was, of course, accrued from the imports of the Hudson's Bay Company, which are very large. The disbursements have been on account of road repairs, and salaries of petty magistrates, constables, and others. The latter must be acknowledged to be on a very low scale.

The members of Council have always been the leading residents in the settlements, and have included those whose wealth and stake in it were greatest. They have always commanded the confidence of their fellow residents, and had the system of representation been in force, there can be little doubt that for the most part the same persons who have held seats under the existing mode of appointment would have been returned.

Of course, it is not to be denied that the system of Government just sketched out was applicable only to a very elementary condition of things. The state of society to meet the wants of which it was devised having undergone of late years the most serious modification, it is fit and right that a rule more in conformity with the new order of things should be organised. The thinking portion of this people hails in the scheme of the Canadian officials the system required. It is, however, unlikely, for several reasons, that any Government can be as powerful as can be desired, unless a military or other disciplined force be stationed here, or an easily travelled road be opened up connecting Red River with the other Provinces of Canada.

It has been urged against the present Council that its members have suffered themselves to be too much swayed by the Company. It is well known here that this is incorrect, but it is undeniable that the wealthiest and most influential members have been in some cases, for a great many years, officers in the service. This has risen from the circumstances that the Fur trade has been the only one in which profitable employment in this country has been possible. Hitherto, no appreciable amount of capital has been sunk in any enterprise except the Fur trade.

I have enlarged so fully on this subject that my space is almost already covered.

The principal event of the past week has been the advent of the Hon. Joseph Howe, who has taken up his headquarters during the term of his residence at the principal hotel in the village of Winnipeg, kept by an enterprising German named Emmerling. Mr. Howe has occupied his time in visiting all the places of interest in the colony, and making himself practically acquainted with the leading features of business and life in it. He has been, I believe, particularly successful in smoothing down disagreeable feelings roused in the minds of residents who, not seeing very clearly before them, and misled by a variety of causes in their estimate of the changes now pending, have eagerly availed themselves of the opportunity afforded by his presence of learning something of the wishes or ideas of Canadian men in office regarding the relations between them and the present population of Rupert's Land.*

---

* Joseph Howe did not talk to Louis Riel or any of the Métis spokesmen.

Although Mr. Howe's visit has been at least ostensibly of an unofficial nature, and all his interviews with people have been in private, I believe the feeling is general that it has been exceedingly useful and well timed, and will probably lead to increased confidence in the success of the opening enterprise.

I regret to have again to report a disagreeable affair which has occurred between some French half-breeds and Canadian Surveyors. In the execution of the system of operations contemplated by Colonel Dennis it became necessary for a party of men under his command to run a line across the property of some settlers. They were warned to desist by a party of half-breeds, who objected to their passing over their lands. A complaint was lodged by the Surveyors with the authorities at Fort Garry, who remonstrated with the offenders as urgently as they could, but I regret to say, without effect. No act of violence was committed, but the operations immediately contemplated by the party when interrupted cannot be carried out.[2] The alteration necessitated by this event in the designs of Colonel Dennis is, I believe, not great. This survey of the settled portion of the colony will proceed and be going on during winter. Very considerable and satisfactory progress has already been made in the preliminary measures relative to the laying out of that portion of the country lying between the United States frontier and the settled parts around Fort Garry. By an ingenious system of boundary making, this region will at an early period be divided into townships and laid off for immediate occupation.

The arrival of Governor Macdougall is the event to which eyes now begin to be turned. It is reported that the preparations are being made by certain of the settlers to receive him with some ceremony. It is understood, however, that he will arrive before his commission has become operative, and consequently will not enter on his official career until the expiration of some time unknown. Many questions of importance wait his consideration. Probably the most pressing in its demands will be the Indian difficulty with the cognate one concerning the treatment of the half-breeds. Should Mr. Macdougall succeed in settling these troublesome questions on a basis of justice, he will have deserved well of his country.

EDITOR'S NOTE

[In addition to McDougall, the Canadian government appointed A.N. Richards as prospective attorney-general, J.A.N. Provencher as potential secretary to McDougall, Alexander Begg of Caithness as future collector of customs, Captain Donald R. Cameron as future military attaché, and Major James Wallace as a councillor. The *Herald* elsewhere described them as "six Canadian adventurers."

In June of 1857, over 500 local residents of Red River signed a petition calling for the extension of Canadian laws and political institutions to the settlement (see Toronto *Globe*, 12 June 1857). Hargrave's comment regarding the perception of the Council, therefore, is not entirely true.]

# J.J. HARGRAVE

## 22 OCTOBER 1869

[At this date, Hargrave was still unable to believe that the Métis would actually manage to mount a resistance to Governor McDougall and the Canadians. Printed in the *Montreal Herald and Daily Commercial Gazette*, 13 November 1869.]

Red River Settlement,
British North America,
22 October 1869

The only approach in this colony to anything of the nature even of a village is the village of Winnipeg, situated about half a mile north from Fort Garry, the intervening space being occupied by the Hudson['s] Bay Company's Land Reserve which is a large quantity of ground round the Fort, lying between the Red River and the Assiniboine which unite at this place.

For many years it had been a subject on which opinions varied whether a town of any size was likely ever to exist in the colony, and another, where, in the event of such an event coming to pass, would be the favoured site. In 1862 the first house of the village was built by Mr. Henry McKenney, Sheriff of Assiniboine. The spot selected by Mr. Henry McKenney was on the frontier of the Company's Land Reserve at the place where the tracks along the Red River and the Assiniboine intersected each other. The former is the highway along the principal farming and grain producing portions of the colony while the latter is the one traversed by the half-breed hunting population on their way to the Plains, to the West of the Settlement where the buffalo hunts are carried on. The locality selected was therefore a central one with respect to the existing trade of the country. It was, however, unfavourable as being the centre of a district reported by the oldest inhabitants to have been little better than a morass for several weeks during every Spring within their recollection. It was certainly situated at a considerable lower level than the ground between it and the river, which accordingly prevented the free flow of the melting snows into a channel by which they would have been carried away, and detained them for a long time in the form of a stagnant mass. The distance intervening between it and either of the rivers was also a serious objection to the site, no one having previously ventured to build at so great a distance back from what had until then formed the sole source of water supply to the colony.

It was universally believed that the cellars of the new establishment would be filled with marshy water during the spring months, while its remote situation with reference to the river would prevent its inhabitants procuring water fitted for use, and the state of the roads about it would render it practically inaccessible to customers. Yet in the face of these dreaded obstacles Mr. McKenney persevered, and before the winter of 1862-63 had completed a long narrow wooden edifice, the lower or ground story of which was fitted up as a shop, while the upper portion was furnished as a dwelling house.

The forebodings of the incredulous have happily not been realized to anything like the degree apprehended. Since the date to which I refer a succession of dry seasons has taken place; and although the part of the highway passing through the village of Winnipeg is undoubtedly one of the most impassable during the transition period from Winter to Spring, men with business on hand, fail not to traverse it on account of its defects, and an artificial improvement on the causeway has of late years been carried out with satisfactory results.

Mr. McKenney having set the example, a number of other settlers followed in his footsteps, cautiously at first, but of late in considerable numbers each season. The highway is now lined for a considerable distance with houses on both sides and several transverse pathways or "streets" run towards the river. There is no general plan of building, and each builder suits his fancy or convenience with regard to frontage. The consequence is that the whole village is a mere jumble of separate huts and houses, the grand feature of which is the highway which runs through their midst. Along it, the principal places of business are erected. All the houses are of wood, some of logs and others of frame work. Of late an attempt has been made to introduce brickwork, but with doubtful effect, as it is by no means certain that the clay found in this neighbourhood is very suitable for bricking &c.

The places of business in Winnipeg are stores, in which merchandise of all kinds is exposed for sale. In only a very few instances are shops set apart for dealing in any one line of business. Liquor selling is here and there carried on in a house devoted entirely to the trade. In fact the great bulk of the licenses issued in the Settlement are held by parties residing in the village. Watch-mending, harness-making, cutter-building and tailoring are done by tradesmen in Winnipeg, but there is I believe still great room for the investment of moderate capital in all these channels of industry.

There are several hotels or Inns. Of these, the one of most pretension is that kept by Mr. George Emmerling, a German American. The others are on a more humble scale. Without any disparagement to any of these it may I think be stated that there is still vast room for reasonable improvement and there can be little doubt that a large and tolerably well appointed hotel in the village would prove a paying investment to any man practically conversant with the business, who possessed the means and inclination to work it out. I cannot doubt that the experiment will be tried at an early date. Two billiard tables exist and are kept in pretty regular employment at "the George." The first of these importations was made about two years ago.

No less than three churches exist in the little village. One is that of the Revd. George Young, Methodist Missionary who arrived about a year since. The Presbyterian one is occupied by the Revd. Mr. Black, whose headquarters are about five miles further down the Red River, at Frog Plain, in the heart of the Scotch Settlement. The third is that of the Holy Trinity, occupied by Archdeacon McLean, incumbent of St. John's Cathedral. The two latter are as yet mere "Preaching Stations," their respective incumbents living at a distance from them.

A thriving Steam Mill is kept in constant employment at Winnipeg. Of Steam Grist Mills there are altogether I believe seven in the colony, two of which are the property of the Company, while the remainder are owned by private individuals. Of these, three are capable of being turned to account as Saw Mills.

Regarding the employment found for the latter it is limited by the small amount of lumber procurable in the neighbourhood of the colony. Hitherto the public wants have been supplied by wood which, cut on the higher tributaries of the Red River and Assiniboine, has been floated down to the spot at which it has been required. These limited supplies have however been found quite inadequate to the demand and the attention of timber speculators has of late years been turned towards Lake Winnipeg and its affluents, as the theatre of their future operations. The difficulty of transport from the latter regions is created by the fact that the passage thence to the colony is *up stream*. A Tug Steamer would meet this disadvantage, and it is reported that some such vessel will be placed on the river in the ensuing Spring, with more direct reference to the trade between the village of Winnipeg and the upper reaches of the Red River in Minnesota.

The distance between the village and the mouth of the Red River is about forty miles. With regard to the other difficulties than that of transport which hedge the local lumber trade, I hope to have a good deal to say by an early future opportunity. Meanwhile I may remark that about one year ago Mr. Henry McKenney, already mentioned in this letter, made a very important experiment. Having built a schooner and imported the machinery for a saw mill, that gentleman selected a spot on the eastern coast of Lake Winnipeg considerably to the south of the narrow part of that Lake called "Dog Head" on which he erected his mill. Throughout the whole of last winter Mr. McKenney's people were occupied with cutting and sawing lumber, which, after being transported into the settlement by the schooner on the opening up of last season's navigation, has found a ready sale at about £8 sterling per thousand feet. As to the quality of the article I am unable at present to speak; but a late sale, reported on a very reliable common rumours to have amounted to £1,000 sterling, made to a Canadian party, would appear to bear favourable testimony. However, I am bound to say that a great deal even of the best lumber hitherto used in the Colony, is of such a quality as would be condemned by Canadian tradesmen, consisting of spruce and bastard pine. Mr. McKenney, in the course of his winter operations, completely cleared the neighbourhood of the spot on which he had erected his mill of all large and valuable trees, and he has I believe, been compelled to change the site of his works to a place near Fort Alexander at the mouth of the Winnipeg river at which timber cutting has never hitherto been practised.

Next to wood the supply of good water will be a subject for grave consideration to the future Red River population. The rivers have hitherto been the great source of supply. In summer they are extremely muddy, and receiving, as they do, a vast quantity of sewage, are positively revolting. This will be understood when the circumstance is considered, that instead of depositing the infrequent cleanings of their cow houses and stables as manure upon their lands, the people here lay them in unsightly heaps upon the river bank close to their own doors. The melting snow in spring or plentiful showers in Summer, wash away these mounds into the common receptacle of all impurities—the river.

The water in Lake Winnipeg is admirable, but being forty miles distant is beyond our reach. A few wells have been dug. One at Fort Garry is about fifty feet deep, but its water is not used, being considered undrinkable. In the village of Winnipeg and elsewhere there are also wells—but the water, though perfectly fit for use, has at some seasons a very perceptible mineral taste. This is observable, I believe, chiefly in the summer. Curiously enough, animals seem highly to appreciate it and drink it with avidity in preference to river water.

The state of the labour market here is very remarkable. Parties requiring to employ servants cannot get them, save at the most exorbitant prices. Twelve shillings per diem is not an exceptional amount for short periods. It was, I believe, the amount paid men who recently were employed to dig certain excavations in the village for the apparatus connected with the Fire Brigade lately formed here. Ten shillings per diem is a common rate of pay to rough Carpenters. The reason of this is that the present local population will not work as hired labourers for short periods. It is expected that employment for this class of people will continue to be plentiful.

A similar inflation is observable in the price required for land by proprietors in the village and its environs, rates varying from thirty to fifty pounds sterling per square chain have been paid by purchasers of ground in the village. The reason of this appears to be the cramped space occupied by Winnipeg. The Hudson's Bay Company's Reserve prevents it spreading in the direction to which it naturally tends—towards Fort Garry, and the community seems to stand in need of some enterprising man to give the example of spreading backwards towards the Plain. In this direction the amount of ground available is unlimited, and so soon as it begins to become used for building purposes, prices will fall.

With regard to current events, I have to record that the Hon. Joseph Howe left the settlement on the 18th inst., on his return to Canada. Some gentlemen who were of his party on the inward journey, have remained behind him and start for Canada today.

Mr. Macdougall's arrival is expected daily, and is at present the occasion of some considerable excitement. For some time past, rumours have been current expressive of deep dissatisfaction felt by the French half-breed community in view of approaching political changes, which cannot fail most seriously to affect their interests, but in which they have had no voice. This dissatisfaction has at length taken a form which, if it contains a large portion of the ridiculous, is likely also to have serious consequences. A number of half-breeds, the leaders of whom are of the more intelligent and respectable of the community, have posted themselves at places of the highway from Pembina with the declared intention of meeting and talking with the Governor, and in the event of his refusing to comply with certain demands they have to make, they express themselves determined to oppose his entrance into the Colony, or, to use their own expression, "to turn him back." The demands they have to make seem to me so ridiculous that I shall not report them until they have been actually made.

People along the route refuse to allow these men to enter their houses, and it is possible the cold weather now commencing may induce them to abandon their absurd design. Meanwhile they have been two entire days at their stations on the highway, along which it is said they have erected barriers. They expose every new arrival to a careful scrutiny, and yesterday they are said to have stopped a German American tailor immigrant, who had some difficulty in persuading them he was not the man they sought.

Settlers and Canadians have a talk of getting up a counter demonstration to this, by going in a large body to meet Mr. Macdougall, and save him from any temporary inconvenience to which he might be exposed by the conduct of these people in an uninhabited country at the close of the travelling season across the Plains. Should these conflicting schemes come to any serious results I shall duly advise you of it.

EDITOR'S NOTE

[Charles Mair, in a letter published in the Montreal *Gazette* on 11 October 1869, wrote of Winnipeg:

Winnipeg (an Indian word signifying "foul water") is a wooden village, the houses being all frame or log buildings, either clap-boarded or lath-and-plastered. The place, so far, is laid out very irregularly, and, if left to its own devices, will end in a stupendous series of *cul de sacs*. The houses angle every way, and have no architectural beauty whatever. They are big, ugly and comfortable. The latter condition, which has been fairly attained, atoning in scanty measure for their utter lack of symmetry. Around it stretches the prairie in every direction, broken alone by the woods on the river, or by an occasional clump of red or grey willows.

Such, then, is the village of Winnipeg, the product of adventurous and enterprising free-traders, and the rendezvous of trappers, half-breeds and Indians from all points of the compass. It is interesting—singularly so—as an evidence of what may be effected by energy and enterprise under circumstances the most unpromising and difficult. Only in a prairie country could such a thing be possible as a comfortable and prosperous village, cut off from the nearest railway by a wilderness of hundreds of miles, and supported entirely by the wild, irregular and engrossing pursuits of the north.

Further details of the barricade from Pembina were supplied by "Nor'West" in a letter to the Montreal *Herald* of 22 November 1869:

Your correspondent found the insurgents camped at a point bearing the not very mellifluous name of Stinking River. The road at this point is laid through a belt of cotton-wood and from side to side of the wood, across the road is laid a barricade of fencing timber with a gate in the centre. The gate is shut and before the barricade are facing two sentries with muskets on their shoulders. One waggon is told to halt and a spokesman comes forward who enquires in French the nature of your correspondent's business in their country. He is very civil and we tell him. He seems to be satisfied but should like to see a letter with your correspondent's name. We have a card and hand it to him and he gives the sentry the word to pass us. Before leaving, however, we enquire as to the force under arms and are told they amount to 100. There is a tent in the wood a few yards from the road, and many of the men are lying there, more are squatted round a blazing camp fire, and a number more are straggling along the road. We ask the spokesman what action they are to take. He says they will have no compromise. The Governor must go back. If he attempts to pass the barricade he will be shot. But will you not hear what he has to say? Yes we will hear what he has to say, but we have made up our minds that he must go back. We will offer him no violence unless he attempts to pass our line. We want to govern ourselves. We will accept of no concessions. He spoke too hard in print in St. Paul. Such were the views I ascertained during a few minutes stay at the camp. On our way here we met a great many going out to join those already there. One man had a seventeen shooter rifle and a seven shooter revolver. Bread, beef, and other supplies are daily sent from this place for their subsistence. There were anxious enquiries as to the Governor's arrival. From what I told them I did not expect to hear of his arrival at Pembina for two or three days. Pembina is the boundary line, and distant 60 miles from their camp. They have selected the Stinking River as it is the only convenient point where a barricade could be erected, and is besides within easy reach of their homes. About two hundred yards on this side of the barricade we found a camp of about 20 half-breeds belonging to the loyal party. This party, I understand, is headed by Mr. Wm. Dease a leading French half-breed and a member of the Council of Assiniboia. He claims to be able to raise a much larger party than those at the barricade, but is in hopes that there will be no occasion for it. Business is in the meantime at a stand still. The leader of the English half-breeds, a very intelligent, influential man, went out yesterday to the camp of the insurgents to reason with them, but has so far been unsuccessful. I hear that the French half-breeds have formed themselves into a republic, and have elected a President and Vice President. The Scotch half-breeds take no part in the quarrel. They are prepared to submit to the new order of things, but seem disinclined to take up arms against their French cousins.

The leader of the English half-breeds may have been James Ross.]

# J.J. HARGRAVE

## 30 OCTOBER 1869

[J.J. Hargrave was still at this point trying to introduce eastern readers to the settlement, although this task was rapidly being overtaken by fast-breaking developments in the insurgency. This letter provides eastern readers with their first detailed description of Louis Riel. Printed in the *Montreal Herald and Daily Commercial Gazette*, 24 November 1869.]

Red River Settlement
30 October 1869

Important among the points of interest, to intending immigrants, is the state of religious facilities and the collateral subject of education.

At present four sections of religious opinion are represented at Red River. The Church of England, the Wesleyan Methodist[,] the Presbyterians, and the Roman Catholics, possess numerous and well attended places of worship, scattered at no great distances apart from end to end of the Colony. The Church of England has been represented in this place since 1821. Missionaries from various of the great Missionary Societies in England, but more especially from the "Church Missionary Society" of London, have since that date resided in the country, and have secured a very strong and well merited hold on the feelings of the existing population.[1] In 1849 a Bishopric having been endowed from a legacy made by a chief factor in the Company's service combined with an annual grant to be paid by that body itself, Dr. Anderson was appointed to the benefice which he held until 1865 when he was succeeded by the present bishop, Dr. Machray. Eleven parishes, each supplied with at least one church, stretching along the Red River and Assiniboine from the Indian Settlement of St. Peter, about twelve miles from Lake Winnipeg, to Portage Laprairie, on the Assiniboine, about sixty-five miles from the confluence between that stream and the Red River at Fort Garry. It is understood that the Portage being one of the most suitable localities for cultivation will be among the earliest settled up by immigrants. The ground included with the above described limits of St. Peter's and Laprairie is that, in other words, extending along the western bank of the Red River and the southern one of the Assiniboine so far as yet settled up. To the South of the confluence between the rivers there are yet no Protestant churches, the local population being Roman Catholic.

The Wesleyan Methodists have as yet been represented in the Colony for only a little more than one year. The Rev. George Young, from Canada, has erected a parsonage on a portion of land granted to him from their reserve about Fort Garry by the Hudson Bay Company, and will doubtless at an early date complete his operations with a suitable and permanent place of worship. Although located at this place as his headquarters, Mr. Young has several preaching stations at various spots throughout the colony, which best suit the convenience of his adherents.

The Presbyterian church has been established since 1850 in the heart of the Scotch Settlement.[2] The Reverend John Black, who arrived about that date, has been since assisted in his work by several clergymen from Canada, who have from time to time resided in the colony. The headquarters of this church is at Kildonan, on the western bank of the Red River, about five miles north from Fort Garry. It possesses also a regularly served preaching station in the village of Winnipeg as well as several others in the Protestant parishes of the settlement.

The Roman Catholic church is that of the French half-breed population, which lives chiefly on both banks of the Red River to the south of its confluence with the Assiniboine, and on the south bank of the latter river. They have been established in the settlement since its formation in 1818, and their priests have penetrated to some of the remotest parts of Rupert's Land, which has been divided into two vast dioceses, comprehending respectively the northern and southern portions of the country.[3]

Bishop Provencher, who arrived at Red River as priest in 1818, was succeeded in his office of Bishop of St. Boniface by the present occupant, Dr. Taché, whose principal residence is in the settlement. The Cathedral of St. Boniface is situated on the eastern bank of the Red River, opposite Fort Garry, and is yet incomplete, its erection having been commenced in 1862, a destructive fire having completely destroyed the original church built on the same site.

While St. Boniface is the headquarters of Catholic operations here, there are a number of smaller establishments scattered up and down the settlement. The whole population attached to this creed number between five and six thousand souls. The ecclesiastical work is conducted by a considerable corps of priests, lay brothers, and a sisterhood of Grey Nuns.[4] The priests belong to the French order of Oblate de Marie l'Immaculée.[5] The whole of the priests in Rupert's Land, with but very few individual exceptions are members of this order.

The foregoing brief sketch of the present position of Church matters in Red River Settlement may show intending immigrants that at any part of the colony at present settled on, church accommodations may be found within a very few miles, connected with any of the leading sects of Christianity.

Respecting Schools, instruction of an exceedingly elementary nature may be obtained at those attached to each of the Protestant parishes. The priests at St. Boniface have a very efficient college at which boarders and day scholars may be entered, and the nuns also conduct a similar institution for girls.[6]

The principal educational institution of the colony, however, is the College of St. John.[7] This establishment was commenced in 1833 by the Revd. John McCallum of the Church of England. It was intended as a school at which the children of officers in the Hudson Bay Company's Service might be educated as those of their rank in life are in other countries. It was exceedingly successful, and men occupying the highest positions at present existing in the country were educated there. Mr. McCallum died in 1849 and the school gradually fell to pieces. The present Bishop of Rupert's Land, on assuming office in 1865, set himself to resuscitate the college.

Under the new arrangements its principal purpose was to act as a training school for theological students. Apart from this, however, a course was inaugurated comprehending the usual studies pursued by boys between the ages of say ten and seventeen years, the principal being Latin, Greek, and Mathematics. The bishop secured as head master of the school the Rev. John McLean, late of London, Ont. This gentleman is Archdeacon of Assiniboia and incumbent of the Cathedral parish of St. John, in which and adjoining the church, the college of which he is warden is situated.

Ever since its renovation in 1866 the school has continued steadily to advance. The bishop himself teaches in it for several hours daily. The Archdeacon, as responsible head master, is assisted by the Rev. Mr. Pritchard, each of these two gentlemen having under his charge a boarding house in connection with the school. The establishment is assisted by a large annual grant from the Church Missionary Society and the Hudson Bay Company has hitherto voted an annual sum of £100 stg. towards its support. Doubtless, as new arrivals crowd in, much advantage will be taken of this well conducted establishment, which will doubtless be greatly enlarged and extended to meet the wants of the times. At present it possesses I believe as many pupils as it can accommodate. The expense of year's residence varies I believe from £25 to £40 sterling.

A well managed Girls' School also exists at St. Andrew's—a place about fifteen miles north from Winnipeg.* It is a boarding school conducted by a lady of considerable experience, and for the last two years has been assisted by the Hudson Bay Company with an annual vote of equal value with St. John's College grant.

The above is an account of the only educational establishments, so far as I am aware, yet existing here.

The past week has been one of great popular excitement at Red River. You may remember that one week ago I advised you of a movement among the French half-breed population, the avowed object of which was to prevent the entrance of Lieutenant Governor McDougall into the Colony. The scheme appeared to my mind so childish and objectless, that I felt considerable reluctance about entering into any detailed account of it. It has, however, now assumed serious proportions and will, I doubt not, lead to a good deal of writing and talking, if not to much more serious results.

On the 22nd instant it became generally known in the Settlement that, after considerable premeditation, the leader[s] of the revolutionary movement had decided on collecting a camp of their compatriots at a point on the Pembina road named La Rivière Sale, about 7 or 8 miles from Fort Garry. At this point a fence was erected across the highway, and a permanent guard was organized to prevent the passage of any one personally unknown, without a pass from their leaders.

A meeting of the Council of Assiniboia was convened on Monday last, at which along with some of his most intelligent assistants, the leader of the French half-breed population attended. His name is Riel; he has been educated in Lower Canada, and is highly respected among his own people here. He attended before the Council at a conference which lasted for eight

---

* Little more is known of this girls' school.

hours or more, but although every possible argument was exhausted to induce him to abandon his project, he remained steadfast to his purpose.[8] The secrecy with which the debates of our local Council are surrounded has of course prevented any reliable report of what occurred being published, but with regard to Mr. Riel's own opinions they may be inferred from the tenor of a speech made by him on Sunday last to the congregation of the Roman Catholic Cathedral of St. Boniface as it was separating after Morning Mass.

He is reliably reported to have told his countrymen that if they were as he could wish to see them, he should propose that by all means Mr. Macdougall should be permitted to enter and comfortably establish himself in the Settlement. But he was aware that in that case his hearers would go on with their accustomed occupations without regarding their political rights, and the only means he could imagine as likely to rouse them was to force them to some such action as that contemplated. Once roused he had little fear of them, and he urged that should any one fall, a handkerchief should be dipped in his blood and used in all future engagements as their national flag. He said their opposition to impending changes must begin somewhere, and it had been determined to commence it by opposing the entrance of the future Governor. It is reported that he professed the same sentiments on Monday before the Council.*

That body tried to organise, through the agency of the French half-breed members of its board, an opposition movement which turned out a complete failure. Riel's men have steadily increased in number throughout the week, and now amount to several hundreds. Their camp is also kept well supplied with food. Parties coming from the States represent the road as being lined with scouts all the way form Pembina, and the arrangements are said to be such that within a very few hours after the Governor's arrival at the latter place, intelligence of the event will be received at LaRivière Sale.

Apart from their alleged designs their conduct has been good. Supplies of provisions and buffalo robes sent hence to meet the Governor were allowed to pass the lines in safety, and the rights of private property are scrupulously respected. These evidences of right feeling increase the regret with which their indefensible conduct is viewed by the well disposed.

---

\* This story is available in no other source.

By the most reliable accounts yet received Mr. Macdougall must now be drawing near Pembina. What course he will pursue on reaching that place we have no idea. His attorney-general and various other assistants are reported as advancing towards the settlement in different parties. They will all be stopped by the insurgents, and meanwhile no Canadian official will I believe be permitted to leave this place to meet them. We are in fact isolated from them.

I shall not fail to keep you advised of the further progress of this affair.

# ALEXANDER BEGG

10 NOVEMBER 1869

[This letter appears at the beginning of Alexander Begg's journal of the events of 1869-70, thus demonstrating that he was indeed "Justitia." The writer sets out to defend the rebellion against reactions by the Canadian government, and he produces what is arguably the most powerful indictment of Canadian policy in advance of annexation ever written. The comments about gaol breaking refer to the release of the Reverend Griffiths Owen Corbett and of John Christian Schultz. Printed in the Toronto *Globe*, 2 December 1869.]

To the Editor of the Globe.
Winnipeg, Red River Settlement
November 10, 1869

Sir,—That which has been foretold for some time past in this settlement has taken place. The discontent that has been brewing amongst a large number of our settlers towards the new order of Government proposed for them has at last culminated in an open and decided resistance by the French half-breeds in preventing Mr. McDougall and his Council from entering the North-West Territory. Great will be the indignation throughout the Dominion amongst a large class of Canadians at this reception of their fellow countrymen, and if it is (as it is very likely to be) put before the public in the light of an insult to Canadian honour, there is no saying what results this feeling of indignation may lead to. But let the public of Canada pause before it accepts the one side of the story until it also hears the other. The days are past for coercing a people into anything that is utterly distasteful to them, and I am sure Canada is not the power that will willingly insist on pushing measures that are found to be unwise, it may be unjust, at all events decidedly unpopular in this case. It is quite apparent to intelligent people here, as it will be generally admitted in Canada when all the facts are known, that the Government at Ottawa have made a serious mistake in the outset of their assuming the rule over the North-West, and only ignorance of the country and the people of the wise heads at the head of affairs will allow it, can be the plea in their self-defence. Can it be that Sir John A. Macdonald and Cartier were aware that there were about 14,000 of a population here who would justly consider it their right to be, at least, acquainted with the steps the new Government proposed taking with regard to their future welfare, and that they in the face of this knowledge have insisted upon throwing in their deputies on the pretext that "We have bought your country—we have paid so much money for the purchase—we expect to spend so much more in improvements—we of course did not exactly buy you as a people, but unfortunately for you, you happened to be born there, and therefore you must just grin and bear with what we intend to do." The action of the Canadian Government looks like this—that it is really this, I cannot believe—I have to fall back on the old plea ignorance. There is reason to suppose in the minds of Canadians, and those conversant with Canadian policy, that the measures of the new Government will be for the benefit of the Settlement, but how are you to convince people here, who have never had proper means of becoming acquainted with Canada and its people, that these measures are to be beneficial to them, when as yet they have never had any authoritative assurance of the same? We are at this present day utterly ignorant of what is proposed for us, by some we are told we are not to have a voice at all in the new order of things; others say our representation at the Council Board of our country is to be very limited; others that we are to be taxed in equal proportion to the people of Ontario and Quebec; others that our taxes are to be light—and so on. Dame Rumour has full sway here, for she has it all her own way. Nothing official has transpired to enlighten us. Everywhere is conjecture, and conjecture is the worst thing to be abroad in a country like this. In the presence of this utter ignorance, can you, free thinking, free speaking, and free acting Canadians, condemn this people for feeling that they have been slighted and forgotten? And can you blame them if their conjectures are apt to take the darkest form, and that they look upon the freedom they have so long enjoyed as about to be taken from them? Were you to see a species of serfdom before you, would you not kick against it? Here is where the Government at Ottawa has made the grand mistake of their new undertaking. Why, if it was known to them that the Settlement contained the population that it does, did they not feel their way before taking such a long stride as they have done? Would it not have been wiser policy for them to have sent up authorized Agents to this country as soon as the transfer of the territory was agreed upon, for the purpose of feeling the pulse of the settlers, find out their ideas on the change proposed, and opening out, as far as possible, the views of the Canadian Government towards them? This, at all events, could not have done harm, and I believe it would have prevented the rupture that has now taken place. The views of the settlers would have been obtained by the Ottawa officials, and measures to meet these views could have been taken, unless, indeed, the wise ones really intended to ignore the fact of there being any people here to consult. The settlers too on the other hand would have been prepared for the change proposed for them, and instead of a barrier to prevent Mr. McDougall from coming to Fort Garry, crowds would have gone forth to welcome him. Now let me give you a short retrospect of late events that have tended to raise and foster the feelings of discontent now prevalent in the settlement.

I can easily imagine that statements from this country, numerous and diversified as they will doubtless be, will be received by most parties with a degree of caution if not of incredulity, nor do I for one moment suppose that my poor epistle will effect any of the changes I would advise for the best; but I am determined to give a truthful statement of facts which speak for themselves, and my opinions on the state of affairs, while they cannot do any harm, are at least those of one deeply interested in the result of this trouble.

For the last two or three years sundry attempts have been made to get up public meetings for the purpose of raising sympathy in favour of Annexation to Canada as it was called, and at the same time to throw discredit on the Hudson Bay Company rule.[*] These meetings, as they actually took place here, were miserable failures. The men engaged in getting them up were unauthorized in their attempts, at least as far as was known in the Settlement. The consequence was that Annexation to Canada became a by word of ridicule. The meetings held were scenes of uproarious merriment instead of sober, orderly gatherings for the public weal. But how were those ebullitions of a few reported abroad? Why as large and influential meetings held, important resolutions adopted and so forth, intended to

---

[*] The most recent public meetings in the settlement, held in July 1869, had dealt with the prospective Canadian annexation and the rights of the natives of the country to land. See my *Red River Rebellion*, 45-48.

lead the public of Canada and the rest of the world to suppose that we were a people tyrannized over and that we were eagerly seeking for a milder and more generous Government to step in and free us from our thraldom. Now this was all erroneous. Whatever may have been the faults of the Hudson Bay Company rule they were light ones, and although I admit there was a feeling in the minds of the settlers that the H.B.C. were not powerful enough to enforce the laws when required, yet there never was to my knowledge a general feeling of discontent towards them or their actions in the government of the settlement. On the contrary, we felt ourselves a free people in every respect. We had privileges that in other countries were not enjoyed by the people. Our Government was, by a Council, appointed from amongst ourselves. It is true we had no direct vote in their election, but the H.B.C. invariably consulted the opinions of a neighbourhood before choosing a Councilman from that part. We, therefore, to a certain degree, had a voice in our own Government, and were content therewith. Our laws, as administered, savoured more of arbitration than law, and in that respect suited our requirements better than if a pack of lawyers had been amongst us, urging us with all the quibbles best known to them to eat each other up in useless suits. While speaking of law, I may add here that in the history of the past few years of this Settlement it was found that one gaol has twice been broken open and prisoners liberated. The first, a clergyman condemned by twelve of his fellow settlers for a crime unmentionable here; the second, a prisoner for resisting the officers of the law.* And liberated by whom? By a small part who, in justice to the law-*abiding* people of this Settlement, be it said, have not to this day recovered from the stigma the act of gaol breaking has cast on their characters. And who were those engaged in the above acts? Principally Canadians—who have railed most against the existing laws of our Settlement, and tried to set them at defiance. Can you wonder, then, that for a time Canadians were generally looked upon with suspicion in this quarter? Be it known now, however, that although for a time the feeling was— Can anything good come out of Canada? Since the advent of better men from your country—since truer specimens of what Canadians generally are, have visited this Settlement, the reaction is altogether in their favour, and the feeling now is that it is not fair to judge the whole flock from there being

---

* The references are to G.O. Corbett and John Christian Schultz, respectively.

one or two black sheep in it. We have many good men here from Canada, and I would be sorry to cast a slur on them. Those for whom my remarks are intended need not take offence at their truthfulness, and those to whom they do not refer need not apply them to themselves.

We now come to another epoch in the tide of events that did much towards causing the present troubles. Our settlement was suddenly devastated, by means of a plague in the shape of the grasshoppers. It is needless to give the already often repeated tale of how our crops were utterly destroyed; how the buffalo disappeared; the fish failed; in fact, how utterly we were beseiged by famine [the famine of 1868]. England came to our aid; the United States assisted us; private contributions from Canada flowed in upon us; and the Hudson Bay Company did more than all the others put together. At this time, the Government in Ottawa, no doubt, for praiseworthy reasons, sent in a party to commence the road to the Lake of the Woods; the idea being to pay for their labour in provisions those from amongst the settlers who were willing to work.* The Ontario Legislature voted $5,000 towards the relief of the settlement, but John Sandfield Macdonald could not see it in the same light, for we never received the amount, and Ontario is that much richer to day.† It will be well, however, to allow the appropriation to stand good, as it is likely to be required next year to assist in feeding those emigrants from Canada who may be hardy enough to settle in Red River next summer; there being every reason to look forward to the grasshopper calamity then, and there is not more than enough in the country to feed the people already here for one year without crops. The two parties sent in charge of this end of the Government road may have acted wisely, but not too well.‡ They employed a certain number of men from amongst the settlers, and when flour was selling at three pounds sterling per barrel in the stores, they charged the poor men, their employees, three pounds twelve shillings and four pounds sterling, per barrel, and, at the same time, only paid them three pounds per month

---

* This project was led by John Snow.

† Red River never received this $5000, which was exactly the sum subsequently voted by the Ontario legislature to put a price on the head of Louis Riel.

‡ The references are to John Snow (1824-1888), head of the construction team building a road from Lake of the Woods to Upper Fort Garry, and Charles Mair (1838-1927), the poet and member of Canada First.

in that ratio for their work—this created dissatisfaction.* The next thing, which caused still more discontent amongst the people, was a concerted plan of a few, in which the Government officials in charge of the road were implicated, to buy up from Indians (who had no right to sell) parcels of land, on part of which people were actually living, in and around Oak Point, the head quarters of the Government works. This raised such a feeling of indignation against the parties concerned, that the head men in charge of the road summarily received notice from the neighbours around to quit the premises forth with; and afterwards, one of the principal actors in the affair (a Government official) was fined by one petty court ten pounds sterling for giving liquor to those same Indians.† These and similar actions on the part of the Government employees, whilst making them unpopular, seriously injured the cause of Canada in the minds of the people here; and matters were not afterwards improved by the doings and writings of the poet, Mr. Charles Mair, who, after having received the hospitalities of many families in the Settlement, saw fit to ridicule in public print those who had entertained him—to speak and write disparagingly of the settlers as a body, and the ladies in particular. These you may say are minor matters, but I only point them out to show the gradual feeling those actions of a few individuals caused of dislike to the Government, who would send such men as samples of their employees. On the top of all the unfortunate occurrences, in comes Col. Dennis, with his party of surveyors, to divide and sub-divide the land into sections as they saw fit. This, at all events, was premature on the part of the rulers at Ottawa, before any arrangements had been made with the people here, regarding the incoming government. And, although Col. Dennis acted in a gentlemanly and proper manner in the discharge of his troublesome duties, still the people looked on the act of his party going to work before the establishment of the new order of rule, as arbitrary and presumptuous. I can believe, however, that if the minds of the settlers had not been prejudiced beforehand by the previous acts of Government officials there would have been no interruptions offered to the Col. and his party in their surveying operations; for everywhere Col. Dennis was received favourably by the majority of the

---

* This was part of the complaint of the "strikers."

† Again, the reference is to John Snow.

Settlement, although he too unfortunately fell into the same trap as his predecessors, and (if I may use the expression) was "gobbled up" by the men who all along have been the principal cause of trouble in the Settlement.* As if everything was fated to be to the disadvantage of Canadian interests, a clique of men, unpopular through their own deeds in this Settlement, have all along taken up the cudgels (it may be unasked) for Canadian Annexation. These men have professed themselves as authority on all subjects concerning the new Government, and have invariably endeavoured to throw discredit on the Hudson Bay Company abroad and at home. Now the fact is the Hudson Bay Company have been misrepresented. It is not, nor has for the past twenty years, been unpopular to the majority of the Settlement. Indeed it has been the best friend to the settler, many of whom have reason to feel grateful to our grandmother, as the Company has been called, by those desirous of being facetious on the subject. The Canadian Government too, will do well not to throw aside the advice and assistance the Hudson Bay Company will surely have in its power to give; that is if it wishes to become popular as a Government with the present inhabitants of Red River. Let the public of Canada beware of reports touching the injustice of the Hudson Bay Company to the people here, for such is not the general feeling in the Settlement. I asssure you, though I am sorry to say it, the *prestige* of the men who have figured so far in connection with the Canadian Government here has tended to make it dreadfully unpopular with the majority of the Settlement.

It may be said, however, that an intelligent people should not have been led into error, by a class of men such as I have described who could not have been vested with any real authority. But you must remember that there was no other authority to consult. Even at this moment no official notice has been received in any way, by either the people here, or their Council, of the proposed actions of Mr. McDougall and his *confreres*—and in the face of that, we must judge from the Government men we have come in contact with—and certainly the specimens produced so far in this case have not redounded to the credit of Canada. Besides, it is known that the clique here, with whom these very employees from Ottawa fraternized, were in communication, personally at times and otherwise, with the chief men at the seat of Government; indeed, so much so that they endeavoured to make capital

---

* The reference is principally to John Christian Schultz.

out of the same here. Was it not then, natural to suppose that the views of the Canadian officials at headquarters were impregnated with those of a certain one-sided, self-interested party here—one too obnoxious in the extreme to the majority of the Settlement? I say, again, these facts, in the face of an utter want of official information as to their intentions from the new Government, invested it with feelings of distrust in the minds of Red River people. This is strong language, you will say; but what is the use of sticking at the meat when the bone of contention is still to come? I have endeavoured to give a few of the causes that have given rise to the present feeling of discontent in the Settlement. A total or complete list of griev-ances I could not give you; the task would be too great. One would require to have lived here, as I have done, to know all. Let me, however, cite one more case before I give you the crowning acts in this political drama. Our community has been cursed, instead of blessed, through the medium of the Press as it has been conducted in the Settlement. A one sided, unpopular mismanaged sheet, in the interest of the clique already referred to in this letter, has endeavoured to mislead the minds of the people abroad regard-ing the true state of affairs here. It has maligned the Hudson's Bay Com-pany by asserting statements of tyrannous actions on their part—actions that never took place except in the brain of the worthy editor; it has uttered the falsehood that we, the people of Red River, have been groaning under the yoke of oppression, when, in fact, we have been all along blessed with the greatest freedom; it has endeavoured to show a party inimical to Canadian interests here, when such a party never existed. In truth, I can hardly wonder at Canadians having such an erroneous opinion of this coun-try and its people as they seem to have, when a great deal of their informa-tion has been gleaned from such a source as this *Nor'-Wester*. I blame it to the men in whose interests it acts for the unwise course they have all along pursued with regard to this country, and I condemn it flatly for the many falsehoods it has served from time to time to circulate. Thank god, we are to have another newspaper here soon, which will, at least, give us the opportunity of vindicating ourselves in the future.* The *Nor'-Wester* has

---

*James Ross (1835-1871), the son of Alexander Ross the historian, had recently returned to Red River with a new press. He printed part of one issue of the *Pioneer* when all newspaper publication was suspended by Riel. The press was later used by *The New Nation*.

continually railed against monopoly in this country. The greatest monopoly that we have had here for the past few years has been itself. Let me here cite a comicality in newspaper experience which cannot but incite a feeling of contempt and pity for such "littleness" in the minds of all honest journalists. The *Nor'-Wester* hearing that the proposed newspaper was to be called the *North-Star,* coolly informed its readers that it (the *Nor'-Wester)* had succeeded in "blowing" the clouds from the horizon to allow the *North Star* to shine forth (the present aspect of affairs in the settlement looks like a clear sky, does it not?) and when afterwards it learned that the name of its rival was to be the *Pioneer* instead of the *North Star*, what does it do but christen itself the *Nor'-Wester AND Pioneer*. Piratical, was it not, forsooth, and impudent piracy at that, eh?

While feeling was rife we had a visit from the Hon. Joseph Howe, and on his arrival the first act of the clique already mentioned was to invite him to become a guest in the house of one of them, who has made himself conspicuous in Canadian affairs here. The old politician, however, was not to be caught with such chaff, and declined the invitation. Fatigued by his hard trip over the plains, Mr. Howe kept a good deal to his quarters at the hotel. He, however, made a couple of trips up and down the Red and Assiniboine Rivers seeing enough to satisfy himself, I am sure, what the country was like. Had he come earlier in the season he would have seen the Settlement to much better advantage than he did, as everything while he was here looked bleak and miserable, preparatory to the change from autumn to winter. Many of the principal settlers visited the hon. gentleman, one who could see and act for himself. A great deal of satisfaction was felt throughout the settlement at Mr. Howe's visit, although it was understood that he merely visited us in the capacity of a private individual irrespective of his public character. This will go to show how much good might have been done had delegates been sent to prepare the way for Mr. McDougall's coming. Although Mr. Howe never favoured us with a speech, or in any way made a public demonstration, and although he would receive nothing of the latter from our hands, I am of the opinion that he left the settlement with a pretty correct idea of the people and the situation of affairs as they then stood. I may say, indeed, that he did much in his short visit here to counteract the evil influence that was abroad; but I am sorry to say the seeds of discontent had been too deeply sown to be rooted up so easily, and after his departure the crisis came.

The feelings of the people then broke out in a manner too plain to be mistaken. One portion of the settlers (the French) avowed their intention of preventing Mr. McDougall from entering the Settlement, and in support of this determination, they erected barriers across the roads leading to Fort Garry. Scouts were posted all along from the Assiniboine to Pembina, a distance of over sixty miles, to give notice of Mr. McDougall's approach. The number of men under arms at one time must have been upwards of six hundred, and this large number was not assembled merely for the purpose of turning back one man and his few friends, but it was done to show the universal opinion of the French half-breeds regarding the question at issue. Many of the French did not take part in this armed protest, but offered their services as soon as they should be required. The English speaking portion of the settlement, in the meantime, quietly remained in the background, nor were attempts to raise them against the French, and in favour of McDougall, found successful. They had no interest in opposing their neighbours, with whom they had lived so long in amity; especially in support of a cause that intended, apparently, to reduce their rights as British subjects to nothing, in fact, when the thing was canvassed, which was done by the friends of Mr. McDougall, there could not be found fifty men amongst the settlers themselves to offer their assistance in bringing the new Governor so far as Fort Garry. Several ideas were afloat as to the propriety of keeping Mr. McDougall out, but the general opinion seemed to be—we have not been justly dealt by, and we will not at all events oppose those who are fighting our battles to bring in a government that has, as yet, given us no assurance nor example of their fair dealing. The universal cry was—we have been overlooked in this matter, and if Mr. McDougall should come in and attempt to force on us a measure distasteful to the community, we will then join in open resistance against him. I give this as the voice of our people. It may not be palatable to Mr. McDougall and his clique, but it is a true version nevertheless. The Council of Red River, in the meantime, had several meetings, and their ultimate decision and advice to Mr. McDougall, and which was forwarded to him in the shape of a letter from the Council, was that it would be better for him, in the existing state of the country, for his own peace and safety and for the public welfare, to remain at Pembina, and not endeavour to force himself into the Settlement, especially as it was found that there were so few favourably inclined towards him. On Mr. McDougall's arrival in Pembina he accepted the situation, and decided on remaining there for the present, but Messrs. Provencher and Cameron thought to press through to Fort Garry. It was a useless attempt on their part, as they were stopped within nine miles of the Fort, and escorted back to Pembina by an escort of 25 or 30 armed men. Provencher spent a number of hours among the rebels, as they are called by the *Nor-Wester*, and, if report speaks true, he had no reason to cavil at their treatment of him. Cameron, however, had no opportunity to parley with them, but was immediately turned back the way he came.

The escort of Messrs. Provencher and Cameron had orders to see Mr. McDougall and party across the lines, and at this present moment our would-be Governor is quietly resting on his oars in Uncle Sam's dominion. Whether he intends to direct his course back to Canada or to persist in entering the Settlement this winter, no one can predict. These are the facts of the case, and where matters will end no one can at this present moment foretell. One half of the settlers are up in arms, sworn to protect the laws as we have been accustomed to have them (what greater denial can there be to the statement of tyranny on the part of the Company) and to repel Mr. McDougall and his ready-made Councilmen; the other half of the people are satisfied to remain quiet so long as there appears to be no desire on the part of the French to lord it over them. The general sentiments of the people is to be allowed to elect their own Councilmen, and have their proper rights as a free people respected by the new Government. We have armed night patrols to guard the property of private individuals from pillage and outrage by adventurers. Fort Garry is guarded in the same way by a force of over sixty men. Some idea can be formed of the earnestness of these French people when you learn that many of them have, at the moment I am writing this, been out on guard eighteen days; sleeping at night on the snow, with no tent or other covering except their ordinary clothes—and this without the least prospect of pay. The food they eat is the only thing they get, and that is furnished them by the more wealthy of their own people. A meeting is called for the 16th inst, at which delegates from all parts of the Settlement are to meet to discuss the present state of affairs, and the best method of providing for the future. Freight carts were watched for guns, which it is reported the Canadian Government are trying to run into the Settlement. A portion of Mr. McDougall's property, in the way of furniture, &c., is in the hands of the French, which they are merely retaining, and have placed away in safety until matters are arranged. No violence has been committed; no outrage taken place; all has been order, and certainly the movement has evinced good management. Colonel Dennis, who went through to meet Mr. McDougall, has been notified that he will not be permitted to return to the Settlement in the meantime. What the object is of keeping Mr. McDougall out, is best known to those who have taken that course. One thing is sure: there is an impression here that he has been at the bottom of all the mismanagement that has already taken place in Canadian affairs here; and they dread his further mismanagement when accepted as their Governor by the settlers.

As I said at the beginning of my letter, there have been serious mistakes committed, and those who have been the cause of them should be held answerable to the public of Canada for the same. Why, instead of rushing things as they have done, did not the Government at Ottawa feel its way with more caution and policy? Was it worthy of politicians at the first to accept statements from one or two invididuals, or from the columns of a newspaper, regarding this country? And were their after-deeds worthy of experienced men? Instead of sending in competent delegates to find out the whys and the wherefores of things in the Settlement—they sent in a couple of road makers under the cloak of charity, and a party of surveyors who, before the country has left the hands of the old rule, go to work under the direction of the incoming Government. They then, from all the reports we can hear, for we have nothing official on the subject, ignore the fact of there being people here at all, and are actually going to place what they call a Provisional Government over us, which, with the exception of one or two chosen from the Hudson Bay Company, are to consist principally of Government hangers on. A fine Family Compact idea, if true, at all events we have no assurance from the Canadian Government that it is not to be so.* Will the people of Canada stand by and see a community of free British subjects there ignored? I cannot believe it. There is one thing sure. The Settlement generally will not submit to their Councilmen being elected from abroad. Every honest freedom-loving Canadian will, I am sure, join me in saying that the people of this country deserve their rights, and the greatest right of a free people is a voice in the Government of their own country. The people here, I am sure, will fight to the end to give this point

---

* The reference is to the Family Compact of Upper Canada, an élite group of politicians who were alleged to be closely related and practitioners of nepotism.

a thorough representation at the Council board, and there is no use for the Government at Ottawa to coerce them into anything else. I have heard it said that as Canada is about to spend about 300,000 pounds in improvement in this country that the rulers claim a right to have that much of a voice in the Government of the Settlement. Answer me this, does England, that advances large sums for the benefit of Canada, ask for that reason the right of having representatives in the Council at Ottawa? Is it not sufficient for Canada that she sends us our Governor? Let emigrants come in here, who, as well as the present settlers, will have a voice in the public affairs, and the £300,000 will be sufficiently represented by Canadian influence.

And now for the future. Who can tell what that may be? It rests altogether on the policy of the Canadian Government, in the adjustment of the present difficulties. It will be useless to split the Settlement on the point of representation. Would it be wise, as we are situated, to endeavour to raise one side of the Settlement against the other? God knows where such a course would end. Extermination on one side or the other would follow; the Indians, heretofore tractable, would be roused, their worst passions inflamed, rapine and massacre would be the result, and, for all this, who would be answerable but the Canadian Government? It will be the same if it is attempted to coerce the Settlement by force. Such an action would be unwise and uncalled for, and the result would be that instead of a profitable acquisition to the Dominion in this country, you would have an expensive and unsatisfactory Government to support here for the next five or ten years, at least I would advise, if so humble a person as myself may be permitted to do so, that proper delegates be sent to this country to find out the exact views of the people. That could be done during the present winter. In the meantime, let Mr. McDougall return to Canada, to await the decision of the House at Ottawa on the report furnished by these delegates. Give the people here their just rights, and no more faithful adherents to the cause of Canada will be found in the Dominion than those same settlers of ours. Take a new start in the spring in a proper direction, and all will be well; but for the sake of the fearful consquences that will ensue—a rising of the people generally, united with the Indian troubles throughout the whole North-West—let your actions be those of peace. At present we are in the greatest uncertainty as to the result of the present difficulties. As long as Mr. McDougall remains at Pembina, the country will be in a state of excitement, especially as he has not yet vouchsafed to send any message as yet to the people as to what his intentions are. If blood be shed in this cause, may God help those who have been the cause of it. I will write you with further particulars as they develop themselves.

Yours truly,
JUSTITIA

EDITOR'S NOTE

[A letter from Charles Mair from Red River, dated 19 November 1868, and printed in the Toronto *Globe* on 1 January 1869, got the poet in all sorts of difficulty in Red River. His comments about mixed-blood women were not appreciated by many in the community, and Mrs. Annie Bannatyne, having waited for Mair to appear from the local post office, proceeded to administer to him an old-fashioned horse-whipping.

The importation of guns into the settlement was sometimes thwarted by peculiar circumstances. A supply of guns—100 Spencer carbines and 250 Peabody muskets, equipped with bayonets and accoutrements—was brought west by William McDougall, but was left in storage at Fort Abercrombie. A collection of Springfield rifles was stolen from storage in Lincoln, Nebraska, in the autumn of 1869 by a Fenian cell. It was shipped to St. Paul collect, but was never picked up and ultimately was returned to Lincoln. See John Sutton to Addison Sheldon, 29 September 1926, Nebraska Historical Society, Ms RG 1449.]

# J.J. HARGRAVE

13 NOVEMBER 1869

[Although he is more favourably disposed to the Hudson's Bay Company than "Justitia," J.J. Hargrave in this letter demonstrates that he shares with his fellow correspondent a critical view of the actions of the Canadian government in its attempts to annex Red River. Printed in the *Montreal Herald and Daily Commercial Gazette*, 4 December 1869.]

Red River Settlement,
British North America,
13 Nov., 1869.

The topic to which the attention of all here at present is turned, is the expulsion of Governor MacDougall, and the revolutionary movement among the French half-breed population, by which it has taken place.

The minds of men are of course in an excited state, though the absence of any violence to life or property is one of the remarkable features of the movement. Opinions conflict with each other, and those who possess houses and property of a permanent character know not what course to take in the turbulent times which have so suddenly come upon the Colony. It is difficult to ascertain peoples' sentiments on political questions, and the declared partizans who attempt to talk, claim the commiserations of their friends for the poor result of their efforts, and with somewhat amusing *naivete* complain that men, to whom they have been long speaking under the full conviction that they carried their auditors along with them, turned out afterwards to have been only "chaffing" them and laughing in their sleeve at them all the time.

At the present moment we may regard local public opinion as being under three divisions. These are the French half-breed insurgents; the whole remaining resident population possessed of property in the Settlement; and thirdly the Canadian new arrivals of the past summer.* These

---

* This tripartite division of the settlement is different from that of Hargrave in his first letter.

three classes, I regret to say, regard the present situation of the Colony with widely different sentiments. In my last letter I mentioned in detail what I understand to be their views and therefore need only repeat they are, respectively, a resolution to maintain what has been already done to oppose the incoming Government on the part of the French; indifference to what [that] Government, so that it only protect them and theirs, on the part of the English; and much professed indignation at the half-breed movement—on the part of the new arrivals.

As much of what in other parts of the British Dominions would be, I think justly, considered positively disloyal, exists in the views entertained by the well affected Settlers, I shall, even at the risk of being accused of dealing with the first principles of very high matters, endeavour to bring before the reader some of the broad features of the subject under consideration. By the term "disloyal views" I mean, for example, readiness, on the call of expediency or the avoidance of personal loss, to change one[']s allegiance from British to United States sovereignty.[*]

A haziness of ideas appears to exist relative to the past position of the Hudson's Bay Company as a governing power. Many regard the Company, Canada, and the Imperial Government as so many independent sources of sovereign jurisdictions. Under this view, allegiance once withdrawn from the Company may, at the option of the governed, be transferred with equal sanction of law to the authorities at Ottawa or Washington. Many therefore err through ignorance. But have the best informed pursued the straightest and most unimpeachable course in this matter?

Canada has been compelled to pay a considerable sum for the extinction of the Hudson's Bay title. The course she long took to evade the performance of this act was, at least by her public voice heard through the Press, if not by the official action of her responsible government, to deny the validity of the said title. The Imperial authorities, however, acting under the unassailable advice of their law officers, have always recognized the disputed title, both directly and indirectly, in acts of Parliament relating to allied subjects.

It appears under this view that the party which ought to have extinguished the Hudson's Bay claim was the Imperial and not the Dominion

---

[*] Much less national loyalty existed at this time than in the twentieth century. Many of the Métis moved from one country to the other without compunction.

Government. The sum in question was voted in compensation for the withdrawal of privileges conferred by an English King on an English Company. The large trade conducted by the Company for the past two centuries has been with the port of London, and only an infinitesimal part of its purchases or sales has taken place in Canadian markets. On the contrary the profits of the great Trade, drawn from the vast wilderness by which she is surrounded, have been systematically placed beyond the reach of Canadian traders, through the operation of the instrument for the extinction of which she is now called to pay, what appears to those who have paid highly for their Hudson's Bay Stock a very inadequate remuneration.

The Hudson's Bay Company in fact, as a political agent, has served its purpose.[1] It has governed for England a vast colony for 200 years in the cheapest and most effective manner. The rule of a Commercial Company is plainly intolerable and inexpedient in a settled and civilized country; but in an inaccessible and savage country commercial occupation benefits the Indians and reserves the Sovereignty for Great Britain. Apart from remunerative commercial pursuits, the expense of paying and maintaining British Magistrates throughout Rupert's Land would have been enormous, even were the plan otherwise practicable. In the absence of some such occupation, American ascendancy must before this have prevailed from Sitka to Fort Garry.

The benefits accruing to England from the Hudson's Bay Company have therefore been, the retention of a vast colony during all the years of its uselessness and inaccessibility; the conduct for two centuries of a large and valuable Fur Trade the mart of which was in her Capital; and the just and equitable treatment of the Indian tribes, which, still in the midst of undisturbed peace, appreciate the difference between their condition and that of their kindred tribes in the hunting grounds under the administration of the American Indian Department.

At the close of its political career, the Company has been offered a sum equal to about one-seventh of its capital stock, in exchange for its right of exclusive trade. I shall not here attempt any argument to show that the treatment has been unhandsome, but content myself with the remark that Earl Granville in submitting the terms ultimately to the parties, admitted that the equivalent proposed would appear inadequate to those regarding it from the Company's point of view.

An additional burden has been imposed on the Canadian tax payer in the necessity laid upon him to extinguish Indian and half-breed titles, and come to an understanding with the civilized inhabitants of Rupert's Land regarding the terms on which they were to enter the confederation.

Now, Confederation is a scheme presumed to emanate from the Colonial Office, and is doubtless an important phase of the altered relation soon likely to exist between Great Britain and her North American Colonies. The plan is magnificent—but the execution is beyond the unassisted strength of any of the Colonies. Petty local interests and jealousies must be attended to and appeased, and English assistance alone can sometimes meet the emergency. Would the temporary expedient of the creation of a Crown Colony, the officials of which would have acted under direct commissions from England, not have been more likely to deal satisfactorily with the troublesome elements affecting the incorporation of Rupert's Land into the Dominion, than the transition scheme provided for in the Act of the Canadian Legislature, which authorized the formation of the Council to be presided over by Lieutenant-Governor Macdougall?

Regarding the advisability of removing the responsibility of government from the Company it can hardly be a matter of doubt that the time has fully arrived for such a step. The action of the Government here for some years past has been grossly misrepresented to the Canadian public through interested agencies, the nature of some of which I may have occasion hereafter to explain. It has certainly been an administration ruled by expediency, inasmuch as men accused and found guilty of criminal offences have been permitted to remain at large after having been rescued from prison by the illegal violence of their adherents—but the spirit of the government has been pure, and its administration most lenient.[2] It wanted, however, the element of strength, to be found only in a material force sufficient to uphold the law.

This being the case even with but a limited population, it will be understood that the steady progress of American population through Minnesota would greatly have increased the difficulty by introducing a foreign element. The country is open to the States, but closed by a formidable barrier of Lake and Morass on the Canadian side. It is therefore desirable that the basis of a strong Government professing loyalty to the British crown should be firmly established at Red River before the arrival of a population American in sentiment and ties.

Since assuming, to a certain extent, connection with Red River, the

Canadian Government has committed very serious errors. These have been, commencing operations of a nature which required the presence of a staff of officials acting under their authority before the transfer of the Territory was effected, and secondly[,] neglecting in the most unaccountable manner, to establish close and direct communication between themselves and the present government of Rupert's Land.

It will be remembered that, in the autumn of 1868, about the period when Sir George E. Cartier and Mr. MacDougall commenced their English Mission, Mr. John Snow, a Canadian Surveyor, was sent to Red River to commence operations at the western extremity of the overland route to Canada. Mr. Snow's mission to Red River was represented as combining the double benefit of expediting a great Public work, the ultimate necessity of which was admitted by both parties, and of rendering timely assistance to a famishing community. As notwithstanding the plausibility of the latter pleas, the measure appeared to be calculated to affect the position of the Company in their pending negotiations, the Governor and Committee, on being advised of it entered a protest against the invasion of their territories; but with regard to the actual works, the Government here countenanced and assisted Mr. Snow.

Respecting that part of the scheme bearing on the relief of the prevailing distress although undoubtedly every barrell of flour imported was an acquisition to the colony, it must be remembered that the Canadian Government supplies were sold to the men employed on their works at a higher rate—to the extent I believe of ten or twelve shillings per barrell—than the then market price of Flour in the settlement, the wages so payable being, I am informed, three pounds sterling per mensem.

Mr. Snow's career all last winter, notwithstanding the favour shown him by the local authorities, was chequered with many unpleasant episodes, the causes and details of which I need not at present relate. The element of Indian and Squatter claims, however, entered so much into them as to have undeceived the most short sighted with reference to the paramount importance of giving them immediate consideration.

In the course of the now expiring autumn, a surveying party under the direction of Colonel Dennis has been occupied in a portion of the Country never hitherto surveyed, and over which the Indian title is still unextinguished. Hitherto, it has been considered most desirable by the Company to restrict colonization within the limits assigned to it by the Indians in their treaty with Lord Selkirk in 1817.* The prospect of immigration on a large scale has already alarmed the Indians, a large concourse of whom is expected to take place here in spring. The half-breeds have also as already stated, in a former letter interfered with Colonel Dennis' party.

The situation of public affairs remains much as it was at the date of my last letter. Mr. Macdougall, I regret to say, has been compelled to quit the Hudson's Bay Post of Pembina, and along with his Council to retire across the Line to American ground. It is reported that his family and servants have gone back to winter at St. Cloud. Mr. Macdougall appears to have been very rudely treated by the French half-breeds sent to meet him, and who, with arms in their hands, marched with him to the frontier.

Fort Garry remains in the oc[c]upation of the insurgents. The guard has however been reduced from 120 to 60 men.[3] They are well behaved, but permit nobody unknown to them to pass unchallenged. I close this letter by inserting copy of a printed proclamation addressed by the Insurgents to their fellow settlers.

"PUBLIC NOTICE TO THE INHABITANTS OF RUPERT'S LAND.

The President and Representatives of the French speaking population of Rupert's Land in Council (the Invaders of our rights being now expelled) already aware of your sympathy, do extend the hand of friendship to you our own friendly Fellow-Inhabitants, and in doing so invite you to send twelve Representatives from the following places viz:

St. John's, 1; St. Margaret's, 1; Headingly, 1; St. James, 1; St. Mary's, 1; Kildonan, 1; St. Paul's, 1; St. Andrew's, 1; St. Clements, 1; St. Peter's, 1, Town of Win[n]ipeg, 2; in order to form one body with the above Council consisting of twelve members to consider the present political state of this country, and to adopt such measures as may be deemed best for the future welfare of the same.

A meeting of the above Council will be held in the Court House at Fort

---

* Selkirk purchased land for two miles on either side of the Red and Assiniboine rivers, and even this purchase was later disputed by the First Nations.

Garry on Tuesday the 16th day of November at which the invited Representatives will attend.

Winnipeg November 6th 1869.
By Order of the President.
(Signed) LOUIS RIEL, Secretary"

EDITOR'S NOTE
[Regarding the proclamation issued by Riel, according to "Fort Garry" in the Montreal *Herald*, 29 November 1869,

> Dr. Bown of the 'Nor'-Wester' was called upon to print this document, but as I understand it refused chiefly on account of the words 'invaders of our rights' being used in it. There are two gentlemen here who are about starting a new paper, but their type is not ready for printing, and the 'Nor'-Wester' office was the only place at which it could be done. The money was offered the Doctor before he should set his printers to work, but he was immovable. The Secretary then placed a force in possession of the building and a guard near the Doctor, and a sometime printer, now bar tender, was obtained who put the necessary type together and struck off the notices by the hundred, to be spread this morning from one end of the Settlement to the other.]

# J.J. HARGRAVE

20 NOVEMBER 1869

[Although the *nom de plume* has changed, the opening sentence of this letter makes plain that the writer is J.J. Hargrave, who offers a dispassionate account of the development of the troubles in Red River, which does not spare the Canadians. His listing of the anglophone delegates to the November meeting with the Métis demonstrates that all the major anglophone interest groups were represented. The delegates included several mixed bloods, an Aboriginal, a number of Scots-born settlers, an American, and a Canadian merchant. All the major anglophone districts were represented, as well as the major religious denominations (Anglican, Presbyterian, and Roman Catholic). This letter was reprinted by Morton in the documentary appendix to his edition of the Begg journal, 415-20. Printed in the *Montreal Herald and Daily Commercial Gazette*, 9 December 1869.]

Red River Settlement,
British North America,
20th Nov., 1869

In my last week's letter I mentioned that the errors of the Canadian Government in its present dealings with the North West Territory are considered to be two-fold, and to originate, first, in the premature mission of Surveyors and road markers; and secondly, in neglecting to open direct communication with the present Government. I adduced the fact corroborative of my first assertion, and beg now to continue the subject, by shewing how the hands of the existing authorities have been tied through the non-existence of official intercourse.[*]

Mr. Snow, in his arrival in autumn 1868, brought with him the intimation on the part of his employers, of a hope that no molestation would be offered him in his road operations, and he forthwith went to work across a

---

[*] Hargrave's position as secretary to the governor of the HBC makes his statements at least semi-authoritative.

tract of country, still the property of the Indians, and, in those portions of it at a greater distance than fifty miles from Fort Garry, beyond the civil jurisdiction of the magistrates of Assiniboia. He met with many troubles on all hands. Indians required compensation; Half-breeds who had settled at a place called Oak Point, at the western terminus of his road, declared their squatter rights had been invaded by self-appropriations of land made by people more or less directly connected with the works. Bad feelings broke out, which resulted in applications to quell tumults among the Half-breeds being made to the authorities at Fort Garry, and on one occasion the Red River Magistrates were pained in having to adjudicate in an action brought against Mr. Snow of liquor selling to Indians—the offence consisting I believe in a dram having been given a Chief who had made a call on New Year's day. In all such matters Mr. Snow was treated as a private individual by the authorities, although his real position was known and appreciated by the Half-breeds. I regret to have to add that the feelings of the latter towards him were not soothed by the circumstance that the individuals with whom he and his party maintained the closest apparent connection, had frequently called down upon themselves the hostility of the French population, and were professedly hostile to the existing Government of which, until the occurrence of the present disturbances the French have been steady supporters.

Early in June immigrants arrived in successive parties from Canada. Some of these people having settled at a place named Muskrat Creek, seventy or eighty miles west from Fort Garry, were peremptorily warned off by Indians, who objected to the further settlement of their lands.* Muskrat Creek is in the opposite direction, as regards Fort Garry, from the theatre of Mr. Snow's experiences of the previous winter. The new arrivals complained to the authorities that they had exhausted their means in coming to the Settlement and were unable to return. If not permitted to farm therefore they would be in a very awkward predicament.

A Councillor in Assiniboia, of very great experience and influence in dealing with the Indians [probably James McKay], repaired to Muskrat Creek, and after some difficulty made such representations of the hardships of the case to the Indians as induced them to consent to the

* Muskrat Creek is in the Portage la Prairie area.

temporary occupation of the lands by these settlers. The point was not, however, conceded without considerable difficulty, the only assurance which the authorities could give being, that the occupation of the lands would in no way prejudice the title of the Indians to compensation, which would probably be made by the Canadian Government as soon as possible after the contemplated transfer had taken effect. Respecting the general scheme of Indian policy contemplated by the Dominion Government, no reliable information could be given.

The recent interruption to the operations of Colonel Dennis' Surveyors, and the outrages offered to Governor Macdougall and others, have filled up the measure of the difficulties of the directors of the old order of things. The French half-breeds demand from the local government an explanation of the measures taken with regard to the country they call their own by the Dominion of Canada. What private information may be in the possession of the Governor and Council has been communicated to them, but of responsible assurances they have yet had none. The fact that the actual government has been practically ignored has contributed to the mainte-nance of a feeling of apathy towards coming events in the minds of the English-speaking population, who, however, wait only an authoritative and reliable exposition of their rights and duties, to demand the one and perform the other. They object to the measures taken by the French, on account of their violent and illegal character, but they feel the necessity of having an explanation on many points from the Dominion Government, and believe that such a communication ought long ago to have been made through the Governor and Council of Assiniboia or the Governor of Rupert's Land.

Such being the relative position of parties here, it will be seen that the occurrence of some demonstration, at least of coldness of feeling towards the incoming governor, was an event which might have been anticipated. In fact so great have been the misrepresentations made through the press of late years respecting the condition, sentiments, and governments of the Red River people that the amount of reliable information regarding the lat-ter in the possession of the inhabitants of the Eastern provinces, is about as small as that regarding the intentions of the Canadian Government now in possession of the Red River people. It was much desired and fully expected that the recent unofficial visit of Mr. Howe would be productive of good effects in opening the eyes of the Canadian Government, through

the personal observation of one of their foremost men, to a great many
things hitherto habitually misrepresented by the professed friends of the
Dominion. There is every reason to believe that the information collected
by Mr. Howe was sound; but, at the time of his departure, shortly as that
was before the date at which the advent of the Lieutenant Governor was
expected, the disturbances which have prevented his approach to the
colony were altogether unanticipated, and the possibility of such movements discredited.

Throughout the Autumn reports were in circulation of movements
among the French half-breeds, and Sunday public meetings were held by
that section of the people which ended apparently in no practical result.
The main movers in these preliminary acts have indeed been among the
opponents of the present demonstration, which appears to have been in
train, silently developing itself since the month of July.

On 21st October, the Settlement was taken by surprise on having [learn-
ing] that the French had taken possession of the highways at St. Norbert,
nine miles south from Fort Garry, and were subjecting outgoers and incomers to a rigid search. The previous interruption offered to the Surveying
party of Colonel Dennis had not been generally received as evidence of any
comprehensive line of action.[*] The authorities here did their utmost by
personal intreaty and attempts at persuasion, to divert the recognized
leaders of the movement from their purpose, but the effort was vain and
the road to Pembina remained guarded day and night, while armed bands
were placed at intervals all the way to Pembina, in order that immediate
intelligence of the arrival of Mr. Mcdougall at the latter place might reach
head-quarters at St. Norbert.

The insurgents had represented themselves as being constituted into a
corporate body, called the "Republic of the Half-Breeds," the President of
which was a man named John Brouse [Bruce] and the Secretary Louis
Riel. On 25th October a meeting of the Governor and Council of Assiniboine was convened, before which these people attended. Renewed
attempts were made by the Council to dissuade them from their course—
but all were unavailing. The Council, finding itself much embarrassed
through the position in which it was placed, being till then practically

---

[*] This was on the land of André Nault at St. Norbert.

ignored by the Dominion Government, and subsequently defied by the half-breeds, opened a correspondence with the incoming Governor through the Governor of Rupert's Land, who forwarded a communication to be handed to Mr. MacDougall on his arrival at Pembina, acquainting him with the serious complications which had arisen here. Attempts to move the half-breeds from their resolution were persevered in through the agency of members of Council belonging to their own class but still without effect. The Roman Catholic Priesthood, as a body, refused to interfere; but the parish priest of St. Norbert [Father Noel Ritchot] openly countenanced the insurgents.

On 30th October Mr. Macdougall reached Pembina, whence, on learning the impending troubles, his family and servants returned to winter, I believe, at St. Cloud. The Lieutenant Governor took up his residence at the Hudson's Bay Post, a short distance north from the frontier. The advanced guard of half-breeds immediately handed him a letter from their leaders. Mr. Provencher, and Captain Cameron advanced towards the Settlement, but were forced to retrace their steps under armed escort after penetrating as far as St. Norbert. Colonel Dennis, as the date of Mr. Macdougall's expected arrival drew near, had gone by a round about route to Pembina, where he still remains.

On the afternoon of 2nd November, Mr. Macdougall was warned by an armed party of half-breeds, which entered the Company's post at Pembina, that he and his party must retire beyond the International line and quit the territory.* He produced his commission and explained its items; but was informed in reply that, by order of the Government they had established, he must withdraw. On the morning of 3rd November Mr. Macdougall was abruptly warned that delay on his part protracted beyond 9 o'clock might occasion bloodshed, as the half-breeds declared their orders to be positive that he should be beyond the line at that hour. Without waiting for breakfast he and his party therefore left the post, and were escorted by the half-breeds to the frontier, which they were warned not to re-pass. The Governor is accordingly encamped on American ground a short distance south from the International Boundary Line. Colonel Dennis, Captain Cameron, Attorney General Richardson, and Mr. Provencher continue to remain with him.

---

* This party was led by Ambroise Lépine.

Meanwhile on 2nd November a party of about 120 armed men, detached from the main body at St. Norbert, marched into Fort Garry, of which they took possession, posting sentinels at the gates and on certain of the platforms. Demands were made for provisions, at first to a very limited amount, payment being promised on the part of the so-called Republic.

It was at first imagined that the capture of Fort Garry was merely a feint contrived to mask the further design of an attack on the village of Winnipeg, in which reside a number of people personally obnoxious to the French. The latter, however, denied any such interior design, and alleged they merely wished to protect Fort Garry by their presence against an impending danger, the nature of which they declined to explain. From 120, their number was afterwards reduced to about sixty, who are relieved at intervals.

The outgoing and incoming mails were repeatedly detained and examined, though no letters were ultimately seized. A considerable quantity of goods have also been detained at St. Norbert, and it is yet doubtful when they may be released. The Government store of guns and ammunition, a considerable quantity of which have been kept in store at Fort Garry since the departure of the Canadian Rifles in 1861, have been seized and distributed among the insurgents.

I mentioned in my last week's letter that an invitation had been issued by the French to the English parishes requesting that delegates should be sent to meet the former at a public meeting to be held in the Court room, near Fort Garry, on the 16th instant. The following delegates were returned by the various parishes:—St. Johns, Morris E.G. Soloman [Lowman]; St. Margaret's, None; Headingly, William Tait; St. James, Robert Tait; St. Mary's, John Garrioch; Kildonan, James Ross; St. Paul's, Doctor C.J. Bird; St. Andrew's, Donald Gunn; St. Clement's, Thomas Bunn; St. Peter's, Henry Prince;Winnipeg, 1. Henry McKenney; Village, 1. Hugh F. O'Lone.[*]

The representation was certainly very fair, and as the deputies were all provided with instructions by their constituents, every security was obtained that a reliable statement of English opinion would be presented to the French.

The meeting took place on Tuesday morning, as arranged. Sixteen

---

[*] Hargrave does not list here the French delegates to this council.

rounds were discharged from the six pounder cannon at Fort Garry, which had been seized by the insurgents, and armed sentinels surrounded the place of meeting. The public was excluded. The English party objected to the show of force used in firing cannon and musketry, and the attendance of armed sentinels, but were assured these demonstrations were meant only to do them honour.

An attempt was made to secure the presence of a reporter, but the French party peremptorily refused to permit it.

A sealed message was handed to the meeting from the Governor of Rupert's Land, which, when opened and read, after a two hours discussion as to the propriety of receiving it, was found to be a solemn protest against all the recent outrages. It has since been printed in the form of a Proclamation, addressed to the inhabitants of Red River Settlement, and widely circulated. It was thankfully received and highly extolled by the English members, whose sentiments it embodied, but it produced no apparent effect on the French.

The meeting between the French and English delegates has already occupied two days. As the Quarterly Court commenced its session on Thursday morning, and the room in which the members were convened was consequently occupied, the temporary Council agreed to defer its further meeting from Wednesday evening last, until Monday morning, when it will resume its deliberations.

There is said to be some hope entertained by the English members that a compromise will be effected between the two parties until Governor Macdougall can be at least communicated with. As yet, however, the French party has preserved a wonderful silence, respecting its ultimate policy and wishes. It merely declares itself determined to uphold its rights. What these are nobody seems to know.

It is at least satisfactory to be able to report that as yet no lives have been lost. The insurgents have been kept in very good order by their leaders, and drunkenness has been prevented to a wonderful extent. The situation, however, even under these alieviating [sic] circumstances, is very embarrassing. Travellers require to provide themselves with "passes" under the hands of the leaders before they can pass the barriers erected across the highways. The outrages of which these are some, may lead to events which may retard the colonization of this country, but their ultimate effect must be to alienate the minds of men from the perpetrators and lead them to long more ardently for the day when a higher stage of civilization shall be established, and barbarism and semi-barbarism shall disappear.[*]

NOR'WESTER.

EDITOR'S NOTE

[The Proclamation of Governor McTavish, read at the end of the session by Henry McKenney, is printed in Morton, ed., Begg's *Journal*, 167-69. In it McTavish rehearsed the various challenges to public order undertaken by the Métis, and charged everyone "immediately to disperse themselves and peaceably to depart to their habitations or to their lawful business under the pain and penalties of law...."]

---

[*] Hargrave, of course, insisted that the Métis were not fully acculturated into European society.

# J.J. HARGRAVE

## 20 [27] NOVEMBER 1869

[In this letter J.J. Hargrave actually becomes an actor himself in the unfolding drama. Louis Riel's actions at Upper Fort Garry involving Hargrave and the records of the HBC obviously made the writer somewhat less favourably disposed to the rebellion. Printed in the *Montreal Herald and Daily Commercial Gazette*, 2 December 1869.]

Red River Settlement,
British North America,
20th Nov. 1869

On Thursday the 18th Instant the Red River General Quarterly Court commenced its sittings. The unsettled state of the colony may account for the very unusual circumstance, that no civil suit was on the List. On Friday a case was tried which may interest Canadians. It may be remembered, that early in October Mr. Snow, the Superintendent of works on the Canadian Road, was assaulted by a party of his men, who demanded certain moneys their right to which the Superintendent denied.* Mr. Snow was seized and dragged to a neighbouring brook to which he would certainly have been cast, had he not at the earnest solicitation of his assistant, Mr. Hamilton, paid the moneys demanded by the rioters, under protest. A complaint was lodged by Mr. Snow with the authorities at Fort Garry, who immediately caused the men to be apprehended, and after instituting a preliminary examination, committed them for trial at the court just held.

The number so put upon their trial was four, but of these only two were found guilty of the charge brought against them, which was one of aggravated assault. Their names were Thomas Scott and George Fortney. They were recommended by the Jury to the lenient consideration of the Court, which accordingly fined them each in a sum of Four pounds Sterling.

As this session is in all probability, the last to be held by the Red River

---

* This is the party of workmen allegedly led by Thomas Scott.

Courts under the authority of the Hudson's Bay Company, it may not be out of place here to give a short summary of their history and constitution.

The tribunal known as the "Red River General Quarterly Court" is presided over by the Company's Recorder, assisted by as many Justices of the Peace as desire to sit on the bench. It was instituted in 1839 when Doctor Adam Thom, a gentleman who has recently been brought prominently before the public in connection with the Overend Gurney & Co. litigations, was appointed first Recorder of Rupert's Land. He was succeeded in the office by Frank G. Johnson, Esq., now of the Canadian bench, who retained it for several years. In 1862 the present Recorder, Mr. Black, was appointed.

Besides the General Court, Petty Courts are held in the various sections of the Colony, in some cases at monthly intervals, but generally once each alternate month. These are provided with their Presidents and Petty Magistrates. Appeals lie from their decisions to the General Court, but it is very rarely that an instance of the kind occurs. A great deal of business is got through at these inferior Courts, and generally speaking with every satisfaction to the parties and the public.

All causes of any moment are of course decided before the General Court. Its forms are very plain. Cases are originated before it and its decisions are final, except, of course, in cases where a new trial is allowed. It is an institution originated to meet the requirements of a very primitive state of society. The parties state their cases, and conduct them without professional assistance of which none is to be had. There are no written pleadings, and as no official of the Court is supposed to know anything about a case until it comes before him unarranged, and without any single point stated as that specially at issue, it often requires a good deal of penetration to see where the weight of evidence actually lies and in what direction it points. The Court sitting with a Jury, it is often necessary for the Judge to show his own opinions, more unmistakably than I understand to be the custom elsewhere, as in fact, what falls from the bench is frequently that which tells more even than the actual evidence, on the minds of the Jurymen, who, generally speaking, are incompetent to form an opinion on the actual merits of an important and intricate case, especially when the parties on each side are unequally matched.

The inconvenience attending this state of matters in criminal cases is quite unfelt. The amount of crime is very small and the punishment slight;

moreover the great design of the prosecutor is always to arrive at the truth. But in civil cases in which both sides have an interest in making the most of their own views there is much room for deception. Although this has sometimes been successfully practised, however, it is undeniable that substantial justice has been generally administered, and the conduct of the Court has enjoyed the public confidence.

The session seldom occupies less than four, or more than eight days. The present one has occupied only two. I mentioned in my last week's letter that the committee of management of the French and English delegates had adjourned their meeting on the evening of the day on which its session commenced, so as to leave the Court-room at the disposal of the authorities. The leaders of the revolutionary movements declared their intention of respecting the authority of the court and disposing of their men so as to ensure the execution of its judgment in the cases coming before it for adjudication. A guard of armed men was stationed at the door of the Court house during the session. Of course although the Court went through the business brought before it[,] it in no way sanctioned the irregular services of its volunteer supporters, nor recognised the authority of their so called government.

On Monday the 22nd Instant the French and English delegates again met according to appointment. The entire day is said to have been occupied by a protracted debate between the leaders on either hand, at the conclusion of which the principal speaker on the part of the French distinctly and repeatedly stated that neither as governor, nor as a private individual, should Mr. Macdougall enter the territory, except over the dead bodies of himself and his adherents.[*]

Early on the Tuesday morning the Accountant in charge of the Hudson's Bay Company's office, at Fort Garry[,] was aroused by an intimation that Mr. Riel, the acting leader of the insurgents[,] wished to talk with him in his office. I may mention that the French had some days previously, taken possession of a chamber and outer central hall commonly known as the "Bachelors' Hall" in the upper storey of the building used as the public office of the Fort.[†] This they had done notwithstanding the remonstrances of the gentlemen in charge of Fort Garry, asserting that they positively

---

[*] The reference is to Louis Riel and James Ross.

[†] Hargrave lived at the fort and so was in a position to know of these events.

required such a room for the transaction of their writing and other private business. Armed guards were stationed at the outside of the door of the private room which Mr. Riel had fitted up as an office.

The accountant [John McTavish] on entering this room was told that he must hand over to Mr. Riel, as representative of the half breed Republic, the Land Register of the colony, along with all the accounts in his possession, relating to the finances of the Governor and Council of Assiniboia. The reply was a refusal. Six armed men were thereupon selected and ordered to convey the recalcitrant functionary below. As no *interior* communication is held between the upper and lower flats of the house in question, the operation of conveying a struggling man from one to the other would have been calculated by its necessary publicity to create a general alarm without being productive of good. Mr. McTavish accordingly prudently accepted the alternative, offered him of proceeding down stairs quietly on foot.

The governor's secretary who occupied a room attached to the public office,[*] was dressing when the accountant stepped in requesting him to make haste and witness a transaction of an irregular nature about to take place on the spot.[†] On entering the office six men with muskets were seen guarding the outer door. Mr. Riel and Mr. O'Donaghue, the father of whom for about eighteen months past and until within the last four weeks has been occupied in teaching, as a lay brother in the Roman Catholic Establishment at St. Boniface[,] were standing in the office. Mr. Riel demanded all the documents and books in the office connected with the Governor and Council of Assiniboia, or the public Business of the Settlement. Mr. McTavish made a formal verbal protest against the outrage, but was informed his protest was of no consequence and the question was whether he would deliver up the said papers quietly, or render it necessary for his interlocutor to search every portion of the room and examine all the papers and books. The accountant said he thought the latter course would be the best, and Riel quitted the office returning a few minutes later, accompanied by two of his satellites carrying muskets with bayonets attached to them.

Laying his hand on the Land Register which lay in its usual place on a

---

[*] This is Hargrave himself.

[†] What follows is a first-hand account unique to Hargrave.

desk, Riel ordered a man to carry it upstairs to his own office, and then commenced his search among a row of books ranged on a shelf, he soon selected the ones he wished, which included a number of volumes containing the accounts for several years past between the Hudson's Bay Company's Fur Trade, and the people resident in the settlement. In these books among many other accounts those between the Company and the local government have been kept. They were all forcibly carried away.

Mean while the guards at the various fort gates were ordered to permit no one to enter or leave the establishment. This regulation extended even to the grooms and servants. At eleven o'clock the committee was again convened in the Court room, and remained in session for about five hours. The French party claimed to be the government, and to have superseded the governor and council of Assiniboia. They requested the English delegates to return to their constituents to report progress, and to invite the latter to send delegates empowered to join them in organizing a Provisional government. The Council was there upon dissolved, with an intimation that it would meet again on Wednesday the 1st December.

Mean while the insurgent leaders have forcibly possessed themselves of the papers kept by the collectors of customs, and profess an intention of collecting all debts due to the governor and council of Assiniboia on account of duty on imports. These amount to a very considerable sum.

The land Register above alluded to is a vast volume and forms the legal basis of all questions relating to titles of surveyed lands in the colony. Its importance is therefore very great indeed and its abstraction from the hands of its legal custodians a matter, of the greatest import. The English portion of the colonists is becoming thoroughly alarmed and the difficulties with which the whole population is surrounded appear even to increase in danger.

Already public meetings have been held in some of the parishes and motions have been made setting forth the expedience of repelling force by force. The populous parish of St. Andrews on the Red River has distinguished itself by the resolution professed by its inhabitants, who declare themselves willing, on the call of the authorities to take to arms. St. Andrews is situated on the Red river about fifteen miles north from Fort Garry; its population are chiefly English halfbreed agriculturalists.[1] Rumours circulate regarding the intention of these people to offer themselves as a garrison to protect the company's post of "Lower Fort

Garry" against any apprehended attack.\* This post is in the parish of St. Andrew's about twenty miles from the Upper Fort now in possession of the insurgents. It is built of stone and in allusion to that fact is also called the "stone Fort." Although not the head quarters of the district it is a place of very considerable size and importance. Situated on the Red River, about twenty miles from Lake Win[n]ipeg, it is much used in the operations of the Company's summer Marine transport business.

As yet it is not known whether the authorities will consider themselves justified at this late hour of their rule in exposing the lives of the colonists to the dangers of an undisciplined internecine war in defence of the Hudson's Bay Company's depots. The invariable policy of the government throughout all the complicated troubles of the past seven years has been, to prevent such a continuance, notwithstanding almost any provocation. The reluctance of the local authorities to adopt any course which might place it beyond their power to protect from harm the lives and property of the scattered population committed to their charge, has exposed them to much annoyance at the hands of scheming and unscrupulous men who have at various times, found it beneficial to themselves to excite sections of the people to commit outrages, of which they have subsequently circulated false and insidious accounts in Canada, where even in the Provincial Parliament they have been commented on as true by officials who must well have known the unreliable nature of the sources whence they drew their intelligence. It is therefore considered improbable that unless driven to extremity, the authorities will encourage the English halfbreeds to resort to armed force.

Last evening a public meeting was held in the botom [sic] of winipeg [sic] with the purpose of ascertaining the popular sentiment regarding the present crisis. It broke up without any result what was, [sic] The most pressing danger is said to exist in the probability of a colison [sic] between two sections of the English speaking population. The majority of the latter believe that the action of Canada with reference to the present inhabitants of Ruperts Land is likely to be high handed and injust. The incoming government has hitherto practically ignored the existing authorities except in

---

\* This is one of the earliest known references to this fort as "Lower Fort Garry."

instances where it has suited their purposes to call on the latter for protection against popular tumult.

As I close this letter a new alarm has broken out. The French insurgents have planted two six pounders so as to command the principal street in the village. It is said that a portion of the English population is at hand with the object of commencing active hostilities against the French. The latter are on the alert, and armed at all points, ready to meet the assailants. What the result will be is impossible to predict.

Men who have anything to lose are of course, very much puzzled what to do. Among the expedients proposed is that of laying a statement of the condition of the colony before the House of Commons, and asking for the rights of representation and others granted to the inhabitants of other parts of the Empire.

EDITOR'S NOTE

[Hargrave's summary of the court proceedings is accurate. No further details are given in the court records. A bit more detail is given by Begg in his journal, where he states that the case against Snow was badly mismanaged by "Mr. Combs" as counsel. Begg adds: "One of the two fined (a Mr. Scott) stated before leaving court that it was a pity they had not ducked Snow when they were at it as they had not got their money's worth." See Morton, ed., *Begg's Journal*, 173.

The reference to Overend Gurney & Co. is interesting. In 1866 the banking firm of Overend Gurney suspended operations with liabilities of more than eleven million pounds. Considerable litigation followed, much of it turning around the question of whether the partners in the firm had full or limited liability. Adam Thom, the former recorder of Rupert's Land, wrote a number of pamphlets dealing with this case that were published in London in 1868 and 1869 and were undoubtedly discussed in the British newspapers read in Red River.]

# ALEXANDER BEGG

## 1 DECEMBER 1869

[This letter of Alexander Begg, writing as "Justitia," provides all the names of the delegates who met in November, and takes the story up to 1 December 1869, at which point he writes in despair of the future. The *Globe* described "Justitia" as "a correspondent tinged with pro-Company and anti-Canadian feeling," but added that the letter "gives the first connected account yet received of the events which transpired in the Settlement after the meeting of the Council of inhabitants on the 16th November." Printed in the Toronto *Globe*, 23 December 1869.]

Town of Winnipeg, Dec. 1

### THE CONVENTION.

On the 16th of this month (November), twenty-four delegates, from all parts of the Settlement, twelve from the French and twelve from the English side, met, by appointment, at the Court House, near Fort Garry. The delegates were as follows:—

### FRENCH SIDE.*

Francois Dauphinie, Pierre Poitras, Patrice Breland, Pierre Laviellier—Parish of St. François Xavier.
    William O'Donohue—Parish of St. Boniface.
    Andre Beaucheman, Pierre Paranteau, senr.—Parish of St. Anns.
    Louis La Certe, Baptiste Touron—Parish of St. Robert.
    Charles Nolin, Jean Baptiste Perrault—Parish of St. Anns.
    John Bruce, president. Louis Riel, secretary for the above.

### ENGLISH SIDE.

Henry McKenney, H.F. O'Lone—Town of Winnipeg.
    James Ross—Kildonan Parish.

---

    * None of these delegates had been members of the Council of Assiniboia.

Maurice Lowman—St. John's Parish.

Dr. Bird—St. Paul's Parish.

Donald Gunn—St. Andrew's Parish.

Thomas Bunn—St. Clements Parish.

Henry Prince—(Chief of Saulteaux Indians) St. Peters Indian Settlement.

Robert Tait—St. James'.

Wm. Tait—Headingly.

Geo. Gunn—St. Ann's.

John Garrioch — Portage La Prairie.

A SALUTE.

As the above gentlemen were entering the Council Chamber the French people outside fired a salute of twenty-four guns, and a *feu de joie* from the small arms of about 60 men, assembled at the door—this was done for effect—and as it may be difficult to understand where they obtained the large guns, I may say here in explanation that they had some days previously seized all the guns and rifles in Fort Garry as a preventative to their being used against them.[1]

After a good deal of discussion as to the propriety of keeping Mr. McDougall out, and the resorting to arms in the cause, the meeting adjourned till the next day without anything definite being done. In the meantime, however, Governor MacTavish, deeming it his duty, issued the proclamation, which you have doubtless already published.

The document in the shape of an address was sent into the Council of delegates by Governor MacTavish with the request that it should be read aloud. The French at first objected to it, but afterwards consented that Mr. McKenney should read it, which that gentleman did.

The meeting of the delegated Council on the 17th resulted in the same way as on the previous day and was finally adjourned till Monday the 22nd.

THE QUARTERLY COURT.

The General Quarterly Court met as usual on the 18th, and finished on the evening of the 19th. The first day was consumed in deciding a case of child murder; the latter crime was not proved, but the woman was convicted of concealing child-birth and was sentenced to six months in the common gaol. The second day was taken up with a case of Mr. Snow, the Superintendent of the Government road, against a party of his men who had rebelled against him and threatened to duck him in the river—alleging as their reason that he would not pay them their just wages and had not fed them in a proper manner. Two of the ringleaders were convicted of assault and recommended to the mercy of the Court, as there had been extenuating circumstances in their favor—two of the party were not convicted—those found guilty were fined £4 sterling each and allowed thirty days to pay it.

### HUDSON BAY COMPANY PEOPLE INDIGNANT AT BEING SUSPECTED.

During the present troubles endeavours have been made by a few—hopeful of Government approval and patronage hereafter—to ignite the smouldering excitement into open feud—slanders have been circulated that private individuals of standing here have urged the French to commit the acts they have done. Even the H.B.C. has been spoken of as one of the prime movers in exciting the people, when it is well known to every sensible man that an amicable adjustment of the present affairs is more to their advantage than to any private individual in the Settlement. A thorough investigation into the cause of the present troubles will soon, however, put the blame on the shoulders that deserve to bear it; and I sincerely hope that one of the first acts of the Canadian Government will be to fully investigate into all the mismanagement that has occurred to cause our existing difficulties.

### ANOTHER MEETING OF THE COUNCIL.

On the 22nd the Council of Delegates again met for the third time to consult, but with no better results. Some of the English argued in favor of allowing Mr. McDougall in on condition that he would promise not to assume his Governorship until the rights of the people were respected and granted. This point was dwelt on to such an extent that at last the French declared in a body that Mr. McDougall should not enter the Settlement unless over their dead bodies. On this the meeting once more adjourned till the next day.

THE FRENCH SEIZE THE CASH.

In the morning a new move had been made by the French, which rather startled everyone who heard it. They had, in fact, seized the cash and books of the Government of Assiniboia, and had closed Fort Garry to all outgoers and incomers. The information was brought to the town by the son of the Rev. George Young, who is in the employ of the Hudson Bay Company, and who had scaled the walls of the Fort to escape.* This news made the English delegates hesitate whether to attend the conference at noon; but finally they determined to go and see what the new aspect of affairs meant.

A BREAK UP IN THE COUNCIL.

At the meeting the question of Mr. McDougall was laid to one side, and the advantages and disadvantages of annexation to Canada discussed. All seemed satisfied that our only course was to go into the Dominion with the rights of British subjects, and the tariff and other regulations of Canada modified to meet the peculiar circumstances of our country. But when the French announced that they wished the English to form with them a Provisional Government to upset the Hudson Bay Company rule (which they asserted was dead already), the meeting broke up, the English delegates agreeing, however, to put their proposition to their several parishes and to return an answer Wednesday week.

ANOTHER SEIZURE.

Mr. Roger Goulait, Collector of Customs, was called upon to hand over all papers and valuables in his hands belonging to the Government of Assiniboia, and was escorted to his house by a guard of armed men for that purpose. These acts of seizing the Government books and papers were preparatory to forming the Provisional Government proposed, whose duty would be to treat with Canada for the terms on which we should enter the Dominion, and in the interim to govern the affairs of the country.

---

* Little else is known of George Young the younger, except that he was later imprisoned again. His father was a Methodist minister in Winnipeg in 1869.

THINGS BECOMING MIXED.

Things were beginning to become exceedingly complicated and apparently diverging from the original idea of merely asking rights from Canada. The present rule of the country was threatened and private interests interfered with; and these facts made people view matters with a great deal of disquietude. A guard of men were sent to Pembina to watch the proceedings of Mr. McDougall. At the same time permission was asked from Governor MacTavish by the residents around Lower Fort Garry to put a force of 100 to 150 men in it, in case of trouble between the two sides of the Settlement.

THE ENGLISH OPINION.

The general opinion of the English side was against forming a Provisional Government in the face of the Hudson Bay Company rule; and feeling began to run so high on the subject that guns and rifles were raked together and distributed amongst all those able to carry them. A general rush was made for lead; and bullets were moulded by the thousands. Companies of men were formed for drill here and there throughout the Settlement, and the utmost excitement prevailed. The warlike preparations were gone into merely in readiness to meet any trouble that might come. Indeed, the slightest provocation on either side resulting in the shedding of a single drop of blood would have cast our Settlement into a civil war, the end of which would have been deplorable.

A CRITICAL MOMENT.

I am sorry to say evil influences at this critical moment nearly caused our ruin. A lot of Government (Canadian) pork lying in the warehouse of Dr. Schultz, was represented to be in danger of confiscation by the French; while the fact was that Mr. Riel, knowing the pork was there, placed a guard over it in the interests of the Canadian Government, lest it should be destroyed or disappear, and the blame be afterwards put to the credit of the French. Men that ought to have known better represented that personal violence was threatened and private property endangered, and called upon the English side to rise and resist such by force of arms. Fortunately, some parties more sensible and with better hearts, succeeded in stopping the excitement before it had gone too far, and those who resorted to arms in behalf of a few barrels of pork are now thoroughly convinced of the insincerity of those who encouraged them to it.

PEACE PRESERVED.

It is the universal opinion that the French have overstepped the mark. The stoppage of the mails, although the letters were not tampered with, was an uncalled for act; the retaining of private property in transit; the seizure of the public books, &c, &c, were acts uncalled for in their cause, and has raised a great deal of indignation against them; but as yet it will be only an act of extraordinary provocation, or the spilling of the blood, that will raise a fight among the settlers.

A NEW PROPOSITION.

For the sake of humanity and peace in the existing excited state of the people, it was deemed prudent to endeavour to unite the two sides of the Settlement by some means that would be legal and constitutional. It was therefore proposed to the French by a few, that the Hudson's Bay Company's rule be allowed to go on as usual until the Queen's proclamation should come out; and that, in the meantime, a sort of executive committee be formed of representatives from all parts of the Settlement, whose duty would be to treat with Canada for the rights claimed by the people.

THE FRENCH AGREE.

This proposition was at last agreed to by the French, and steps were taken to acquaint the rest of the Settlement with the fact. A universal feeling in favour of the movement was evinced; resolutions were adopted agreeing with it; and the English delegates arrived in Winnipeg town on Wednesday morning, fully prepared to coincide with the French in the formation of an executive committee as has been described, when it was found that

THE FRENCH HAD BACKED OUT,

and still stuck to their idea of forming a Provisional Government. All were taken aback; and as hopes were entertained that the French might divide amongst themselves on the question, the English delegates were deciding upon going to attend the appointed conference, when news was brought in that

## THE QUEEN'S PROCLAMATION

had arrived and was out; and that Colonel Dennis had come into the Settlement by a round-about way, and was then stationed at Lower Fort Garry.

## A GLOOMY PROSPECT.

But here I must leave you for the present. No one can tell the end; but certainly the prospects look gloomy. Should some fanatics arise, and blood be spilt; should Colonel Dennis succeed in inducing any of the settlers to try and bring in Mr. McDougall before some arrangements are entered into with the French—either between them and the balance of the Settlement, or with the Government representatives—blood will be spilt, and when that happens, the fight will be between father and son, brother and brother, and may God forgive the one who commences such a civil war. It would be horrible in its nature, and those who cause it will be inhuman— our Settlement will be devastated. What is now a garden will be a waste.

# ALEXANDER BEGG

2 DECEMBER 1869

[In the following letter, Alexander Begg attempts to disabuse easterners of their misapprehensions about the Red River Settlement, particularly in terms of its mixed-blood population, but also in terms of its government and economy. The *Globe* headlined this letter "Red River People/Their Origin and Progress/Description of the Settlement." Printed in the Toronto *Globe*, 24 December 1869.]

TOWN OF WINNIPEG DEC. 2 [1869]

In my former letter I stated that a meeting of delegates from all parts of the Settlement had been called for the 16th of this month, but before giving you the results of that meeting and others that followed it, I will endeavour to give you a short description of our Settlement and the different classes of settlers that reside in it.

The settlers are divided as follows: French, English, Scotch, Canadian, and American; the three former are what may be termed the old inhabitants of the place; the two latter are principally new comers, although there are some Canadians and Americans who have lived here a number of years. The greater part of the French reside between Pembina and Fort Garry, on both sides of the river, and also on the Assiniboine, as far as Portage La Prairie. The English are on the Assiniboine, principally on the north side of the stream as far as the White Horse Plains, about half-way between Fort Garry and Portage La Prairie, as well as some miles this side of the latter place, and a distance beyond it towards Lake Manitoba; they are also on the Red River, beyond the Scotch Settlement, as far as eight miles the other side of the Stone Fort, or Lower Fort Garry. The Scotch Settlement extends from Winnipeg town about six or seven miles down the Red River. After passing Lower Fort Garry about eight miles there is the Indian Settlement extending as far as Lake Winnipeg.

The distances are as follows:—

From Pembina to Fort Garry, about 60 miles

From Fort Garry (going in a westerly direction) to Portage La Prairie, about 65 miles

From Portage La Prairie (going in a northern direction) to Lake Manitoba, about 12 miles

From Fort Garry (going in a northerly direction) to Lake Winnipeg, about 60 miles

The town of Winnipeg is about a quarter of a mile from Fort Garry.

The residence—"Silver Heights"—engaged and prepared for Mr. McDougall as the Governor's House, is about five miles from Fort Garry.[*] The above table of distances shows the extent of our Settlement, as it is, to be about 120 miles north from Pembina to Lake Winnipeg, and striking off in a westerly direction along the Assiniboine River, about 65 and 12 to Lake Manitoba—77 miles in all.

THE POPULATION.

It would be almost impossible to give a correct idea of the number of our population; but it is estimated to be at present somewhere between 12,000 and 14,000 people. If the large number of settlers, however, who are generally out on hunting or trading expeditions were numbered as well, the latter sum might be materially increased. The French half breeds are estimated to be the most numerous—then come the English—after them the Scotch—the Canadians follow next, a good number of whom are now to be found comfortably settled on farms around Portage La Prairie. The Indian Settlement is a reserve made over to the Saulteaux, and which is now inhabited principally by those Indians who have given up their wandering mode of life and taken to civilized habits, many of them possessing good farms and houses. The Americans are not very numerous, but most of them are in good circumstances, and make respectable and thrifty settlers. Having now given you to the best of my ability the extent of our Settlement— the nationality if I may call it so of our settlers, with their priority as far as numbers go, I will give as far as my space will allow me a description of the country itself and the characteristics of the several classes living in it.

FARMING.

The farms and farm-houses of the settlers line both banks of the Red and Assiniboine Rivers, but the plains in the back ground are as yet unpeopled

---

[*] This house belonged to James McKay (1825-1879) and was in St. James.

and uncultivated; each settler holding land bought from the Hudson Bay Company has the right of running out their farms from two to four miles on the prairie—their frontage, therefore, on the river bank is small, but a narrow strip of from two to four miles in length, will contain a good number of acres. The soil is good, indeed very good, and it is as well that it is so as the keen winds from the prairies in the spring would often otherwise prevent the reaping of average crops in the Settlement. We experience those keen winds in the spring only when it blows from the North and drives the cold from the floating ice on the surrounding lakes down on the tender crops when they are first sprouting. When one plague, the grasshoppers, see fit to leave us alone the yield of the land, as a general thing, is far above that of Canada, or even the most fruitful of the United States. Manure is seldom used by the farmers on their land. All sort of cereals grow here, with the exception of white or winter wheat, which I have never seen, but I cannot say whether it could be grown or not. Wood, for fencing purposes and fuel, is not plentiful, but not what might be called scarce. We do not often see the large sticks of cordwood one is accustomed to in Canada. It is generally small trees, about six to eight inches thick, that are cut down and brought in for fuel. Hay abounds, anyone can go out and cut on the open prairie as much of that as he may require. I think, therefore, that this country is peculiarly adapted to stock raising.

BUILDINGS.

The farm houses are generally built of logs, mudded with the clay from the river banks, which hardens and sticks fast, when dry, to the sides of the houses. In the fall it is customary to whitewash the dwellings, and then they present a clean and tidy appearance; thatch is mostly used for the roofs. Brick has been successfully tried here; indeed, the clay found in the Settlement is of a very fine quality, and the best description of brick can be made from it. Stone is not found in abundance, but there is enough for ordinary purposes for some time to come. The mineral resources of the North West, outside of the settlement, from accounts brought it, must be great. Lumber is scarce at present, but with energy and enterprise, I am of opinion, we could have sufficient of that article for years to come, even should there be a large demand for the same. Lake Winnipeg abounds with spruce and some of the tributaries of the Red River have large pineries on their banks. The general appearance of the Settlement is one of thrift and comfort. The farmers are not behind the times, I assure you, and although you do not see the well built farm houses and barns you are accustomed to in Canada still there is a look of tidiness and comfort round the settlers' houses that is creditable to them, as far removed as they are from the outside world, and from the markets that foster advancement in farming.

THE CLIMATE.

The weather is generally pleasant and the climate healthy. Winter begins in November and ends in March or April, and when the cold once sets in we have no more thaws or rain till spring time. The spring is very bright and cheerful—the summer not too warm and the fall is the most pleasant season of the whole year.

TRADE.

The trade of the Settlement can be comprehended in one word, "fur," and the Hudson Bay Company has been, and is, the chief promoter of the business in every farm throughout the Settlement. The surplus of grain or provisions, over what is required for consumption by the settlers themselves, is taken by the Hudson Bay Company and fur traders, at fair prices from the farmers, and used in feeding the many men who are engaged in bringing in the furs. A great deal of money is expended amongst the people in paying for freighting goods across the plains from St. Cloud and from Fort Garry to the interior posts of the Hudson Bay Company. The money of the Settlement is kept abroad, chiefly in England. The Hudson Bay Company have their own notes for five shillings and one pound sterling, as the currency of the country, which they redeem by granting bills of exchange at sixty days' sight on their House in London, England; and to meet those bills, as well as other liabilities for goods, to carry on their Nor' West trade, the Company here ship home their furs to London, which always meet with ready cash sale. So that everything we own here in the way of cash, with the exception of the little gold and silver in circulation, consists altogether of drafts on account of "fur," shipped abroad either on H.B.Co or private account. There are of course sales of furs in the United States and Canada, but it amounts to the same thing; the only way we can meet our liabilities is through drafts drawn against "fur," sold or unsold. "Fur" is the back stay of the country at present, and is likely to be so for some time to come, notwithstanding the fact that we are drawing nearer every year to eastern markets.

FREIGHTS.

Our Customs regulations have been very light and easy; the rate of duty being 4 percent on all goods consumed in the Settlement, and one shilling per gallon on all wines and liquors. But in lieu of light duties, we have had to pay extremely heavy freights—sixteen shillings sterling per 100 lbs. being the rate from St. Cloud to Fort Garry. Goods therefore are sold at high prices, and I do not see how they can allow of any heavier duty that [than] the present one until a cheaper mode of transportation than by ox carts is effected. The Hudson Bay Company have expended the revenue, collected from the Settlement in repairing roads, running mails, and any other improvements deemed necessary—it will be long ere we find so economical a Government. And really all was done that was requisite for our comfort in a public way—for what need had we of any costly improvements in our small Settlement, isolated as we have been. When we become closer connected with the outside world, and in proportion have an increase in our population, new wants will spring up, which, as yet, have never been dreamt of; and proportionately as we obtain advantages, so will we be the more able to pay for them. But this will necessarily require some time, and it will soon be seen, that, situated as we are, improvements and changes will have to be gradual, as the Settlement is not in a position to have things rushed along at railway speed.

THE PAST GOVERNMENTS.

As I stated in my previous letter, our Government consisted of a Council appointed by the Hudson Bay Company, from amongst our settlers. It was mild in its measures, and, to a certain degree, not very powerful. It reflects the more to the honour of our settlers that, weak as it was known to be, they stood by its rules and regulations, endeavouring to obey them; indeed, any one who was a law breaker had little sympathy from the generality of the Settlement, and in fact was universally looked down upon with suspicion and distrust by his neighbours. I have already shown you how, on several occasions, our laws were broken and defied; but the guilty ones were few in number, and stood alone in the acts they committed. It was on account of the weakness of the ruling powers, and consequent danger to personal interests, that a number of the settlers, at different times, were induced to seek for a new order of things. The means used were in the form of petitions; some were in favour of a "Crown Colony," and others Annexation to Canada; but these petitions sought that all the acknowledged rights of British subjects should be respected, neither did they represent that we were tyrannized over, for they went to show that our Government, as administered, was weak, and a weak government can never be a tyrannical one. Can you wonder then at the opposition of the settlers to the plan on the one hand of having strangers as their Councilmen, and on the other of having the power to appoint Councilmen, vested in one man (the Governor), and that man supposed to be a prejudiced individual. Why, it is stepping from the frying pan into the fire indeed. I have not heard a single word of opposition to going into the Confederation under proper terms; nor do I believe there is any hostile feeling to Canada. It is merely the terms of the junction that are objected to.

CHARACTER OF THE POPULATION—THE FRENCH HALF BREEDS.

Now that I have given you some idea of our Settlement as to its length and breadth, &c., let us take a cursory glance at the people in an intellectual, social and religious point of view. The French half-breeds are mostly given to hunting, fishing and trading for a livelihood.* They are a quick and excitable class of people. As a rule they are law-abiding and honest in their dealings. Where any of them have had educational advantages they profit by them, being quick to learn and intelligent at grasping ideas. Where they pay attention to agriculture, they generally turn out good, thrifty farmers. Indeed we have no better farmers than amongst some of the French half-breeds; but farming as a general thing is distasteful to them; their wants are not numerous and easily supplied; and trained, as most of them have been from infancy to hunting, trapping, trading, tripping, fishing, &c., their nomadic habits have become part and parcel of their nature. They are not, moreover, a lazy people—nor are they dishonest—on the contrary,

---

* This, of course, is the stereotyped view of the Métis, not very different from that of Hargrave.

they are active, fair as a rule in their dealings, and I feel sure that should they turn their attention to farming or other more settled pursuits than that to which they are now accustomed, they will not be behind their neighbours. There are many intelligent clever men amongst them; their women make good, faithful wives, and I must say I have seen some of the handsomest faces, I ever met with on my travels, amongst the French half-breed girls of Red River. The French are noted here for their love of gaiety and fun—their homes are models of cleanliness; altogether they are a people that the longer you know them the better you like them. They are brave as a rule—their religion is the Roman Catholic, and their Cathedral and Convents &c. at St Boniface, would be creditable to any country. Unfortunately for Canadians coming to this country, they are impressed with the idea that half-breeds are a sort of half-and-half specimens of humanity, hardly entitled to the privilege of being called rational beings. This idea of the people of this country is not only unfortunate but uncalled for, as those who come here to judge for themselves soon see. The word half-breed merely signifies where there is a tinge more or less of Indian blood—but whoever started the term Breed ought to have been choked before he had time to apply it to human beings. There are very few [among] us now-a-days who have not a mixture of blood in our composition—our mother, perhaps, being an Englishwoman, and our father a Scotchman or Irishman—therefore the term is as much applicable to us as to those who have Indian blood in their veins—and for this reason I would advise strangers to attach no erroneous idea to it, for I have seen as good half-breeds as I have seen white men. Some of the finest ladies in the Settlement have Indian blood in their veins, and more lady-like, courteous and pleasant gentlewomen I never met in my life.

THE ENGLISH.

The English half-breeds are more inclined to farming and trading, more staid in their character, and more settled in their habits than the French. The generality of their farms and houses show therefore to better advantage than those of the latter. The English half-breeds are, as a rule, industrious and intelligent, but not as quick as the French. They are, moreover, frugal, hospitable and kind, and will not be likely to fall in the rear when newcomers flock into the Settlement. Their religion is mostly

the Episcopal. The English Cathedral is a fine stone structure. The Settlement, in fact, can boast of a number of Churches, all of which are good
substantial buildings. The Roman Catholic, Anglican, Presbyterian, and
Methodist, are all represented.

### THE SCOTCH.

The Scotch settlers are a close fisted, canny, thrifty set of people, all well
to do.[*] Their farms are models of careful management. They are not enter-
prizing; but steady going, and very conservative in their ideas. They are,
as a rule, fine-looking, "real Scotch" looking men and women—better educated, as a class, than any other in the Settlement.

### THE CANADIANS.

The Canadians we have here are, generally speaking, a good class of men—
especially those who have lately come into the Settlement; most of them
having brought means, have bought farms and settled down. The young
men have shown themselves industrious and sober. A few of them have
acted unwisely in taking it for granted that there is a feeling antagonistic
to Canadians generally in the minds of the settlers, when in fact no such
feeling exists. Those Canadians who have helped to create the present
troubles by their own wrong acts are well known and appreciated.

The Americans, unlike some of our Canadians, have minded their own
business by keeping aloof from the present troubles altogether; and in fact,
have shown themselves in that respect, good sensible men.

I have dwelt thus long on a description of our Settlement, and the people that live in it, for the purpose of disabusing the public mind in Canada
that we here are not of sufficient importance, either numerically, intellectually, or socially speaking, to warrant granting us the proper rights of a
free people—an elective voice in the management of our own affairs; and
also, that we are not a people inferior, in any single respect, to the general
community in Canada.

---

[*] This appraisal of the Scots is typical of most observers, but quite different
from that of Hargrave.

# J.J. HARGRAVE

## 4 DECEMBER 1869

[This letter from J.J. Hargrave offers the most detailed account known of the Winnipeg meeting at the fire hall, and Hargrave's story about the revolvers is a telling one. Printed in the *Montreal Herald and Daily Commercial Gazette*, 25 December 1869.]

Fort Garry
Red River Settlement
4th Dec., 1869

In my last letter I explained that the delegates representing the English and French sections of the Settlement had separated on the afternoon of the 23rd November, appointing the 1st December as the day of their next meeting, in order to give the former an opportunity of meeting their constituents and receiving their sanction to act in the formation of a temporary or "Provisional Government".

Meetings of a public nature had, in accordance with this design, been held in the various parishes inhabited by the Protestant population of the Colony. I mentioned that one had also been held in the village of Winnipeg, and I would now begin to trouble you with a few matters of detail regarding it. It was held in the Fire Engine House in the village, on the evening of Friday, 26th ult.

The room was well filled with a crowd of American citizens, local residents, and Canadian new arrivals and others late of the Government. The Post Master, Mr. Bannatyne, was chairman. Louis Riel, the most active spirit among the French half-breeds, was present, with his body guard. He did not, I believe, intend to take part in the debate; but Mr. Michael Powers, a Chelsea Out-Pensioner of the rank of Sergeant from a regiment of Dragoon Guards, requested him to state to the people the source whence he drew the authority under which he is at present acting.

After some apparent reluctance, overcome by the encouraging demonstrations of those present, Riel stepped forward, and in the course of a somewhat protracted speech in English, stated substantially that he drew his authority, as did all other constitutional rulers, from the people. He said the French did not wish to impose their Provisional Government on any or all of the English, and that any one who did not wish to own allegiance to it was at liberty to remain beyond its pale. He and his friends wanted no money, and were ambitious only to serve their countrymen. He stated that his widowed mother was suffering the consequences of the action he was taking, as they were very poor; and his was by no means a solitary case, for all his assistants and followers were poor men and their families were suffering while their time was occupied with public service and duties. Above all, the government was not one of religion, as he said had been rumoured.

Mr. Power replied that his question about authority had not been answered. His remarks were interspersed with quotations of a practical nature about the "Meteor Flag," which his soldierly instincts appeared to have led him to feel had been instituted. He was, however, a better patriot than speaker, and his rambling remarks were, I suspect, unintelligible to the majority present, who received them with much laughter. I mention his appearance at this length, because he was the only man who in any way, in my hearing, alluded to the fact that the country was in a state of armed rebellion and that a gentleman had been stopped on the highway and grievously annoyed, because he was the bearer of a commission from the Queen.

The speech of the evening was, however, made by a shoemaker named Macpherson, who objected to the formation of the proposed "Provisional Government" on the ground that he had already, some years before, been a victim of a scheme of that kind, attempted in this neighbourhood. Thomas Spence, a gentleman from Canada, had been placed in the Presidential chair of an institution called the "Republic of Manitobah," the seat of which was at Portage La Prairie, on the Assiniboine River, about sixty-five miles west from Fort Garry, the Republic itself embracing a vast tract of Prairie country west from the Portage.[1] The incident of which Mr. Macpherson was the victim, and of which he gave the following narrative to the meeting proved I believe the death blow of the infant Republic.

Early in 1868, an oath of allegiance having been administered to the inhabitants of that portion of the Hudson's Bay Territories included within the limits of the said Republic of Manitoba—which was entirely in the Indian country beyond the circuit of the municipal district of Assiniboine—this preliminary step was succeeded by an attempt to levy taxes on imports, to the same amount, of four percent *ad valorem*, leviable by the constituted authorities on the settlers of Assiniboine. The result was a misunderstanding between the President and the gentleman in charge of the Hudson's Bay Trading Post of Portage La Prairie, situated within the bounds of his self asserted authority, and an intimation to Mr. Spence from the Governor of Rupert's Land that no Hudson's Bay duty would be paid him, and any one so inclined might refuse to comply with his demand.

Mr. Macpherson not only refused to pay duty, but accused the President of having misappropriated half a crown already levied on account of Customs by expending it for whiskey for private consumption at a house of call in the Republic.

"Macpherson, I'll *hang you*," said the President. About two days afterwards two constables called on the complainant bearing a warrant from the Government for his apprehension on a charge of "treason." The result was an attempted flight on the part of Macpherson; a spirited and protracted chase in carrioles, on horse-back and on foot, off the track and out on the plains; a desperate struggle in the snow, and finally, the conveyance of Macpherson, bound before the "Governor and Council." The poor man had been stripped of his clothes in the struggle, and after a long drive, appeared before his judge attired, he assured his audience, only in his shirt.

Spence and his abettors had not proceeded far with the hearing of the case of treason, when an armed mob of Macpherson's friends appeared on the scene, and after abusing the captive as a fool for not using his firearms, turned on the "Governor and Council," and with insulting expressions expelled them from the house in which they were assembled, and unbound the prisoner.

Mr. Spence subsequently addressed the Imperial Government on the affairs of his Republic, but receiving a reply from the Colonial Office, warning him of the danger he was incurring by his conduct, and repeating what the Governor of Rupert's Land had previously told him. Before the answer came, however, the whole scheme had collapsed, and Mr. Spence had turned his attention to the manufacture of salt.

Macpherson's account of his sufferings was received by his sympathizing audience with great laughter and applause. The meeting, however, separated without any result being arrived at with respect to the object for which it had been convened, which was to consult about the attitude to be maintained towards the French insurgents.

As an instance of the state in which society exists here at present, I beg to mention the following facts: Talking over the events of the meeting with three friends, with whom I spent the subsequent part of the evening, I rather ridiculed the idea expressed in my hearing, that almost every one present at the meeting had been armed, and that there had been certain critical moments when a general discharge of pistols had been imminent. I must confess, however, to a modification of opinion when my three friends pulled, each man from a belt concealed under his coat, a revolver pistol. In one of these three instances, certainly, only one chamber was loaded, and as the hammer was laid down on the corresponding nipple, the instrument, on being cocked, would, of course, have turned, so as to let it fall on any empty chamber, and the person covered by *that* instrument would probably have run no very serious risk; but the other two were fully charged and capped, and had only to be cocked, after which, to use the expression of one of the parties, "one trigger, sir, would do the business." After such a demonstration I affect not to doubt the truth of the assertion that more than fifty revolvers were in readiness for use at the meeting; but the position of a non combatant spectator, in the centre of such a shower of leaden hail as might have burst forth in a crowded chamber from all these instruments, would have been far from pleasant.

On Saturday a collision between the two sections of the settlement was apprehended. Some government pork and provisions which had been permitted at various times to pass the barrier at La Riviere Sale, were stored in a house in the village of Winnipeg.* The Canadian Government officials, to whom it belonged, had set a guard over it, and the insurgent leaders had also stationed several of their people armed at the place, under the pretext that they believed it might be surreptitiously removed by others, for whose action they might subsequently, though innocent, be blamed. The Hudson's Bay authorities, at the request of the Canadian officer in charge of the merchandise, had also stationed some constables on guard over it. It was understood further that the pork was, in spite of the precautions, to be conveyed, for greater security to Lower Fort Garry—a step which the French half-breeds were determined to oppose. It was with this design that they

---

* The house of John Schultz.

pointed two field pieces at the store where the articles were, and took other steps which appeared preparatory for immediate collision. Before dusk, however, all fear of such an attempt was dispelled, and the colony was again quiet.

On the forenoon of 1st December the delegates again met according to appointment, and it was whispered that, from intelligence received by mail on the preceding day, it was known that something of consequence would transpire in the course of the day. In the afternoon it was known that Col. Dennis had arrived from Pembina, bringing with him the Royal proclamation, which was forthwith published, and was to take effect from that day. It was distributed in written form, it being impossible to put it in type, as both the printing establishments now here had previously been seized by the insurgents.

Colonel Dennis, it appeared, had arrived by a somewhat round about way, selected so as to avoid the obstructions at La Riviere Sale, on the evening of 30th November. His journey was a brave undertaking, as he certainly ran a narrow risk of his life, being already regarded with a evil eye by the insurgents, in consequence of having passed their lines in a similar manner, on his journey to meet Mr. Macdougall at Pembina. His exertions at the latter place, in rendering the position of the Lieutenant Governor as tolerable as possible, are also very highly spoken of, and will doubtless be appreciated at their proper value in official quarters.

Louis Riel and his Council were served with a copy of the Proclamation on Wednesday afternoon. The English members who attended had already become convinced of the practical impossibility of concurring with the French in any project such as that of a "Provisional Government," and had determined on withdrawing from the movement. An evening session was however agreed to, and after a recess of two hours the assembly met at six o'clock, and continued in session till a late hour. The course of the proceedings with which the delegates were occupied is only slightly known [to] outsiders. I believe, however, that a series of proposals, to be made to Mr. Macdougall, was drawn up, and at least tacitly agreed to, by a majority of the English delegates. When the question rose, however, as to which of the latter should represent their party in a commission to be forwarded to Pembina to meet Mr. Macdougall and lay the terms of compromise before him, the whole English party declined to go. Their reluctance is scarcely surprising if it be true as reported, that one of the acquisitions [] was, that

Mr. Macdougall should give the deputation an "Act of Parliament" to assure them of his good faith in the matter, which would be more than doubtful were he to refuse so straight forward and simple a guarantee. I think, however, the project of English cooperation with the French is at an end, and the deputies have gone home. The French deputies however remain together and the party is growing stronger than ever.

Yesterday a guard was placed over the two local newspaper offices, the forthcoming issues of both journals being seized by the French.* Colonel Dennis, assisted by Captain Boulton, late of the 100th Regiment, is now near Lower Fort Garry, engaged in raising and drilling a corps of English half-breeds. He is said to have full powers from the Governor to organize a corps and fight. The whole French body are collecting about Upper Fort Garry, and are resolved on preventing the entrance of Mr. Macdougall, which is the only point on which they seem able to agree.

I enclose a lampoon which has been written and circulated among the half-breeds.[2] The feeling of dislike towards Mr. Macdougall, apparent in it, I cannot explain. The gentleman's name I believe to have been totally unknown here previous to his connection with recent events. An attempt was made, on the part of his professing friends, to represent him as the desired of all in the Settlement. The prevailing expression of dislike to him may be only a counter demonstration. Any inordinate liking or dislike to him as an individual, seems to me quite absurd and misplaced, seeing he is yet quite unknown. But the party which arrogates to itself the character of being representative of Canada is most unpopular here, and the fact that Canadian incoming officials have openly allied themselves with it, I believe to be explanatory of the dread with which the advent of their rule is generally regarded. This song given below was sung in public by a clerical gentleman on a recent occasion:†—

* The *Nor'-Wester* and the *Pioneer*.
† Possibly Father Noel Ritchot.

CHANSON

"Des tribulations d'un
roi malheureux."

Est-il rien sur la terre
Que la tragique histoire
De McDoug'l et ses gens:
Je vous la conterai
Veuilles bien m'ecouter

Sur notre territoire
Devenu ses Etats
Il venait—ce bon père
Regner au potentat,
Ainsi l'avait réglé
Le Ministre Cartier

Le coeur gros l'espérance
Partant du Canada
Il dit j'ai confiance
Qu'on vive a bien là-bas
Ah! quel bon heur!! ma foi!!!
Je suis donc enfin Roi!

Comptant sur les richesses
Qu'il trouverait chez nous,
Il eut la maladresse
De ne pas prendre un sous, Meme
            pour traverser
Un pays étranger.

Le juif errant—plus sage—
En portait cinq au moins
Dont il faisant usage
Dans un case de besoin.
C'etait mieux fait, on dit
Que de prendre à credit.

Mais trève de remarque
Allons droit au plus court,
Suivons notre Monarque
Entouré de sa cours—
De bon roi Dagobert
Traversant le désert.

["BALLAD OF THE TRIALS OF AN
UNFORTUNATE KING"

Is there anything on earth
Of an interest more grand
Than the story—check your mirth—
Of McDougall and his band!
But listen to me well
And the tale I will you tell.

Upon our broad and noble land,
Now become his realm of state,
He has come, this worthy man,
To hold sway as potentate,
As him did command and say
The wily Minister Cartier.

His bosom swelling out with pride,
Down in Canada, all over,
"I am right sure," he loudly cried,
"That I shall be deep in clover!
And, my word, what luck does bring!
Now at last I am a king!"

Counting on the easy money
He among us here would spy
He thought the idea merely funny
To have a single penny by,
Even for to pay his way
And o'er a foreign land to stray.

The wandering Hebrew—much more
            wise—
Bore with him a dime at least,
With which he could, should need arise,
Purchase crust or hire a beast
As is better far, 'tis said
Than to borrow, or beg bread.

But no more of persiflage!
Let us take the shortest way
And pursue our Monarch sage
And his court in its display,
This right royal Dagobert
Wandering on across the desert.

Il parait que l'orage
Dans son gouvernment
Durant tout le voyage
Eclata fort souvent
L'union qui rend plus fort
Etait loin de ce corps.

Mais malgré la tempete
Camerons a son bord?
Voulait decrire la fete
Qui l'attendait a porte
Et la voir imprimée
Avant qu'elle fut passée.

Ce ministre fidèle
Etant loin de prévoir
Qu'elle ne serait pas telle
Qu'il avait cru la voir
Funeste illusion!
Quelle déception!!

Déjà de son royaimé
Le sol il va toucher
Quand tout-a-coup un homme
Lui défend d'avancer
Lui disant—"mon ami,
"C'est assez loin ici."

Etonné de l'audace
De ces hardis mortels
Il emploie les menaces
Pour vaincre ces rebels.
Mais cela fut en vain
Il ne put gagner rien.

Obligé de reprendre
Sa voie du Canada
Il lui faudra attendre
De l'argent pour cela.
Car, pour manger ici
Il prend tout à crédit.

It does seem that passions wild
Raged within this royal court
And through all that journey piled
Rage on rage, and tempers short
Drove the union which is strength
From that cortége a great length.

But what if tempests intervene—
The bold Cameron for his part
Wished to depict the future scene
Which awaited man and cart
And to see set down in print
What was in morrow's eye a glint.

That tried and trusty officer
Was far from coming to foresee
That nothing would in fact occur
Of all that he had hoped would be—
Illusion of the hopeful eye,
Deception of most dismal dye.

Just as our king was setting foot
Upon his realm's fair soil
A man at once sprang up and put
A stay unto his progress royal,
And to him said—"Hold hard, my friend,
You find right here your journey's end."

By the boldness set aback
Of these mortals bold enow,
He uses threats, and worse, alack,
Such rebellious folk to cow,
But 'tis all in vainest vain;
Not an inch can he thus gain.

Forced to wend his weary way
O'er the Plains the way he came,
He finds he must a period stay
To collect some cash for same,
For, to eat while here at all,
He did upon his credit call.

Aujourd'hui sa couronne
Est un songe passé.
Le trone qu'on lui donnee
Est un tronc percé
Mais il dit qu'a présent
Il est bien suffisant.

MORALE.

Adieu! Chateaux d Espagne
Déjà si bien bâtis!
Beau pays de Cocagne!
Acheté a grand prix.
Il faut laisser les plans
Tires depuis longtemps.

Trouver de riches mines
Ouvrir un long chemin,
Pour pénètrer en Chine,
Et voire même au Tonquin,
Etait pour tous ces gens
De petits jeux d'enfant.

Aujourd'hui que va dire
Monsieur le Gouvernement,
Sera t'il noir de rire
Quand il verra ses plans
Déjà tous culbutés
Par tous les Bois brules.

And today his royal crown,
 Is a dream the dawn dispensed
And the throne to sit him down
Is a throne with bottom pierced,[*]
But he says that for a spell
It will do him very well.

MORAL

Farewell, castles, then of Spain,
All so well and truly built,
Farewell, land of bright Cockagne
For which so much gold was spilt;
He must now his blueprints shed
Drawn up so far ahead

To open up mines rich in ore,
To build a highway broad and fair,
To drive to China's distant shore
Or to Tonkin the rich repair
Was for these folk athirst for fame
The merest children's idle game.

And lord and master Government,
What will it say, what will it do,
Will it be with laughter spent,
When it sees its plans askew,
All askew and tossed away
By every daring Bois-Brule!]

---

 [*] A reference to the rumour that McDougall had brought his own toilet seat cover with him from Canada.

EDITOR'S NOTE

[The Fire Engine House had only recently become the home of a new fire engine. In the sketch of the town of Winnipeg in Morton, ed., *Begg's Journal*, 206-207, the house is listed as "Engine House MacTavish Fire engine Company No. 1."

Colonel Dennis's proclamation was, of course, quite illegal, since the Canadian government had decided to postpone the transfer of the territory until it was pacified. The text of the proclamation is in Morton, ed., *Begg's Journal*, 193-95. Although the proclamation originally circulated in handwritten form, it was soon printed. The printing of this proclamation, wrote Bruce Peel, was one of the most exciting episodes in the history of Canadian printing. According to George Winship, who was a young printer in the *Nor'-Wester* office at the time, he smuggled type out of the office, secreted on his person, first in his pockets and then under a long overcoat. He added:

> I have forgotten just where Mr. Laurie and I located our improvised printing shop, but it was in some back room on Main Street, not far from the old Emmerling Hotel. It taxed our ingenuity to devise a plan to distribute the type without having 'cases,' but finally enough small paper boxes were procured to serve our purpose, and the work of 'setting up' the proclamation began. We expected to have it ready for the 'press' before the following morning, but running out of 'sorts' compelled us to stop work until I could make another raid on The Nor'-Wester office, which I successfully accomplished during the forenoon of the next day. While the setting up of the proclamation was laborious, the printing of it subsequently was a painfully slow, tedious job. It was printed by the 'planer process,' and took us all the afternoon and most of the night to print 300 copies.

See Bruce Peel, *Early Printing in the Red River Settlement 1859-1870* (Winnipeg: Peguis Publishers 1974), 25-27.

According to Louis Riel's own notes of the convention, when A.G.B. Bannatyne brought him the purported Queen's Proclamation, he handed it back, saying, "Take that big sheet (pronouncing the double 'e' very short)." See Morton, ed., *Begg's Journal*, 427.]

# ALEXANDER BEGG

9 DECEMBER 1869

[The titles and subtitles were presumably added by the editors of the *Globe*. This letter of Alexander Begg must be read in conjunction with his journal for this period (pp. 192-225). In this letter Begg does his level best to persuade the people of Canada that the villains of the piece in Red River are the Canadians, especially those representing the government of Canada but also the party led by John Christian Schultz. Printed in the Toronto *Globe*, 31 December 1869.]

The Troubles in Red River.
THEIR ORIGIN AND PROGRESS. [No. 3]

THE QUEEN'S PROCLAMATION.

My letter of the lst instant terminated with the announcement of the Queen's Proclamation being issued. Such indeed was the case—to the surprise of a great many, although a few of the more knowing ones now say that they expected it on the day it came out. There being no printing press at the command of Mr. McDougall, he had a number of copies written out by members of his staff, and certified to; these were distributed amongst the people, and posted up in conspicuous places.

While this was being done, the French Council were sitting in conference; and, as it was thought advisable to do so, a gentleman was commissioned to go and lay a copy of the Proclamation before them.[*]

THE COUNCIL.

The French Councillors have received the Proclamation with due respect, although they did not admire the slovenly manner in which it was written out, and certainly you would not blame them if you saw some of the miserable daubs that were issued from the office of Col. Dennis. The

---

* This gentleman was Henry McKenney.

English delegates being notified to visit the Council, now did so, and after a good deal of discussion on various subjects, the French proposed having the meeting adjourned for an hour, when they would be in a position to speak definitely on the subject of the rights claimed by them.* This was agreed to, and at six o'clock in the evening the delegates met once more for the last time. The French then placed before the meeting a list of the rights they claimed from the Canadian Government.† These were discussed one by one and were nearly all agreed to as fair by the English side.

A BREACH.

But when Mr. Riel stated that before Mr. McDougall should enter the settlement he would have to get an Act of Parliament passed securing these rights to them, the delegates from the English side stated that they were not in a position to take that ground, they deeming the words of Mr. McDougall a sufficient guarantee that they should get the rights claimed if he gave a promise to that effect. It had been almost agreed to on both sides of the Council to send delegates to confer with Mr. McDougall, but this point of an Act of Parliament split the meeting without the two sides uniting, as had been expected.

ENDEAVOURS TO HEAL THE BREACH.

The next morning, several persons of influence endeavoured to heal the breach by trying to persuade the French to give way on the "Act of Parliament" for the present, as it would necessarily follow. Some good was being done as certain of the French party were inclined to take that view of it when news came in that Col. Dennis, who had been created Deputy Governor by Mr. McDougall, in his stead, was organizing a force to attack Fort Garry. This upset everything, and nothing but resistance to the coercing power was thought of or acted upon. Those of the French, who had been lukewarm in the cause a few moments previous were amongst the first to come forward to oppose the expected force.

---

* During this interval Louis Riel apparently met with the American lawyer Enos Stutsman (1826-1874) and drafted a "list of rights."

† The "list of rights" was made public on 5 December, and is reproduced later in this letter.

THE RUMOUR FALSE.

The rumour, however, turned out to be a false alarm; but the injury was done, the French being now determined, in a body, to keep Mr. McDougall out of the settlement until the rights claimed were fully secured to them. It appears that a party of about thirty Canadians or over, resident in the town, drove down during the night to the Stone Fort, and offered their services to Col. Dennis; he, it seems enrolled them, but sent them back to the town with instructions to remain quiet until called upon. It was the return of these men that gave rise to the rumour that an attacking force was on its way against Fort Garry. False rumours have done a great deal of harm in exciting the people and keeping up the present difficulty.

FEARS.

Companies of men have been formed all over the settlement, for the purpose of protection, and the fact of these meeting regularly for drilling purposes has given rise to reports that a hostile feeling existed towards the French, when in fact it did not. So long as the rest of the settlers remain undisturbed by the French, there will be no rising of one side against the other. The evil consequences of such a step is too fully realized by the settlers in general. The only thing we fear is that some overt act of evil disposed persons may draw us into a civil war.[*]

MOVEMENTS OF DR. SCHULTZ.

How nearly already we have been plunged into what we feared, will be seen by the following incidents related in this letter. Communications had been carried to and fro between Mr. McDougall and Col. Dennis, by one Cline [Klyne, Kline], and in order to capture the envoy, hearing he was in town, Mr. Riel undertook to search certain houses, Dr. Schultz's amongst the rest. Unfortunately it happened that the Dr. was away from home at the time. On his return, and hearing of Mr. Riel's visit, he naturally felt exasperated, and report goes to say that if the two gentlemen had met I might have to chronicle a duel, and perhaps an end to our present troubles, or a general fight of one race of people against another. But they

---

[*] In Begg's view, the chief danger comes from Colonel Dennis.

did not meet, and no harm was done. Dr. Schultz, however, collected in his house between 30 and 40 of those Canadians who had enrolled themselves under Col. Dennis, and barricaded his premises against an attack from the outside. Schultz had moved away a portion of his goods, and was known to have visited Col. Dennis at the Stone Fort. The fact, therefore, of his collecting these 30 or 40 men around him behind barricades led the French to think that it was done as a menace to them, and for the purpose of forming a nucleus for a future attack on Fort Garry.

FURTHER COERCION.

The French guards in town, and especially around the house of Dr. Schultz, was [sic] materially increased. The printing offices of the *Nor'-Wester* and *Red River Pioneer* were in the meantime taken possession of, and the issuing of the newspapers stopped for the present. The several roads leading to the town were guarded, and everything looked as if under martial law.

THE SIOUX REPORTED TO BE COMING.

While all these things were going on, a report came in that a half-breed name of "Shamon" was on the way from Portage La Prairie at the head of a band of eleven hundred Sioux Indians to devastate and plunder the settlement. A meeting of the townspeople was immediately held and a company raised for the sole purpose of resisting these savages. The rumour, however, turned out, like many others, to be false; but the fact of "Shamon" having left a short time ago for the plains, with a very small outfit, and being a sort of desperado the report was too readily believed.

GOVERNOR M'TAVISH DOES SOMETHING AT LAST.

Governor McTavish has, I believe, placed men so as to be able to watch any Indian movement, and we feel safer from the knowledge of this fact. There is no doubt that the neighbouring Indians would fall upon the Settlement were they sure of success, but the French half breeds have great control over them, and would not, I am sure, call in their aid, unless driven to an extremity. The French party in Fort Garry having been refused the keys to the provision warehouse broke open the door and helped themselves, on the plea that circumstances necessitated their doing so; they declare that the Company will be paid for everything they use from the H.B.Co's stock, but the manner of payment I have not learned.

THE BILL OF RIGHTS.

The following List of Rights was posted up around the Settlement in conspicuous places; it speaks for itself, and is the basis on which the people are agreed upon entering into the Confederation. Parts of it will have to be modified, no doubt, but in the main there is nothing unjust in these demands.

LIST OF RIGHTS

1. That the people have a right to elect their own Legislature.

2. That the Legislature have the power to pass all laws local to the Territory over the veto of the Executive by a two-thirds vote.

3. That no Act of the Dominion Parliament (local to the Territory) be binding on the people until sanctioned by the Legislature of the Territory.

4. That all Sheriffs, Magistrates, Constables, School Commissioners, etc, be elected by the people.

5. A free homestead and pre emption land law.

6. That a portion of the public lands be appropriated to the benefit of schools, the building of bridges; roads and public buildings.

7. That it be guaranteed to connect Winnipeg by rail with the nearest line of railroad, within a term of five years; the land grant to be subject to the Local Legislature.

8. That for the term of four years all military, civil and municipal expenses be paid out of the Dominion funds.

9. That the military be composed of the Inhabitants now existing in the Territory.

10. That the English and French languages be common in the Legislature and Courts, and that all public documents and Acts of the Legislature be published in both languages.

11. That the Judge of the Supreme Court speak the English and the French languages.

12. That Treaties be concluded and ratified between the Dominion Government and the several tribes of Indians in the Territory, to secure peace on the frontier.

13. That we have a fair and full representation in the Canadian Parliament.

14. That all privileges, customs and usages existing at the time of the transfer be respected.

All the above articles have been severally discussed and adopted by the French and English Representatives without a dissenting voice, as the conditions upon which the people of Rupert's Land enter into Confederation.

The French Representatives then proposed, in order to secure the above rights, that a Delegation be appointed and sent to Pembina, to see Mr. McDougall, and ask him if he could guarantee these rights by virtue of his commission; and if he could so so, that then the French people would join to a man to escort Mr. McDougall into his Government seat. But on the contrary, if Mr. McDougall could not guarantee such rights, that the Delegates request him to remain where he is, or return, till the rights be guaranteed by Act of the Canadian Parliament.

The English Representatives refused to appoint Delegates to go to Pembina to consult with Mr. McDougall, stating they had no authority to do so from their constituents, upon which the Council was dissolved.

The meeting at which the above resolutions were adopted was held at Fort Garry, on Wednesday, Dec. 1, 1869.

COL. DENNIS' PROCLAMATION.

Thus matters stood—every day looking gloomier than the previous one—affairs seemed more and more threatening around Dr. Schultz's premises—some say that Col. Dennis never ordered the men into the Doctor's house, and that when they did get in he ordered them to disperse. Be this as it may, the following proclamation was issued by Col. Dennis, and which was read by Mr. Riel to his men in front of Dr. Schultz's house, so excited the French that the fate of the people inside was evidently sealed.

THE NORTH-WEST TERRITORIES.

By his Excellency the Honourable William McDougall, a Minister of our Privy Council for Canada, and Companion of our most Honourable Order of the Bath, Lieutenant-Governor of the North-West Territories.[*]

To JOHN STOUGHTON DENNIS, Esq, Lieut. Colonel Military Staff, Canada, Greeting.

Whereas large bodies of armed men have unlawfully assembled on the high road between Fort Garry and Pembina in the Colony or District of Assiniboia, and have, with force of arms, arrested and held as prisoners numerous private and official persons, and prevented them from proceeding on their lawful journey and business, and have committed other acts of lawless violence, in contempt and defiance of the magistrates and local authorities;

And whereas Wm. McTavish, Esq, Governor of Assiniboia, did on the sixteenth day of November last publish and make known to those armed men and all others whom it might concern, that the lawless acts aforesaid, and which were particularly set forth in his proclamation, were "contrary to the remonstrances and protests of the public authorities," and did therein himself protest against all of the said unlawful acts and intents, and charged and commanded the said armed persons to immediately disperse themselves and peaceably to depart to their habitations or lawful business under the pains and penalties of the law;

And whereas, since the issue of the said protest or proclamation, certain of the armed men aforesaid, have taken possession of the public records and papers at Fort Garry, and have seized and held as prisoners public officers or persons having charge of the same, and as I am creditably

---

* This proclamation was, of course, utterly improper and illegal, since McDougall did not have any authority.

informed, still keep unlawful possession of the said records and public property, and with force of arms continue to obstruct public officers and others in the performance of their lawful duty and business, to the great terror, loss and injury of Her Majesty's peaceable subjects; and in contempt of her Royal Authority;

And Whereas, Her Majesty, by Letters Patent under the Great Seal of the Dominion of Canada, bearing date the twenty-ninth day of September, in the year of our Lord one thousand eight hundred and sixty-nine, has been graciously pleased to appoint me to be, from and after the first day of December instant, Lieutenant Governor of the North-West Territories, and did thereby authorize and command me to do and execute all things in due manner that should belong to my said command.[*]

Know You, that reposing trust and confidence in your courage, loyalty, fidelity, discretion and ability, and under and by virtue of the authority in me vested, I have nominated and appointed, and by these presents do nominate and appoint you, the said John Stoughton Dennis, to be my Lieutenant and a Conservator of the Peace in and for the Northwest Territories, and as such to raise, organize, arm, equip and provision a sufficient force within the said Territories, and with the said force, to attack, arrest, disarm or disperse the said armed men so unlawfully assembled and disturbing the public peace, and for that purpose and with the force aforesaid, to assault, fire upon, pull down, or break into any fort, house, stronghold, or other place in which the said armed men may be found, and I hereby authorize you as such Lieutenant and Conservator of the Peace, to hire, purchase, impress, and take all necessary clothing, arms, ammunition and supplies and all cattle, horses, waggons, sleighs or other vehicles which may be required for the use of the force to be raised as aforesaid, and I further authorize you to appoint as many officers and deputies under you, and to give them such orders and instructions, from time to time, as may be found necessary for the due performance of the services herein required of you, reporting to me the said appointments, and orders as you shall find opportunity for confirmation, or otherwise; and I hereby give you full power and authority to call upon all magistrates and peace officers to aid and assist you, and to order all or any of the inhabitants of the said

---

[*] McDougall did not realize that his appointment was invalid.

North West Territories, in the name of Her Majesty the Queen, to support and assist you in protecting the lives and property of Her Majesty's loyal subjects, and in preserving the public peace, and for that purpose, to take, disperse, or overcome by force, the said armed men, and all others who may be found aiding or abetting them in their unlawful acts.

And the said persons so called upon in Her Majesy's name, are hereby ordered and enjoined, at their peril, to obey your orders and directions in that behalf; and this shall be sufficient warrant for what you or they may do in the premises, so long as this commission remains in force.

Given under my hand and seal at arms, at Red River, in the said Territories, on this the first day of December, in this year of our Lord one thousand eight hundred and sixty-nine, and in the thirty-third year of our reign.

(Signed),
WILLIAM MCDOUGALL.
By command.

(Signed)
J.A.N. PROVENCHER,
Secretary.

By virtue of the above commission from the Lieutenant-governor, I now hereby call on and order all loyal men of the North-West Territories, to assist me by every means in their power, to carry out the same, and thereby restore public peace and order, and uphold the supremacy of the Queen in this part of her Majesty's dominions.

Given under my hand, at the Stone Fort, Lower Settlement, this 6th day of December, in the year of our Lord one thousand eight hundred and sixty-nine.

(Signed) J.S. DENNIS, Lieutenant and Conservator of the Peace in and for the North-West Territories.

## THE EFFECT ON DR. SCHULTZ.

It may be doubtful whether Col. Dennis was right in issuing the above document, but one thing is certain it was very unfortunate that he did so. Every sensible man felt this and trembled for the fate of those cooped up in Dr. Schultz's house. A party of gentlemen, therefore, met together to do all in their power to avert the threatened calamity. Riel had offered protection to the men if they gave themselves up, but this, it appears, Dr. Schultz refused to consent to unless under certain conditions. The French, on the other hand, would have no conditions, but stated as their ultimatum that they had to either fight or surrender unconditionally. The party of gentlemen who had interested themselves in the matter now deemed it their duty to go and see Schultz, which they immediately started to do, to see if they could persuade him from causing blood to be shed.

## THEY MEET RIEL.

As the party were nearing Dr. Schultz's house they perceived a band of about three hundred armed men coming from the Fort, and knowing well their purpose, they, instead of going into [in to] see Schultz, passed on and met Riel at the head of his men. On stating their purpose to him, he professed his willingness to do everything in his power for peace before taking extreme measures.

## UNCONDITIONAL SURRENDER.

Mr. A.G.B. Bannatyne then (being spokesman for the party) entered Dr. Schultz's house, and laid the matter before that gentleman.* The Doctor, however, still objected to an unconditional surrender. This seemed tempting Providence, and unwarrantably risking the lives of those men who had stood so nobly by him, and it was only on the peremptory refusal by Riel of all or any conditions that at last obliged the Doctor to consent to surrender on the terms "unconditional" with the assurance of their lives being spared.

---

* Some sources have Thomas Scott acting as a messenger from Schultz to Riel.

DREADFUL SUSPENSE.

While this delay was occasioned the suspense was dreadful. Here were over forty men confined inside of three houses fully armed with abundance of ammunition sufficient in themselves to destroy a great many lives; outside were over three hundred men also carefully armed and equipped, and possessed of cannon, powerful enough to blow the buildings to atoms. Had a shot been fired—had the delay lasted much longer, the fight would have broken out, and then the carnage would have been dreadful; but the results afterwards to the whole Settlement would have been still more disastrous. There was a great mistake made by having these men in the houses so exposed and unsupported as they were; but where the blame rests will certainly be seen hereafter.

THE PRISONERS.

Dr. Schultz before giving himself up was assured by several citizens present as well as by Mr. Riel that his property would be protected. There were Mrs. Schultz, Mrs. Mair, and Mrs. O'Donnel, in the house all this time, and although several attempts were made to induce them to leave, it was of no avail; they would not part from their husbands. Mrs. Schultz fainted on the approach of the attacking party, and her condition during the time of settling for the surrender was very trying. As soon as all the preliminaries were gone through the prisoners were marched out and taken to Fort Garry, to the number of 45; the wives of the married men insisting on accompanying their husbands. Dr. Schultz drew his wife along in a sleigh, she being too ill to walk, and credit is due to Mr. Riel for the gentlemanly and kind manner in which he treated the ladies of the party, as one instance he threw off his own coat to wrap round Mrs. Schultz as a protection from the severity of the weather.*

---

* According to Mrs. Bernard Rogan Ross, who was at Fort Garry a few days later when the flag of the provisional government was raised, after the ceremony Riel escorted her to her "cutter," bowed and said, "Ladies always have the first consideration, in war as in love." See W.J. Healy, *Women of Red River: Being a Book Written from the Recollection of Women Surviving from the Red River Era* (Winnipeg: Women's Canadian Club, 1923), 228.

A FEU DE JOIE.

As the prisoners reached Fort Garry, the French, to the number of over six hundred, inside and outside the walls, fired off their guns in a volley. The scene was a wild one, and many thanked their stars that the hundreds of leaden bullets were not flying about their ears instead of in the air.

A HUDSON'S BAY COMPANY VIEW OF CANADIANS.

Thus ended this uncalled for, foolish piece of business. What induced these Canadians to put themselves in the position they did, was unaccountable. Men of family actually left their employment and those dependent on them to look after themselves, while they went to protect another man's property, and that property not endangered any more than the rest of the town. Some of the men now state they did not consider they were there for the protection of Dr. Schultz's houses, but that they believed themselves only doing their duty as being enrolled under Col. Dennis, and that they expected to be reinforced. This is very strange, as Col. Dennis denies having ordered them to take the stand they did, and, in fact, repeatedly ordered them to disperse. Who, then, is to blame for keeping these men cooped up in the position they were in? Be that as it may, however, all honour is due to them for the noble stand they took. They were ill advised; but, as far as they were concerned, I believe they thought they were doing their duty, and they stood nobly by it. It was certain death to them had a fight occurred, although they could, and would, no doubt, have sold their lives dearly.

Let not the fact of these Canadians being taken prisoners influence the public of Canada, either for good or bad. In a few words, it was simply their own fault that has been the cause of their present situation. The people of the country were trying for their rights, and not in opposition to Canadian annexation. The French being in arms for their side of the cause, it was natural for them to suppose that influence might be brought to bear to induce the balance of the Settlement to resist the armed formation. On the point that one part being armed and the other not, it was an unequal demand on Canada, and a menace to the rest of the Settlement.

### THE FRENCH THE LAMB—THE CANADIANS THE WOLF.

The French, then, considered that Canadians had no right to interfere, and were exasperated at Col. Dennis and his staff in virtue of their commission, endeavouring to raise one half the Settlement against the other. This is why they took the stand they did against the armed men in Schultz's house.

### THE FRENCH PEACEABLE.

The French are not anxious for war, neither are the other settlers; but it seemed as if the so-called Canadian party here, headed by Mr. McDougall and his staff, desired nothing else but to plunge the Settlement into ruin and devastation, and this has caused a great deal of indignation all over the land.

### A SALVE TO CANADIAN HONOUR.

Do not, therefore, I say, take the act of confining the Canadians in Fort Garry as an insult to Canadian honour, for it is not intended as such. They were merely in arms against the people of this country, and by being so were unwarrantably seeking to plunge the whole Colony into destruction. They were as if standing between the people and their rights so considered, and it is only to prevent their doing further mischief that they are now confined.

### PRISONERS' QUARTERS.

Their quarters are none of the most comfortable, the room being spare inside the Fort; but they are confined in the bedrooms lately occupied by the officers of Fort Garry, and everything is being done by the citizens of the town for their comfort. How long they are to be confined I have not heard; but I feel certain that nothing harsh nor inhuman will be perpetrated on them. It is not the character of the half-breeds to be cruel unless in a fight, and then their nature becomes fierce in the extreme; and it is for this reason that a civil war in this country would be deplorable in its consequence.

DISCOVERY OF ARMS.

After the capitulation, Dr. Schultz's premises were searched for arms. Weapons of all descriptions were found in abundance, as well as ammunition. Guns, rifles, and pistols, were found concealed in every direction, and in every possible manner—even in the beds six-shooters and rifles were found hid.* Indeed, a desperate resistance was evidently intended.

THE FRENCH LAMBS AGAIN.

Now why this accumulation of arms and ammunition? And who were they to be used against? Why, against a people who had never harmed a Canadian, or anyone else, to my knowledge; whose actions have been universally kind towards strangers; peaceable until roused, and simple in their natures. Oh, fie, shame on the one who caused this demonstration against a people whose only fault seems to be the wish to secure their just rights for themselves and their posterity.

ANOTHER M'DOUGALL PROCLAMATION.

A Proclamation now came out from Mr. McDougall, in the course of which he says, "I do hereby require and command that all and singular the public officers and functionaries holding office in Rupert's Land, and the North-Western Territory at the time of their admission into the Union as aforesaid, excepting the public officer or functionary at the head of the administration of affairs, do continue in the execution of their several and respective offices, duties, places and employments, until otherwise ordered by me, under the authority of the said last above mentioned Act; and I do hereby further require and command that all Her Majesty's loving subjects, and all others whom it may concern, do take notice hereof, and govern themselves accordingly."[1]

---

* This sounds worse than the report in Begg's journal, where he says that "2-14 shooting Rifles 1 Breach loader 5 6" Shooter Revolvers 1 Double barrel pistol 100 Cartridges" were found under the bed where Mrs. Schultz had been lying, and other arms were found elsewhere. See Morton, ed., *Begg's Journal*, 223.

GOV. M'TAVISH.

Will you believe it, that actually our loved and respected Governor McTavish has not even been advised of the actions of Mr. McDougall, or his intentions? He had no notification of the Queen's Proclamation, but had to borrow a copy of it to see what it was like. Was it courteous, [to] say the least, in Mr. McDougall so utterly ignoring a man in the high position of Governor McTavish, his predecessor? Is it customary for a Governor coming into office to so treat the one going out? What does it mean? The first thing Governor McTavish knew was an ill-written dirty-looking sheet lent him by a friend, and said to be a copy of the Queen's Proclamation; the next thing is the above Proclamation, telling the people that he (McTavish) is no longer Governor; and all this time our old chief lies on his sick-bed utterly ignored by the big man who is to take his place, and treated as Governor going out of office was never treated before. But Mr. McDougall's Proclamation came out too late; for the following declaration was issued and posted all over the Settlement: "It being reported that Mr. McDougall had taken up his quarters at the H.B.C. post in Pembina, a guard of men left at once with instructions to see him once more across the lines. We have not heard from them."

NO ANNEXATION.

We observe that the American papers speak very strongly on our present situation and strong hints of annexation to the States are intimated, but allow me to disabuse your minds if such an error has crept into the public mind of Canada. There is not the least sympathy (unless amongst a very few) with annexation to the United States. We cannot but look in a friendly manner on the Americans individually and collectively, as they have been good friends on their part to the people of this country in many ways, and indeed it will be found that our future progress will be more indebted to American enterprise in one direction than perhaps even to Canada itself. We are naturally bound by close ties to the Americans, as only an imaginary line separates us, and at present our only outlet and inlet are through American Territory. But that there is any feeling in favor of annexation to the States I deny, as far as my knowledge goes. The only cause of the present troubles is the blunders that have been committed towards the people of this country by the Colonial office at home and the officials at Ottawa—let these blunders be rectified and more loyal subjects to the Dominion of Canada will not be found throughout the whole Confederation.

COL. DENNIS' PROCLAMATION.

After Col. Dennis had tried his utmost to raise a force to put down the French, and failing in his endeavours, as far as we are informed, he comes out late in the day with the following proclamation:—

LOWER FORT GARRY,
RED RIVER SETTLEMENT,
DECEMBER 9, 1869,

*To All Whom it may Concern:*
By certain printed papers of late put in circulation by the French party, communication with the Lieutenant Governor is indicated with a view to laying before him alleged rights on the part of those now in arms.

I think that course very desirable, and that it would lead to good results.

Under the belief that the party in arms are sincere in their desire for peace, and feeling that to abandon for the present the call on the loyal to arms would, in view of such communications, relieve the situation of much embarrassment, and so contribute to bring about peace and save the country from what will otherwise end in ruin and desolation. I now call on and order the loyal party in the North-West Territories to cease further action under the appeal to arms made by me; and I call on the French party to satisfy the people of their sincerity in wishing for a peaceful ending of all these troubles by sending a deputation to the Lieutenant-Governor at Pembina without unnecessary delay.

Given under my hand at the Lower Fort Garry this 9th day of December, 1869.

(Signed) J.L. DENNIS,
Lieut. and Conservator of the Peace in and for the North-West Territories.

BLUNDERS ALL THROUGH.

Blunder! blunder! blunder! it seems to be a blunder from beginning to end. It was a blunder issuing his call to arms. He ought to have known it, for he acknowledges that if it had been successful and acted upon, it would have resulted in ruin and desolation to the Settlement. Is it through ruin and desolation that Canada would come amongst us. [?] Oh! no; I cannot think so. Why did Col. Dennis then seek, as his call to arms plainly intimates, to call one part of our settlers to oppose and massacre the other? What stopped him? He says it is the list of rights circulated around; but in reality it was nothing more or less than the finding out of his mistake, and the unwillingness of the people to join in it. The last proclamation of Col. Dennis is worse than the first—for although it speaks peace; war is evidently at the heart of it.

SIOUX STORIES.

Reports are still abroad regarding the Sioux Indians, and it has been said that Canadian officials are concerned in endeavouring to bring them into the Settlement. This I do not believe; but the truth or falsehood of the report I will be able to give you in my text. It is too barbarous to think that Col. Dennis would warrant calling in the aid of savages. If he did, however, he would find that the Indians would side with the half-breeds and desert him at the first opportunity.

THE REMEDY.

Now, after giving you these particulars, you may say what is to be done? The answer is this:—If the delegates to arrange this present difficulty have not been sent up already, let the Government lose not a single moment in dispatching competent qualified men at once to meet the people of this country; let these men see for themselves, and on their return to Ottawa take such steps as are necessary to secure the claims (if granted) of this people.

They will not treat with McDougall, this is certain now. Let him remain where he is until these matters are arranged, and in the meantime the French are determined until arrangements are made with Canada to stick to their Provisional Government, and I would not be surprised if in my next letter I would have to inform you that the whole Settlement for the mutual protection of all had joined in the said Provisional Government already professedly formed.

Yours truly,
JUSTITIA.
Winnipeg, 9th Dec., 1869


EDITOR'S NOTE

[The numbers that occasionally appear in the Begg letters as published in the *Globe* do not agree with the actual appearance of the letters. This one is labelled "No. 3," although it is the fourth missive from Begg.

Colonel Dennis was supplied with a commission from William McDougall dated 1 December 1869 "to raise, organise, arm, equip and provision a sufficient force within the said Territories and with the said force to attack, arrest, disarm, or disperse the said armed men so unlawfully assembled and disturbing the public peace and for that purpose and with the force aforesaid to assault, fire upon, pull down, or break into any fort, house, stronghold or other place in which the said armed men may be found...." The full text of the proclamation is given later in this letter. In an editorial comment on a letter from "Fort Garry" written on 11 December 1869 and published in the Montreal *Herald* on 31 December 1869, the newspaper wrote: "We have another interesting letter from Fort Garry, with a copy of the very warlike instructions given to his General in the field by MacDougall the first, whose royal style loses nothing from the fact that it is so extremely recent, and directs the siege of Forts, Castles, strongholds, &c., in a comprehensive manner that would have become Louis 14th in a campaign in Flanders, where such places are plenty as blackberries."

This Bill of Rights was the first of a number to be produced in the settlement over the winter of 1869-70. According to "St. Norbert" in a letter dated 18 December 1869 to *Nouveau Monde* and printed in translation by the Toronto *Globe* on 14 January 1870:

We see by some journals that the discontent of the people of Red River is attributed to certain undertakings and acts of the employees of the Canadian Government. Although some of these undertakings and acts have undoubtedly disposed the people against Canada, I can assure you, having observed, with the most minute attention, all the elements which have produced the actual movement, that the people of Red River do not contend against personal misdeed. They have examined with their customary *sang froid*, the principles on which Canada has relied to introduce itself as sovereign in this country, and having found them false, they refuse to allow her domination. Moreover, these people, having been abandoned by a kind of government which they had been accustomed to support from a respect to authority, will never accept a government which is not based on justice. If reports are to be believed, the Council would have passed a resolution, not to answer Canada until a year after propositions for an arrangement had been made. In that case, Canada might find the time too long; but the North Westers think that so important a matter merits reflection, and they will take time to reflect. A journal says that the intention of the Government is not to take away their rights from the North-west people; is that all the advantage that Canada offers to a people to induce them to accept a foreign yoke? Does she believe that for that price the North-westers will renounce the liberty which they have so long desired and that to day they possess? No, no; this people, more enlightened and more civilized than is wished to be believed, understands its position and will know how to maintain it. The principles on which its operations are based are to-day published and warmly approved.]

# J.J. HARGRAVE
11 DECEMBER 1869

[This letter was printed without separation from another letter by the newspaper, but this one is clearly from J.J. Hargrave, and is indicative of the good will that Riel and his rebellion enjoyed in Red River in December of 1869. *The Montreal Herald* had long been critical of William McDougall, and loses no opportunity in its editorial introduction to be hostile. Printed in the *Montreal Herald and Daily Commercial Gazette*, 31 December 1869.]

"LIST OF RIGHTS

1. That the people have the right to elect their own Legislature.

2. That the Legislature have the power to pass all laws local to the Territory, over the veto of the Executive, by a two-third vote.

3. That no Act of the Dominion Parliament (local to the Territory) be binding on the people until sanctioned by the Legislature of the Territory.

4. That all Sheriffs, Magistrates, Constables, School Commissioners, &cv., be elected by the people.

5. A Free Homestead and Pre-emption Land Law.

6. That a portion of the public lands be appropriated to the benefit of Schools, the building of Bridges, Roads and Public Buildings.

7. That it be guaranteed to connect Winnipeg by Rail, with the nearest line of Railroad, within a term of five years; the land grant to be subject to the Local Legislature.

8. That, for the term of four years, all Military, Civil, and Municipal expenses be paid out of the Dominion funds.

9. That the Military be composed of the inhabitants now existing in the Territory.

10. That the English and French languages be common in the Legislature and Courts, and that all Public Documents and Acts of the Legislature be published in both languages.

11. That the Judge of the Supreme Court speak the English and French languages.

12. That treaties be concluded and ratified between the Dominion Government and the several tribes of Indians in the Territory, to ensure peace on the frontier.

13. That we have a full and fair representation in the Canadian Parliament.

14. That all the privileges, customs and usages, existing at the time of the transfer, be respected."*

RED RIVER SETTLEMENT, BRITISH NORTH AMERICA,
11 Dec., 1869.

The above is a copy of a placard posted at Church doors and other public places of this colony on Saturday last, and which forms I believe the first public announcement, issued by the leaders of our present *de facto* government, of what they considered the basis of any arrangement to be made with Lieutenant Governor Macdougall.

In my last week's letter I mentioned that the above list had been drawn up and submitted to the votes of the English and French delegates on the evening of 1st December; but, that the various items it contained were still unknown to the public. I have no desire at present to make any comments on them, further than to remark that the demand on which most stress seems to be laid is that which provides for the election of functionaries of

---

* Begg notes, in his *The Creation of Manitoba* (Toronto: A.H. Hovey, 1871), 157, that this document differs slightly from that passed by the Council meeting.

various kinds by the people. An impression has gained ground from the boastful words of certain public servants already here, and the damaging indiscretion of a knot of men who make pretensions to be the friends of Canada, that certain leading men among the latter are already virtually appointed to important offices, the holders of which will be nominated by the incoming Governor. The effect of the formation of an entire staff of officials, selected on the principles which would have secured the appointment of the parties referred to, would be to force the existing population to submit to the possible caprices of those who have hitherto rendered themselves publicly obnoxious, until when a more permanent order of things, inaugurated by the dreaded men, should be at last established, the present population and natives of the country will find themselves in a hopeless minority, swamped by the advancing wave of immigration.

There is said to be evidence, in the contents of the list, of American ideas and American suggestions.* I think it very probable that the demands may have been largely influenced by citizens of the United States, but the French party denies any wish for annexation such as that attributed to it by incoming newspapers in which events of late occurence here are commented on.

It may be remembered that I stated in my previous letters that some Government provisions deposited in a store in the village of Winnipeg, belonging to Doctor John Schultz, the contractor for their inward freight, had led to some excitement in consequence of the guards having been placed over them by the insurgents, the Canadian officials and the Governor of Assiniboia. On the arrival of Colonel Dennis, bringing with him the Royal Proclamation, that gentleman immediately proceeded to Lower Fort Garry, which he required from the Hudson Bay Company's officers as a basis of military operations. and commenced enrolling and drilling a force which he collected by authority of a commission given him by Mr. McDougall, a copy of which I enclose, and which I beg you will insert, as its publication, which took place in printed form, has led to grave results, and has been much censured as a rash and ill-advised measure.

On hearing of Colonel Dennis's action a party of Canadians resident in

---

* The first four clauses are a direct lift from a Dakota bill of rights written by Enos Stutsman a month earlier.

the village of Winnipeg proceeded to Lower Fort Garry, and enrolled themselves under his command, but were ordered to return home without delay. Louis Riel and his party issued instructions to the entire body of insurgents to assemble on Monday last at Upper Fort Garry, and having heard that a courier had arrived, bringing despatches from Governor MacDougall, accompanied by about twenty of his men, searched every home in the village from garret to cellar, with the object of finding the messenger, who was said to be in concealment somewhere in Winnipeg. This visit, which took place during the night, created a considerable panic, but was quite fruitless.

The two newspaper offices were next seized, and the facilities offered by one of them used for printing certain documents connected with the operations of the insurgents. The forthcoming issues of both journals were also confiscated, I understand, because the narratives of certain events which they contained were considered by Mr. Riel to be unsatisfactory.

On the morning of Sunday it was generally felt that some event of importance was impending. French half-breeds from all quarters poured in crowds towards Fort Garry, where every house and room, already appropriated to their purposes by the insurgents, was densely filled with them, as they stood and lay in all sorts of places and positions. The parties in the Settlement, recently from Canada, collected in a house in the village of Win[n]ipeg for unusual protection and support. Rumours were also in general circulation of drilling and other operations being carried on under command of Col. Dennis at Lower Fort Garry, with the view of attacking the insurgents on an early day, and expelling them from their present position at the Upper Fort. The movement, it was thought, would take place by surprise. Other rumours stated that a formidable party of English half breeds from Portage la Prairie, a place about sixty-five miles from Fort Garry, assisted by a number of Sioux Indians, for some years resident at the same place, would make a descent, in combination with the principal movement under Col. Dennis' immediate direction.

The house in the village of Win[n]ipeg, in which the Canadians had taken refuge, was that belonging to Doctor John Shultz, and was the same in which the pork and other supplies belonging to the Canadian Government were already deposited. Besides those of its inmates, whose object was simply mutual assistance, there were those composing the body which had, as above mentioned, visited and been enrolled by Col. Dennis at the

Lower Fort. These men had, it is understood, been ordered by the Colonel to watch and defend the Government property, holding themselves in readiness to join and assist him in his attack on the Fort. Capt. Boulton had visited them in the course of a tour he was making through the English speaking parishes for purposes of enrolment, and had constituted them into a company, of which Dr. Lynch, a medical gentleman recently from Canada, was appointed Captain.

On Sunday morning it was asserted that Doctor Schultz intended hoisting the Canadian flag, with a view to precipitate an encounter before the French party had collected in full force. In explanation of this rumour I may here mention that, for a long time past, it has been the habit of the Doctor to go through this form on Sundays. His house is situated on the public highway at the spot where the village of Win[n]ipeg abuts on the Hudson Bay Company's Land reserve, extending thence to Fort Garry. It is, therefore, in a very prominent position. The hoisting of a flag of Canada, at a date long anterior to the actual transfer of the territory, though a matter insignificant enough in itself, was well understood to be intended as an expression of malevolence towards the out-going government, and was regarded by the French half-breed community as the harbinger of their coming humiliation.

On hearing the report of the intended demonstration, Riel stated that he did not mean to permit his men to take further notice of it than to raise the St. George's flag on the flag-staff at Fort Garry. The provocation—as such it must be unhappily considered—was not, however, offered, and the Sunday passed without any event of importance. On Monday morning a large and permanent guard of Frenchmen were posted round Schultz's house, and throughout the entire day negotiations were carried on between the party within it and Riel. The party of Canadians were ordered to disperse before a given hour, but refused to do so, although it has since been discovered that instructions had been received from Colonel Dennis to the same effect. The hour having passed, Riel intimated to the party that, unless they surrendered at discretion, they would not be permitted to leave the house alive. Several Canadians in the Settlement were taken prisoners, and a courier carrying dispatches from Mr. MacDougall was also intercepted.

On Tuesday morning the entire French force was put under arms; the six pounded field pieces at Fort Garry were got in readiness, the doors of some of the Company's depots were forced, and all the guns which could be discovered were abstracted. The result was that about 600 insurgents were armed.

Throughout the preceding night Schultz's house had been surrounded by the half-breeds, who yelled, charged and went through a series of evolutions, the object of which appeared to be to keep the garrison awake, and by depriving them of rest, and subjecting them to long suspense, so to demoralize them as to unfit them for fighting when the decisive moment should arrive.

Isolated prisoners were brought in during Tuesday forenoon, and about one o'clock p.m. it became known that the given time had elapsed, negotiations failed, and nothing save a collision appeared inevitable. At two o'clock Riel and his men started for the village and surrounded the house in which the Canadians were assembled.

The latter numbered more than forty men, well armed with breech-loading rifles, "six shooters" and revolver pistols. The house was a mere "lath and plaster" structure, with a smaller edifice of brick adjoining it. Neither building could have offered much resistance to a volley of musketry.

The Rev. Mr. Ritchot, curé of the parish of St. Norbert, accompanied the French, who drew up when they reached the scene of action, unwilling to fire the first shot but waiting only for one from the party within the house. At this juncture some of the inhabitants of Win[n]ipeg, by earnest solicitations, prevailed on Riel to offer the beleaguered party a final alternative of unconditional surrender.[*]

Meanwhile the Venerable Archdeacon McLean coincidentally passed the spot on his way to Fort Garry. His efforts to gain an opportunity of speaking with the party in question were repulsed, but he was permitted by Riel to pass onwards to the Fort, accompanied by an armed insurgent as a fellow passenger in the gutter. The Revd. George Young was also on the ground. His [son] was one of the garrison, and he was fortunate enough to secure him free exit without being treated as a prisoner.

The upshot was that the entire Canadian party was compelled to surrender at discretion. There was in fact no choice left them. The house they occupied was quite isolated. They were entirely unsupported. Mounted

---

[*] The citizens were led by A.G.B. Bannatyne.

half-breeds were in readiness to pursue any who might attempt escape by night, and although they might have done much execution among the French, they must have been cut off to the last man, and their women and children would have shared the same fate. Their neglect of orders given by Colonel Dennis to disperse, while such a course was yet in their power is certainly to be regretted, but, as respects their ultimate surrender, the only feeling is one of approval.

A procession was formed and the prisoners were marched up to Fort Garry and housed in the rooms over the Company's public office, already appropriated by the insurgents. As a special favour the women and children were permitted to live in some of the houses still occupied by the Company's officers. The French party collected in one of the squares in the Fort and discharged their muskets in the air. Many of them dispersed at once to the homes, but a party of twenty men was dispatched to Pembina, to expel Mr. Macdougall who was said again to have taken up his quarters at the Hudson's Bay Company's post.

A Declaration of the people of Rupert's Land and the North West, was subsequently published by Messrs. Bruce and Riel. I enclose a copy of it which I beg you will append to the documents already advised as enclosed. I need, I presume, make no comments on it, as it speaks its own story.

Yesterday a large body of the French collected in Fort Garry, and went through the ceremony of "Raising the National Flag" on the Fort flagstaff.* Speeches were made by Riel and others, and the brass band of the scholars at the Roman Catholic school at St. Boniface played a series of airs, after each of which a volley of musketry was fired, the Company's Field Pieces, which were stationed at intervals outside the Fort gates, being also discharged at various periods of the performance. The device on the banner consists of three *fleur de lys* on a white ground with a shamrock underneath. The insurgents subsequently marched to the American consulate in Winnipeg, which they saluted with music, cheers, and volleys of musketry. This is said to have been done as a compliment to the only foreign power having a resident representative here.

Two proclamations, issued respectively by Lieutenant-Governor

---

* Hargrave does not note that a provisional government was declared at this ceremony.

McDougall and Col. Dennis, have been published within the last few days. I enclose them herewith.* The one issued by Col. Dennis is bitterly commented on as an admission that, had his first operations been successful, the Government of Canada would have inaugurated its rule amid carnage and desolation.

The prisoners are yet in ignorance of their fate. It is said a "court martial" will sit on some of them so soon as the party dispatched after Mr. McDougall shall have returned from Pembina. Col. Dennis, who is still at the Lower Fort, is reported to be on the eve of returning to Canada with all the Canadians connected with his party who are still at large.

I have no doubt that the prisoners will be treated with the utmost leniency, as there appears to be every disposition on the part of Riel to allow them an indulgence compatible with his designs. The houses and property of those among them resident here are guarded, and will, doubtless, be restored intact.

EDITOR'S NOTE

[According to "Fort Garry" in a letter dated 6 November 1869 and published in the Montreal *Herald* on 27 November 1869: "Dr. Schultz has been in the habit of hoisting on Sundays and holidays the British flag with the word Canada written on the red ground. I hear it is the Doctor's intention to hoist it as usual to-morrow, and there are predictions of evil if this should be the case." In the same letter, "Fort Garry" describes the flag adopted by the Provisional Government. "A flag has been adopted, which is composed of a white ground, upon which are displayed three crosses— the centre one large and scarlet coloured, the side ones smaller and gold coloured. A golden fringe binds the white ground thus [woodcut of flag]." Apparently a different design was subsequently selected.

For another account of the affair at Schultz's house, the following is from "Fort Garry" to the Montreal *Herald*, 14 December 1869, and printed in the newspaper 5 January 1870:

---

* The proclamations are printed in Begg's letter to the Toronto *Globe*, 9 December 1869, and are not reprinted here.

On the issue of the proclamation the Canadians here thought they were placed in a position to take action in favour of the new Government, and at the request of Col. Dennis, a number of them went over to join him at the Stone Fort. They were, however, on their arrival there sent back to remain in town. In the meantime a report got abroad that the provisions belonging to the Government, stored in a warehouse belonging to Dr. Schultz, were to be taken away by the French, and a considerable number of Canadians gathered at the Doctor's house to watch the progress of events. Some, I believe, continued all night there, and on the next night or night after, while they were gathered there, Major Bolton, late of the 100th, arrived with a message from Colonel Dennis requesting them to retire to the Scotch Settlement, four miles below. On the first night of their assembly large parties of the French came down from the Fort and watched the houses all night. This they continued to do until the arrival of Major Bolton, when it was deemed by the parties in the Doctor's houses impossible to retreat through the large body stationed outside, and the leaders having been consulted, it was determined to remain where they were. In the meantime I believe they had elected officers, Dr. Lynch being captain, Mr. Miller, lieutenant, and Mr. Allen (late of Port Hope), ensign. Guards were appointed to watch outside while others watched the windows. This state of matters continued until Monday the 4th ult., when hearing that an attack would be made on the house that night, a message was despatched to the Fort to learn if the women (5) and children (2) would be allowed to get out of the house. This was refused, from which it was inferred that no attack would be made that night. News I believe had reached the beleaguered that no hope of relief could be expected from Col. Dennis, and as they knew that the guns at the Fort could be directed on the house at any moment they determined to seek for terms. Mr. Snow, superintendent of the road, volunteered to see Governor McTavish in order that he might negotiate with Mr. Riel, the Secretary of the Provisional Government. Mr. McArthur, of your city, at the suggestion of the Canadians was requested to accompany Mr. Snow. The deputation saw the Governor, who, in turn, saw Mr. Riel, but without coming to any agreement. The terms desired by the party in the doctor's house were that they should be allowed to walk out with their arms and disperse. After a long interview with Mr. Riel, a written paper was handed to Mr. Snow, requesting an unconditional surrender. This on being submitted to the party in the house was accepted. In the meantime the French, to the number of 250, surrounded the house, and while the negotiations were going on inside, it was feared that at any moment hostilities might break out from the thoughtless conduct of any on either side. The party, to the number of 44, were then marched to the Fort, where they have since remained prisoners. They have made no particular complaints of ill-treatment, but are too much crowded together. They have plenty [of] blankets, and are supplied with food from the town twice-a-day, provided by Mr. Snow, the only official at all connected with the Canadian Government, who is free, out of the Government supplies.

# ALEXANDER BEGG

## 17 DECEMBER 1869

[In this letter Alexander Begg describes events in the settlement from the arrest of the Canadians in Dr. Schultz's house to the date of writing. He denies any Fenian influence in the rebellion, despite the presence of the shamrock on the Métis flag—and no scholar has ever found any. He then provides the first detailed descriptions of the Métis leaders for his Ontario audience, and, despite his avowals that the decision is up to Canada how to react to the rebellion, Begg clearly has his own views. Printed in the Toronto *Globe*, 6 January 1870.]

NO. IV*
(To the Editor of The Globe)


THE PRISONERS

SIR,—

Since my last, other arrests of suspected persons have been made, until the number of prisoners now in Fort Garry amount to over sixty men.[1] The rooms in which they were confined being found too small for the purpose, about thirty-eight were transferred to the jail in the Court House adjoining. This was an improvement, as it gave the men more room, and made their position much more easy and comfortable; indeed the captured ones appear to be in good spirits, for yesterday a visitor found some of them busy at cards, sitting in their shirtsleeves, joking with each other; while their captors outside were playing a game, the stakes, however, being bullets instead of specie—queer comparison. All seemed jolly enough on the surface, but inside, I have no doubt, there were aching hearts and discontent at the confinement. The prison discipline is rather strict, no parcels being allowed to pass in without first being searched, and no letters or

---

* As previously noted, numbers appear on several of Begg's letters. To what they refer is not clear, since they do not coincide with the number of letters that was published.

papers are permitted to be conveyed to or from the prisoners. We have no knowledge yet as to what is to be done with them, but it is the general opinion that they will be parolled on giving their word that they will not again take up arms against the French or other settlers in the present cause; but nothing is known, as a certainty, what will be their fate, except that their lives are in no danger.

## DEPARTURE OF COL. DENNIS

Col. Dennis, after issuing his peace proclamation, and finding that the French would not treat with Mr. McDougall on any terms, hastily vacated the lower Fort Garry, and left, it is said, for Pembina and Portage la Prairie.

## REDUCTION OF THE INSURGENT FORCE

All the companies who have been in the habit of meeting for drilling purposes, are now disbanded, and everything seems once more on a peace footing.

## STONE FORTRESSES ERECTED

When it was found that Dennis had really left, the Committee of Defence in the parish of St Andrews held a meeting and resolved that the following arms and ammunition then in the Stone Fort, say—200 60lb kegs gunpowder, 120 cases ball ammunition, and a lot of guns and rifles should be distributed privately in places only known to the Committee, for future use, if necessary. This accordingly was done, and the six pounder cannon of the Fort has been secretly stowed away, its whereabouts, at present, being unknown, except to the members of the Defence Committee. These precautions are merely taken for protection to the homes of the settlers, as no one at present can tell where these troubles are going to end.

## HOISTING THE FLAG

The Friday last, the 10th inst., the French went through the ceremony of hoisting the flag of their Provisional Government. About four o'clock in the afternoon, a number of armed men assembled in the Court yard of Fort Garry, and were addressed by Mr. Riel, who called upon them to support the new flag until their rights, as free born subjects of Queen Victoria, were respected. The idea of this movement is simply another step towards the grand scheme of a Provisional Government—an emblem, as it were, of its actual existence. After Mr. Riel's address, the flag (the design of which is the *fleur de lis* and shamrock combined) was hoisted, and a salute fired by the men in the Fort, at the same time the brass bands from St. Boniface, struck up some lively tunes; again and again the salutes were fired, until at last they thought they had wasted powder enough. The bands accompanied by a guard then proceeded to the town and serenaded the citizens. The shamrock on the flag looks significant; but on inquiry I find that it is merely in compliment to Mr. O'Donoghue, an Irishman, who has greatly assisted Mr. Riel in the present undertaking. This, at all events, is the only version of the matter I have heard. I sincerely hope there is no deeper meaning to the emblem. I am sure there is not so far as the general body of the French are concerned.[*]

AVERSE TO FENIANISM

Fenianism is to be dreaded, and, I assure you, the mass of the people here, both French and English, are as much adverse to the inroads of that body of adventurers as you are in Canada, and if I thought for one moment that Fenianism had the slightest influence in the movement amongst the French, I would be only too ready to acquaint you with the fact. At present (I cannot speak for the future) I believe there is no feeling in common between the people of this country and the Irish republic.

REPORT ABOUT MR. MCDOUGALL

It is now expected that Mr. McDougall will shortly return to Canada, if the state of his son, who lately broke his arm, will admit of his removal. In the meantime rumours reach us that our would-be Governor is likely to get himself into trouble with the American authorities, he being accused of endeavouring to enlist Indians and others to fight in his cause. That Mr. McDougall is really guilty of this I cannot believe, but sworn statements, accusing him of infringement on the international laws, have been made at Pembina, but whether these are sufficient to lead the hon. gentleman from Ottawa into difficulty I do not know. But I trust the American

---

[*] A letter in *L'Evenement*, dated 10 January 1870, argued that flags were common in the Hudson Bay region and that nothing was unusual about this one.

Government will be careful not to allow any quibbles got up by parties antagonistic to Mr. McDougall to inflict unwarrantable annoyance on that gentleman in his already trying position. The fact is, he is in a strange country, on a rough frontier, and unwittingly he may have been led to trespass on the laws of the country he has sought refuge in. If, however, it is true that he has tried to employ men on the other side of the lines to fight his battles in Red River he has done an act unaccountably foolish, and one which he might have been sure would bring him into trouble.

THE NEWSPAPER

Dr. Bown, "late Editor of the *Nor'-Wester*", since the departure of Col Dennis from the Stone Fort has mysteriously disappeared, either having left the Settlement for parts unknown, or he has hid himself, at all events his most intimate friends are unaware of his whereabouts. Mr. Riel, it is reported, is about putting the Dr's printing office to a different use. The guard lately in charge of the *Nor'-Wester* office has been withdrawn, and Dr. Bown's late printer has been put in charge by Mr. Riel for the purpose, it is supposed, of getting the place in readiness to bring out the coming newspaper. The *"Red River Pioneer"* in the meantime remains locked up, the proprietors not being allowed to print nor circulate their paper.

THE SIOUX

The Sioux excitement has subsided since the surrender of the Schultz party. I cannot learn definitely whether Colonel Dennis or any of his party were mixed up in it. It is not probable. One rumour is that the reason given to the Sioux Indians to induce them to fight against the French was that they were trying to turn over the country to the Americans. One thing is certain. "Shamon" left for the plains with the avowed purpose of bringing in the Sioux to the Settlement. It is also well known that "Shamon" of late has been on very intimate terms with, and a warm supporter of Dr. Schultz; and when the latter was besieged in his house, he sent up messages for assistance to the Portage, where there is a large band of Sioux Indians encamped.

### ANXIETY FOR THE FUTURE

The past week has been quiet, and the feelings of the people are becoming more settled in their character; but a deep solicitude is felt for the future of our Settlement. Fort Garry is still garrisoned by the French, and their supplies taken from the Company's stores; in fact, not only provisions, but articles of clothing and other creature comforts are taken as required by Mr. Riel and his men, without asking the sanction of the H.B.C. officers. A strict account, they say, is kept by the Provisional Government of all supplies thus acquired; and it is to be hoped the Company will be reimbursed for what is taken by the French, for I assure you their only position at present is to grin and bear it.

### A SETTLEMENT PROPOSED

The Provisional Government seems to be the sticking point between a union of the two sides of the Settlement, and yet I would not be surprised should it be found necessary for the mutual protection of all parties to take some steps toward uniting, so that some such sort of temporary government as that proposed by the French will be formed by the whole Settlement as a body, for the sole reason that the people would then be in a better position to effect an arrangement with the Dominion. Under the circumstances, it would be far better, both for Canada and the Settlement, for the present as well as the future, that there should be a feeling of unity amongst the settlers, as it would be likely to effect a more speedy and durable arrangement of the existing difficulties.

### THINGS 'MIXED'

The English speaking people are more cautious than the French, and they are not certain how far the latter have compromised themselves in the present movement, and are therefore in doubt as to whether it would not be complicity in its late acts should they now join the Provisional Government. As it is, things are decidedly mixed and muddy. There are large sums of money due the old government of Assiniboia for duties, &c.; the collection of these amounts by a Provisional Government in which only a portion of the people are represented would necessarily be attended with much difficulty and confusion. Debts have been already contracted by the French party, the payment of which will be apt to cause dissension should both sides unite, and the English be called upon to pay a share of them. The French now have the upper hand, having in their possession all the books, records, and due bills belonging to the late government of Assiniboia. Amongst other valuables they hold the Land Register, which, in itself is a tickler; for should it be destroyed, or done away with, the title of every man in the country to his land would be lost. Thus matters stand, I have no doubt you will say decidedly mixed, and as we are placed, I do feel that it would greatly assist a speedy settlement if all parties would throw aside their difference of opinion for the meantime, and endeavour to unite in one body for the common good; but at the present moment such a union seems a great way off. God knows where the complications of to day and those likely to follow in the future are to end. It is indeed worthy to be called a prize riddle. Babel must have been a paradise to the position we are in.

MR M'DOUGALL

One thing is certain should Mr. McDougall ever succeed in becoming our Governor, he will never be popular with a large majority of the settlers. But were the present difficulties once got over, I do not think there would be any decided objection to him on either side—but will it be wise policy for the Canadian Government, considering the late events and the feeling of the people, to place a man at the head of our affairs who has been so attended by trouble on his first introduction to us? The disaffected generally look upon him as overbearing in his manners and despotic in his feeling; he is described as being haughty and proud, but whether the description is a correct one I cannot say. But such, at all events is the character he bears amongst a large portion of the people here, most of whom, however, have never seen him. A proud, haughty, overbearing despotic man will never do for Governor of the North West—the people have never been accustomed to such individuals, and it will take a long time to change their present ideas on that score. We want a man who can be affable and kind to the poor as well as to the rich. Remember this has been a free speaking, free thinking country—rough but honest in all its institutions—haughtiness will not do on the frontier where the poorest man in the land does not consider it too presumptous nor too familiar to shake hands with a Governor when he meets him. The truth is, shaking hands is one of the institutions of the country.

THE PRINCIPAL ACTORS

It may be interesting to have a description of the principal actors in the present movement, and therefore before closing my letter I will attempt to describe to you what they are like. To commence with Riel, the first and chief promoter of the French affairs. Louis Riel is a young man about twenty five years of age, stout, and of medium stature. His face, at first sight, at once indicates great intelligence and strength of character; his forehead is rather massive, and surmounted by an abundance of brown, curly hair; his nose is Roman; his eyes, which are dark, are however the most remarkable of his features. When not excited, they have a sort of dreamy look about them, but when interested in a conversation or discussion, they flash in quick, rapid glances, giving zest and piquancy to his remarks. He was born in this country, but when quite a lad he was sent, under the patronage of Bishop Taché, to one of the Catholic colleges in Montreal, where he received the finishing touches to his education. He at one time, I believe, intended studying for the priesthood, but afterwards changed his mind. He was, when at college, and is now, noted for his oratorical powers; and indeed it has been due a great deal to his eloquence that the present movement amongst the French has been universal with them; and his good guidance has made it so far successful. Until he interested himself in the affairs of the country [which] resulted in our existing difficulties, he was not much noticed amongst his own people; but now he is the idol of the French. He can only speak broken English, but very good French. His utterance is rapid and energetic, and his remarks at times are very sarcastic. He is not rich; in fact his circumstances are not good. He lives with his mother, when at home, and until the present outbreak, he supported himself and her by farming a small piece of land. Riel by his energy and perseverance, has, you may say, conducted the whole of this movement; and, if he does not now overstep the mark, he will doubtless bring his people out safely yet. He declares his loyalty to Queen Victoria, but says he cannot stand by and see his people trampled upon as they apparently were to have been. He was elected Secretary of the French, which although only a secondary position, was given to him so as to allow him full scope to use his powers on behalf of his party. He comes from a revolutionary stock; his father before him having been mixed up in some troubles in this country during the time of Judge Johnson, but from what I hear the present Riel is more persevering, energetic and clever than his father was.

BRUCE

John Bruce, the President of the French, is rather tall, very dark features, intelligent, but rather of a morose countenance; in fact it is hard to move even a smile on his sober looking face. Before he took part in the present movement, he worked at his trade as a carpenter; but at the same time he tried his hand now and again in acting as lawyer for his friends in their lawsuits at our petty and general courts. For that reason he was looked upon by his own people as above the ordinary run of the French half breeds in intelligence. He always appeared to me a cautious man, very quiet and retiring in his disposition. He has not given any very material assistance in the present movement; in fact his name only has chiefly been used, for he himself is not always consulted by Riel and the rest of the councillors in matters of importance. However it is likely he will not long fill the office of President, as he is at this moment lying on a bed of sickness and is not expected to recover.

O'DONOGHUE

Wm O'Donoghue is the next, and as he is the right hand man to Riel, his influence amongst the French is strong. At the commencement of the rising, Mr. O'Donoghue was acting as schoolmaster in St. Boniface, in connection with the church. Indeed he was taking the three years' preparatory steps towards assuming the vows of the priesthood; but when the outbreak arose, he threw off his gown and declared himself heart and hand in the movement. He was appointed to represent St. Boniface in the Council on the French side, and from that time he has taken an active and conspicuous part in proceedings, although he does not occupy any specified position other than being a councillor. Mr. O'Donoghue is a young man about the same age as Riel, I should say an Irishman as will be seen by his name and hailing from New York previously to his coming to this country. He is tall and thin, of a light complexion, with long straight flaxon hair. He has shown himself a man of untiring energy, and certainly since he joined his party he has evinced the greatest zeal in their cause. His knowledge of the

English language is of great service to Riel; but farther than that I do not think he influences the Secretary one way or another. During the first sitting of the Council of French and English delegates, O'Donoghue gave expression to sentiments that were considered rather Fenian than otherwise. But he has since declared himself as misunderstood in the matter, and that it was only in the excitement that he, being an Irishman, was induced to refer to the state of his native country. He denied any Fenian feeling on his part in connection with the present movement. In speaking, O'Donoghue's accent smatters considerably of the brogue. He is what would be called a good speaker, and although I am not sufficiently acquainted with him to judge of his character, I can give him credit for showing himself a clever young man.

RICHOT

Last on the list, but by no means the least, is the Rev. M. Richot, a Roman Catholic Priest in charge of the Church at La Rivière Sale—from the first this Rev. gentleman has shown a great interest in the undertaking of his people—being, it is said, wealthy in his own right, he has supplied means from his own pocket to assist the movement. About a quarter of a mile from his church the barrier was raised to prevent the entrance of Mr. McDougall. At one time Mr. Richot became so excited over the French cause that fears were entertained of his becoming deranged. He is rather remarkable in appearance, dressed in his clerical garments, tall and well built, dark complexion, handsome face, with large black piercing eyes, and flowing beard reaching nearly to his waist. He is slightly bald. In speaking his manner is rather excited; but his eloquence is touching at times, and his language very expressive. For instance, on one occasion when speaking of the injustice of Canada, he remarked: "The big sister (Canada) would take all the blanket from her little brother (Red River), but we will let her know that little brother has been feared by the wolf, and will fight if necessary for what is justly due him." Mr. Richot has given as his reason for mixing so much in the present troubles that he wishes to control his people as far as possible from going to excess. But as far as their just rights he is with them to aid them by his counsels and advice. He is a half-breed himself, I believe; hails from Lower Canada, where, it is said, he was mixed up in some political trouble; but I cannot vouch for the truth of the report.* Mr. Richot has no doubt a great influence over his people, and is a good deal consulted in the present difficulties. Indeed I may say that the Catholic clergy have openly shown a decided interest in and taken part to a great extent in this movement amongst the French, so much so that it has given rise to the idea that it is a religion question; whereas I honestly believe it is nothing more nor less than a political one, risen from the fear that the French people were likely to be utterly ignored under the incoming Government. I see too that a mistaken idea is afloat in Canada that the question is one of land. This is a complete error, as you will see at once on referring to the List of Rights sent you in my last Letter.

THE GLOBE BLAMED

Let me here say a word on one subject that has come to our knowledge in Red River. We find in some newspapers called Ministerial that THE GLOBE is actually blamed as being partly the cause of our troubles here. We will give you credit for coming out and advocating the rights of a free people; you were right in prophesying that there would be trouble should the Government at Ottawa attempt to force their injudicious policy on this people; but that you, or anyone there influenced from the first the rejection of that policy, I do not believe. It was spontaneous from the commencement arising only in the feelings of the people who considered themselves injured, and you were only so far right in prophesying, instead of being the instigator of the movement.

CONCLUSION

You will see by this time the perplexing position in which the Settlement is now placed. Col. Dennis, after arriving with full powers from Mr. McDougall to act as our Governor, and issuing proclamation on proclamation without any success attending his literary efforts; after calling on a portion of the settlers to rush to arms and actually forming companies of men for drill for their own protection as the ostensible reason, but in reality [to] try and put down the French; after all this I say, Col. Dennis, one

---

* Begg appears to be wrong in asserting that Ritchot was of mixed blood.

fine night, to the surprize of everyone, and especially those who looked on him as their head, coolly walks off leaving his supporters to stare at each other and wonder where their leader had gone. Now we hear that Mr. McDougall is about starting back for Canada.

We in the Settlement are a people divided amongst ourselves; a larger portion of the settlers recognize the Provincial Government inaugurated by the French, the balance of the inhabitants are of various opinions; some are deeply actuated by their feelings of loyalty (to the Queen, not to Canada), and the uncertainty as to whether it would be wise to [ ] in the Provisional Government; others are perfectly careless whether the ship sinks or swims. It amounts to this however, treason or no treason, the people here will have to unite in some way or another or else nothing will be accomplished but ruin and next to starvation in the Settlement by the Spring.

In the meantime, I beg to reiterate my belief, that the only plan to further a speedy arrangement of our existing difficulties, is to send us immediately, proper, authorized men in the shape of Commissioners, to treat with and satisfy the settlers; let them not come here with half and half powers, but fully empowered to settle matters. A Governor sent with complete authority to grant the people what they ask would suit the same purpose, but I do not know whether McDougall would suit in this instance.

The Government must be aware of the rights claimed by the people; let them take that as the basis, and instruct their agent what to do when they arrive here. The customs duties will also be a matter likely to be considered. Our cost of transportation is so high that it will be but justice on the part of the Government to moderate the tariff for this part of the Dominion, until we are brought in closer and cheaper connection with the East. If the Government attempts to send troops here before matters are settled to coerce the French, let me lay before you what will happen. The French (leaving out the question [of] the rest of the Settlement, for one portion will never rise against their countrymen even were troops here), are desperate, and are bound to have their rights as a people secured to them before they will consent to join the Dominion. You may believe this or not, but I am speaking honestly and candidly what I feel, and it is of no use mincing matters at this critical moment. Where Fenianism is not thought of now, if the French are driven to bay, the aid of that body of adventurers, as well as many others from the United States, will be called in. Aid in the shape of arms, men, and money, will not be wanting. Savage tribes, now dormant, will be roused on the one side or the other. Although troops, when once got here, will be able to clear the country in open fight—do you suppose for one moment that this will end the matter, or that it will establish the Government on a sound and durable basis? By no means. Where are you going to find emigrants who will come to this country to settle when they will be subject to massacre or plunder at any moment? Troops will be the means perhaps of ultimately conquering the country; but they will do so at an immense expenditure, and the complete devastation of our Settlement.

I have said my say; you in Canada now act as you think best.

Yours truly,
JUSTITIA

Had Bishop Taché been consulted when he was last in Ottawa, our troubles here would not have occurred. Were he consulted now, our troubles would soon end. J.

Winnipeg, Dec. 17th, 1869

EDITOR'S NOTE

[A letter of "Rivière Rouge," written on 17 December 1869 and published in the Montreal *Herald* of 7 January 1870, describes the prisoners' situation:

> The prisoners are still supplied with food from the town, but it will be utterly impossible to continue this when the weather gets colder. The distance is about three-eighths of a mile, and with the thermometer at fifteen below zero as it was this morning, there is no chance of keeping even the tea warm. Clean clothing is regularly sent in to them from their own supplies, and with the exception of being rather crowded, there seems to be little or no complaint. The food supplied by Mr. Snow consists of fresh beef, pork, beans, bread, tea and potatoes, while some of the prisoners send money out for molasses or other articles which are sent to them. They are not allowed to receive letters or newspapers, and any memorandum sent out by them has first to be submitted to the secretary. Novels, cards, tobacco, pipes, &c. have been sent in

and were allowed to pass. Brandy was sent in by friends for the first few days but this was not allowed to be continued. The letters from this quarter which have appeared in your paper are eagerly read and quietly discussed.

There was some concern that the Fenians might have influenced members of the Provisional Government. The Fenians were an Irish paramilitary organization, formed in the United States among disbanded soldiers after the American Civil War. Their plans included invasions of British America, which could then be held as hostage for the independence of Ireland. See W.S. Niedhardt, *Fenianism in North America* (University Park, PA: Pennsylvania State University Press, 1975). One Fenian branch attempted to invade Manitoba in 1871. Consult John Perry Pritchett, "The So-called Fenian Raid on Manitoba," *Canadian Historical Review* 10 (1929): 23-42.

In an interview published in the *Globe* on 28 January 1870, Stuart Mulkins, one of the former prisoners at Upper Fort Garry returned to Canada, described Riel:

> He is about 26 years of age; has light hair, is clean shaved, and has a restless eye. From his appearance a stranger would not be likely to take him for a half-breed. When in conversation he looks his man straight in the face with a searching eye, and it would be difficult to deceive him. He is smart, beyond a doubt, but his nature is very changeable. When Fort Garry was captured, he displayed his want of firmness on several occasions. At first he ordered the gates of the Fort to be closed, but hardly had the order been executed when he countermanded it, and had them thrown open again. Another time he sent a patrol through the Settlement, but it was not kept up for many hours, owing to his want of pluck. Like a Frenchman, he has a great deal of dash and show about him, and when he does anything he lets the world know of it.

In its emphasis on Riel's pretentiousness, this description confirmed the account by the *Globe*'s own reporter of a meeting with Riel in Red River, published in the newspaper on 17 January 1870, although the reporter was far more malicious:

> He was a man about thirty years of age, about five feet seven inches in height—rather stoutly built. His head was covered with

dark, curly hair; his face had a Jewish kind of appearance, with a
very small very fast receding forehead. This, I was sure, was M. Le
President Riel, and he stood gazing at me in the most piercing
manner, at least, there is no doubt, he thought so. I did my utmost
to realize in him a Napoleon or an Alexander, but it was a failure—
a dead signal failure,—I could not get beyond the fact that there
stood before me a Linen Draper's assistant. There could be no mistake about that, and though he stood looking at me full ten minutes, he could not put the Linen Draper out of my mind, and if he
had continued to gaze till now, the result would have been all the
same. He was clad in a light tweed coat and black trousers, and he
seemed exceedingly proud of them—and well he might, for it is as
certain as the fact that he wore them, that these clothes were purchased with the price of his poor widowed mother's only cow.

In a letter dated 18 December to *Nouveau Monde*, reprinted in translation
in the Toronto *Globe* on 14 January 1870, "St. Norbert" wrote concerning
John Bruce:

> There is a wish to discredit the men who are at the head of the
> nation. This is another matter of insult; but what will be the
> result of it? Simply, in attacking the President, to furnish us with
> an occasion to eulogise the gentleman. Mr. John Bruce is one of
> the most distinguished lawyers of the country, and could be well
> called the most esteemed by the court before which he has exer-
> cised his profession for many years. In pleading, as in conversa-
> tion, Mr. Bruce is grave and precise; his elocution is easy in style,
> terse and elegant. Mr. Bruce formerly occupied a seat on the
> Judge's bench; there also he distinguished himself by the justice
> of his decisions. Mr. Bruce speaks French and English, and the
> several languages of the natives of the country, which is not an
> unimportant circumstance in this movement now taking place.

Begg's concerns about aid from Fenian or other organizations were not
entirely far-fetched. In 1926 the former Fenian John Sutton wrote to the
head of the Nebraska Historical Society that in the late autumn of 1869, he
and a few fellow Fenians had broken into a storage room in the state capital building in Lincoln and made off with a number of Springfield rifles
being kept there. The rifles were shipped collect to Minnesota, where they

were intended to arm Fenian volunteers who would help the Métis in Red River. The arms were never picked up and were eventually returned to Lincoln, where they were stored until they rusted in the basement of the home of one of the local Fenian leaders. See John Sutton to Hon. Addison E. Sheldon, Ms RG 1449, Nebraska Historical Society, Lincoln.]

# J.J. HARGRAVE

18 DECEMBER 1869

[The editorial note after a letter from "Rivière Rouge" and before this one from J.J. Hargrave reads: "From another of our Correspondents." As one would expect from a trusted employee of the Hudson's Bay Company, Hargrave is very concerned about the impact upon the trade of the consumption of the foodstuffs stored in Upper Fort Garry. He is also concerned about a potential bloodbath resulting from the alliance of Métis and Indians to defend the country against any Canadian armed invasion, and he makes clear how badly, he believes, Canada has managed the transfer. Printed in the *Montreal Herald and Daily Commercial Gazette*, 7 January 1870.]

December 18th, 1869

To the stormy scenes recorded in my last week's letter, a period of comparative repose has succeeded. The chief sufferers from the unsettled state of things are, of course, the prisoners, but the most serious losses fall on the Hudson Bay Company. The numbers of the former have been increased by successive captures effected from day to day, isolated individuals, to whom suspicion of disaffection is attached in the minds of the insurgent leaders, being seized and deprived of liberty without any form of law whatever. Some of the captives are housed in the rooms over the Company's public office in Fort Garry, while the remainder are detained in the Court House and Common Gaol.

Between captives and insurgents, a standing body numbering more than two hundred men, is kept at Fort Garry. Provisions for this assembly are daily required from the Company's stores, when pem[m]ican, flour, leather, tea, sugar, dry goods and minor luxuries are carried off without remorse. The direct loss inflicted by this system of pillage is, of course, very large, but is relatively small in prospect of the damaging effect it will produce on the approaching season's trade. To understand this, it is necessary to remember that the provisions these people are consuming have been stored at Fort Garry to be transported to the North in spring, to supply the posts and brigades of boats, by means of which all the complicated operations of the fur trade are carried on, with the means of existence. The purchase of provisions by the Company from the settlers, which is usually conducted on a large scale about this season, is entirely suspended, because in the first instance, the disturbed state of the colony has interrupted all business, and moreover, such purchases made by the Company would only be instrumental in collecting further supplies for the insurgents.

It is generally believed that so soon as the supplies at Fort Garry shall have been consumed, the stores of private individuals in the village of Winnipeg and other parts of the colony, will be appropriated by the French. Hitherto, the only articles which have been seized, beyond the walls of Fort Garry, have been guns and ammunition; printing presses, and the goods of prisoners are represented as being kept in trust until the advent [?] of more settled times. The pretext [?] under which the levies will be made will, doubtless, be the collection of Customs dues from merchants, whose accounts with their creditors [?] may be outstanding. Some American citizens in this position have declared their intention of refusing to disburse money required in such a manner, and, if necessary, of applying to Mr. Malmros for protection. Of course, the representations of the American Consul will be treated by the insurgents with the same contempt with which the remonstrances of all the other constituted authorities have been received, and his only resource will be, I presume, to report the cases to his headquarters. Such a case has not, as above mentioned, yet occurred, but the supplies to be obtained at Fort Garry are steadily diminishing, and their entire consumption will, it is fully expected, be the commencement of endless complications.

As matters actually stand, the situation is bad enough. Such scenes as are here of daily occurrence must inevitably retard the flow of immigration, and entirely suspend the influx of capital to the country. It is considered extremely doubtful that even the Hudson Bay Company will venture to import to any extent during the coming season, and in the event of the disturbances extending to the districts in the interior, a withdrawal of their supplies already in the country would probably be effected. It happens that, at present, an unusually large number of manufactured goods exists in the colony. Merchants have, of late, imported very largely, with the view of escaping the immediate effects of the high Customs tariff expected to be imposed by Canada. It is much to be feared that the profit contemplated to be secured by the adoption of this course, will prove to have been a bait luring many to heavy loss.

The proceedings of Governor Macdougall and the Canadian officials still at liberty are but imperfectly known in the Settlement. It is understood, however, that the former with the members of his party who have passed the last few weeks with him at Pembina, have returned to Canada. Twenty men of the party of forty dispatched last week by the insurgents to Pembina, with the intention of driving the Lieutenant-Governor back, in the event of his having again crossed the frontier, have taken possession of the Hudson's Bay Post at that place. Colonel Dennis, accompanied by all the Canadian officials still at liberty in the Settlement, with the exception of two, has left Fort Garry, with the intention of proceeding by a round about route, so as to avoid the insurgents at La Riviere Sale to Canada. Messrs. Snow and Grant, the latter of whom is still Treasurer of the party, are still permitted to remain at large. The Government Stores and Provisions, of which there is a great quantity in the Settlement, are still respected.

In view of the probable results of the events of the past few weeks, I may mention that, should this winter pass without such active opposition to the rule of the insurgent party, it [as?] may lead to bloodshed, complications of a serious nature will probably take place in Spring, when it is possible there may be a large gathering of Indians from the West in the Settlement, and almost certainly an influx of the whole half breed population of the Plains. The latter may, I am credibly informed, produce two thousand men capable of carrying arms.

The French half-breed party lying in Red River is certainly accustomed to the performance of rough works, but I think it is unquestionable that the most formidable portion of the fighting population will be recruited from the party known as "Winterers," who live upon the Plains. They are thoroughly inured to all the privations of camp life in all seasons, experienced in savage warfare, adept in all the arts of horsemanship and management of the gun, and at home almost everywhere on a battlefield extending from Red River to the Rocky Mountains. Their organization for purposes of the chase is quite susceptible of adaptation, with the utmost possible advantage, to those of war.

It is, therefore, a matter for the most serious consideration, in the event of the Canadian Government determining to put down the present rebellion with a strong hand, that the commencement of military operations at Red River will be but the beginning of disturbances throughout the entire Indian

Country. The Settlement is connected by so many ties with the whole of Rupert's Land that the lighting up of the flame of Civil War within it will be the breaking out of a conflagration which, like the Prairie fires, will devastate the Territory, gathering strength with its outward progress, and growing more irresistible as the circuit of the ravages expands. The distinction between combatant and non-combatant will become unknown, as has occurred even in the present disturbance; unwilling recruits will be impressed, and compelled to shoulder a musket in the common cause. The result may be the extermination of human life on a large scale.

Already the most serious errors have been committed by the parties to whom has been entrusted the management of the North West extension of the Dominion of Canada. Even under the most favourable auspices, the task of establishing Canadian rule in Rupert's Land, was one requiring a high administrative talent in the person undertaking it. The vast distance intervening between the newly acquired territories and the older Provinces of the Dominion; the absence of any communication between them, except that passing for many hundreds of miles through a foreign state; and the paucity of information possessed by people in Canada relative to the country or its inhabitants, ought to have warned the Government and its officials of the absolute necessity of tact and caution in dealing with North West affairs.

It was surely to have been reasonably expected that on the conclusion of negotiations for the transfer of the country to the Canadian Government, it would have put itself in close communication with the officials who had administered the affairs of Red River under the Hudson's Bay Company. By so doing matters might have been made to work so smoothly that, when the day formal transfer at length arrived, every thing might have been found to settle imperceptibly into running order, and the new condition of things have been inaugurated without noise or bustle.

The course actually pursued was one quite the reverse of this. Successively arriving officials seemed altogether unaccredited to those of the old order of things, and attached themselves to a party, which, while professing itself peculiarly representative of Canada, had always openly gloried in throwing difficulties in the way of the old administration. This party, what influence soever it may have in Canada, never possessed any in Red River. Indeed, the conduct of several of its leading members has been such as altogether to preclude the possibility of their possessing value influence with the well disposed. Among Governor McDougall's most zealous partisans one has been imprisoned twice,[*] and the others once within the last six years, while another has twice assisted at scenes of prison breaking.[†] The offences for which the former have been incarcerated, have been assaults on the officers of the law, in the execution of their duty, and refusal to respect the righteous judgments of courts of justice. False reports of the various causes which led them into trouble have certainly been zealously circulated in Canada by these people, and it is very likely that Canadian officials may have been conscientiously misled. It is also true that the latter may have desired in some way to recompense those men whom they believed to have been persecuted, for the evils of the past; but common prudence might have suggested the expediency of testing the truth of improbable tales, by consulting court and other official records, which would inevitably have come into their possession at the date of the transfer of the territory; and self respect and public decency ought to have forbidden incoming officials to sanction by intimacy the proceedings of men who gloried in defying the authority of the still existing Government, which their own was so soon to replace.

The above are a few of the causes which have given rise to the events of the last few weeks. They are, of course, very far from being *all* the causes, but they account very much for the apathy of the English portion of the colony. The results of the indiscretion of his friends have been highly detrimental to the official career of Mr. McDougall in Rupert's Land, and the circumstances under which the introduction of Canadian rule into the country had taken place form a spectacle of merriment to Americans, and of humiliation and dismay to the friends of English influence.

It is a very grave question to what extent the influence of the Company has been affected by these occurrences. Hitherto it has possessed the confidence of the people to a very great extent. Its professed so called "political" opponents in its Government here have never had anything like the sympathy of any large section of the Settlement. The utter novelty of recent proceedings has, however, been such as to overthrow all old standards of

---

[*] The reference is to John Schultz.

[†] This reference is to James Stewart (b. 1827), an Orkneyman who helped free Reverend G.O. Corbett in 1863 and Schultz in early 1869.

opinion, and may be expected seriously to disturb the entire system of business in the country. Such a disruption was the one thing which ought to have been avoided in the interests both of the Company and the Canadian Government.

Reports have reached us of the probable appointment of Commissioners to enquire into the causes of discontent, and endeavour to effect a peaceful arrangement of the difficulties which beset us. It is the opinion of experienced men here, that this course ought to have been at first adopted. It will be necessary, however, that proper men be selected for the work, and no name which has yet become public in connection with the appointment raises any hope in the minds of those conversant with the difficulties to be surmounted of a successful termination of the mission. Men *are* to be found in this Country of very considerable influence with the Indians, and have been engaged by the Company, at various critical junctures, to employ their good offices in their favour. It is, however, doubtful whether the same persuasion which might amicably settle difficulties between Indians and a Fur Trading Company, could negotiate with equal success in the class of matters to be dealt with between the former and the Canadian Government. But, if the business is to be arranged in a peaceable manner, men who have lived among the Indians are those who can best perform it, and I have no doubt the most reliable information attainable respecting the people it would be most advisable to employ, would be furnished by the officers of the company. Hitherto, I have heard of no step having been taken likely to secure the services of efficient men in this very important department of Dominion affairs—on the contrary, incoming officials seem altogether "at sea" in their knowledge of people, or the choice of those whose confidence they invite and whose representations they trust.

I enclose a list of prisoners in the hands of the insurgents. It is incomplete, containing only 42 names, whereas, it is said, there are more than sixty in confinement.[1] There has been no further rumour of a Court Martial, but a Council of French leaders is to be convened, to deliberate on their fate. Probably the greater number will be liberated on parole. Beyond the fact that they are deprived of liberty, and confined in somewhat close quarters, they are subjected to no severity of treatment. They are permitted to receive their food from the village of Win[n]ipeg, and consequently undergo no privation in that important particular.

Lists of prisoners detained by the insurgents at Red River Settlement;—

FROM CANADA.—Doctor Lynch; Doctor O'Donnel, wife and two children; Stewart Mulkins, Arthur Hamilton, Charles Mair and wife, Mr. Miller, Peter McArthur, Russell Smith.

RESIDENTS AT RED RIVER.—Charles Garrett, James Mulligan (pensioner); Thomas Franklyn (do); Charles Stodzeall (do); William Hallett, John Hallet, James Stewart, Rollin P. Meade, Doctor John Schultz and wife, H. Gomez Fonseca (liberated).

MISCELLANEOUS.—George Klyne, Frank Larose, George D. McVicar, Scott, John Eccles, F.C. Mercer, Charles Palmer, Henry Woodington, George Parker, William Kitson, D.H. Campbell, Angus B. Chisholm, George A. Bubar, William Nimons, John Latimer, Walter F. Hyman, Daniel Cameron, Mathew Davis, George Brandon, James Ashdown, Spice, Combs, Wright, and Stocks.

MEM—The ladies and children named in the above list are not regarded as prisoners, but stay at Fort Garry from choice.

# J.J. HARGRAVE

## 25 DECEMBER 1869

[This chatty letter from J.J. Hargrave is distinguished mainly for its conclusion, in which the author adopts a *nom de plume* for the first time, to
avoid confusion with other correspondents. Hargrave also makes a good
deal of the false assumption of power by Governor McDougall and its
consequences. Printed in the *Montreal Herald and Daily Commercial
Gazette*, 29 January 1870.]

Red River Settlement, British North America
December 25th 1869

Early this week intelligence reached this place of the departure of Mr.
Macdougall and his family and party on their return to Canada. The
weather throughout the week has been piercing cold, but fine; and it is to
be hoped that he should have been able to make reasonably rapid progress,
Mr. Macdougall ought now to have reached the advanced settlements at
Fort Abercrombie.

Since the date of my last letter current events in this place have been
developing themselves. Towards the close of last week it was reported that
an Indian chief named "Grands Oreilles" and his band had been pillaging
the Canadian Government provisions stored by Mr. Snow at Oak Point.* A
case of aggravated assault also occurred in the Settlement, in which a
woman walking home with a boy, her son, was mercilessly beaten to the
ground to the effusion of blood and serious damage to her person.† A case
of murder also occurred at St. Andrew's, near Lower Fort Garry, where, during a drunken debauch, a discussion arose concerning local politics, and
pistols, with which everybody is now provided, were drawn.

---

* Little more is known of Grands Oreilles and his band.

† This is probably the trial of Mrs. Rodway vs Mrs. Meeken, reported by Begg
in his journal, in which the result was "damages all round 10/- to 20/-each." See
Morton, ed., *Begg's Journal*, 239.

All these cases were dealt with by the insurgent leaders, as the Governors of the Country.* A guard of half-breeds is reported to have been stationed at Oak Point. The case of assault was duly heard, and as the complainant was proved to have commenced hostilities on a previous occasion, fines were imposed on her and her son, as well as on the defendant and her husband, who was also mixed up in the case under more immediate consideration. In the case of murder, the legal coroner of the Settlement held an inquest, and the evidence pointed very directly towards one of the individuals present at the debauch, who, however, had quitted the colony before steps were taken to apprehend him.

Nothing definite has yet been done about the cases of the "Political" Prisoners. It is understood that a full "Council" of the Insurgents met for the purpose of deliberating on what should be done with them at least once, during the past week. The particular individuals whose cases are said to have been taken into consideration, are William Hallett and his son John, two leading English half-breeds, resident in this place. If any conclusion was arrived at regarding them it has not transpired.

On the morning of the 22nd instant Louis Riel, the Insurgent Leader, called on the Governor of Rupert's Land, and made a demand for a very large sum of money, to be paid him on account of his Government.† The Governor refused to comply, whereupon Riel threatened to seize the Fort more effectually than by merely maintaining his previous hold on it. Receiving no satisfaction from the Governor, he repaired to the public office of the Sort accompanied by his coadjutor, Mr. William O'Donoghue, and two sentries with fixed bayonets. Disregarding the protests of the accountant, whose pockets they searched for the key of the safe, they opened that box, and having carefully counted what money it contained they carried off both safe and contents to their own office. The result is that the cash and banking business of the Company is at an end.

While ignorant of the peculiar mode of unlocking the safe, they were tampering with the locks, hesitating as to the expediency of blowing it open with gunpowder, the Insurgents repeatedly remarked how strong

---

* Hargrave thus underlines the point that the provisional government was the *de facto* government of Red River.

† This report is obviously first-hand.

their inclination was to compel every officer and servant of the Company to quit the Fort the same evening "before six o'clock." While the search was going on the sentries at the Fort gates were doubled, and no one was permitted to pass out or in.

On the following day Riel assembled his men and addressed them, I am informed, substantially as follows: He thanked them for their previous services, but said what had been done was only a commencement; a permanent guard of fifty men would be kept for the remainder of the Winter at Fort Garry, and their pay as soldiers would commence from that day.

While the foregoing is a brief summary of the chief events of the earlier part of the week, I feel they would lose much of their significance were I to be silent regarding a very painful rumour which has within the last few days begun to be circulated in the colony. It will doubtless be remembered that a few weeks ago I advised you that Colonel Dennis had on the 1st December arrived from Pembina, bringing with him the "Queen's Proclamation," written copies of which he at once distributed, one of which I had myself seen and read.

The Insurgent Leaders and others in the Settlement, on reading the document, declared their unbelief in its authenticity as far as the Queen was concerned. Believing that, in the case of the former at least, incredulity was merely feigned, I could not for a moment consider myself justified in mentioning to you that the document was in any way out of order. It certainly was very different from anything for which I had looked; but the fact that it had emanated from Mr. Macdougall through Colonel Dennis, I had thought sufficient to guarantee its authenticity. It was well known, and much commented on, that the outgoing Governor, Mr. Mactavish, had received no advice whatever of the advent of such an instrument, and that he had not obtained even a copy of it without some trouble. Under all the circumstances however, I deemed it superfluous to enclose you a copy, as I believed it had doubtless already appeared in official Canadian papers, though I forwarded copies of subsequent proclamations issued both by Mr. Macdougall and Colonel Dennis, apparently on the authority conveyed in the original Instrument.

The Proclamation is of course Mr. Macdougall's own; but the gentleman who gave it publicity in the Settlement gave no one with whom he came in contact to understand that Mr. Macdougall had forwarded it before hearing, in the most authentic manner of the formal transfer of the Territory to his Government having been effected. On the contrary Colonel Dennis took possession in the Queen's name of a Fort belonging to the Company, in which he proceeded to enrol and drill recruits, a very considerable number of whom have since been seized with arms in their hands and are held as prisoners by the Insurgents. On learning that they had been enrolled and urged to fight in consequence of our official mistake, and that the Canadian Government had failed to meet the responsibilities under which the Transfer would take effect, some of the prisoners are reported to have expressed extreme indignation, and complaints of having been misled.

I may mention that at the close of November, there were some appearances that the more violent proceedings of the Insurgents were about to be discontinued. Riel and his principal companions declared their intentions of retiring from Fort Garry, where only a very small body of them remained. They contented themselves with asking rations only for the passing day, stating on each occasion that it would almost certainly be the last. Difficulties of various kinds prevented the harmonious working together of French and English deputies in the work of creating a temporary government; and dissensions of a serious character seemed to be rising among the French themselves.

The advent of Colonel Dennis was an event which wrought an immediate change. The French collected with one mind to resent and oppose his threatening proclamation. They crowded to Fort Garry in hundreds, and compelled the Colonel's recruits in the village of Winnipeg to surrender at discretion.

There remains of course the alternative that the apparent dispersal of the insurgents may have been merely a feint, practised to mislead the outside world, and to throw the responsibility of renewed troubles on the Canadian officials, whose mistaken action may have been anticipated. Looked at in this light, Colonel Dennis may only have fallen into a trap with the connivance of the Insurgents. But, if, on the other hand, Riel and his party were sincere in their professions of an immediate peaceful retirement, on the Canadian authorities must be cast the odium of having caused more than sixty men to be exposed to forfeiture of liberty for a length of time yet unknown, as well as having driven the Hudson's Bay Company, and the entire mercantile community of this place to a frightful pecuniary loss.

Yester-night the usual annual celebration of Midnight Mass took place at the Roman Catholic Cathedral of St. Boniface. A line of insurgents was drawn up round the Church, it is said with the object of guarding it against some apprehended danger of incendiarism. At one o'clock in the morning a salute of eighteen guns was fired from the Pieces of Artillery at Fort Garry.

RED RIVER, January 1st, 1870

On the evening of the 26th ultimo. the Rev. Mr. Thibeault arrived from Canada and took up his residence in the house of the bishop of St. Boniface. It is currently reported that Mr. Thibeault is not permitted to move and speak freely among the insurgents. Colonel De Salaberry remained at Pembina, to which place a message was sent early in the week by the malcontents, requesting him, it is said, to come down to the Settlement. No response, so far as is known to the public, has come to this message.

On the 27th, Mr. Chief Factor Donald A. Smith, along with another officer of the Hudson Bay Company, reached Fort Garry.[*] They were immediately notified to report themselves at the office of Mr. Riel where they were detained for nearly an hour. At the expiry of that time they were permitted to go to their own quarters on the understanding that they were to confine themselves in the meantime within the walls of the Fort.

Doctor Tupper of Nova Scotia had left Pembina on the way to the Settlement before Mr. Smith.[1] On the same evening on which the latter gentleman arrived, about ten o'clock, a stranger reached Fort Garry, and after a few minutes conversation with the insurgent leaders is said to have voluntarily returned on his way to Canada. It is thought the stranger must have been Doctor Tupper, who has not since been heard of.

In the course of the week reports from various quarters have been reaching the Settlement that, in consequence of certain action taken by Mr. MacDougall while at Pembina, the Red River Settlement, as well as the Settlements on the American frontier at Pembina and St. Joseph are in danger from the Sioux and other Indians. It is reported, on very good authority indeed, that formal charges of a serious nature have been made, and transmitted, through the hands of the American Consul resident here, to Washington, along with an urgent demand for the immediate presence of a powerful American Military force at Pembina.

---

[*] The other man was Richard Hardisty.

Under the influence of these reports, it is scarcely surprising that the public mind was much agitated on learning the presence of about fifty Sioux armed with guns, within twenty miles of Fort Garry. Being warned to come no further they paid no attention to the message, and the American residents in the village of Winnipeg formed themselves into a corps with the avowed intention of going to meet the Sioux and exterminating them without parley. It was said that the Indians had already committed depredations on the way down. Matters seemed to have reached another crisis, when Riel interfered, and advising the village troops to desist, himself went to meet the Sioux at Sturgeon Creek about six miles west from Fort Garry. It appeared they had come only on one of their ordinary mendicant visits and begged some provisions. They fraternized with Riel for a night and returned westward this morning. Their arms were carried not as an offensive demonstration, but as a necessary means of defence when passing over the grounds of Indians in this neighbourhood, with whom they are on hostile terms.

Regarding the assertions against Governor MacDougall, they are discredited as a matter of course. It is however unfortunate that a person named "Shawman" or George Racette, should be on Mr. MacDougall's side. He is, I believe, the only "Loyal" French half-breed and he is a most dangerous ally. He is at present understood to be among the Sioux.

A rumour, circulating in the American papers that Mr. Macdougall had used the "Swampy Indians" about Lower Fort Garry as his allies against Christians, needs only to be explained at length to be explained away. These people are themselves Christians and Settlers, and Colonel Dennis, when enrolling other Settlers, doubtless did not consider himself justified in refusing their services merely because they were Indians. They belong to the Anglican Indian Mission of St. Peter on the Red River, they are agriculturists and man the Company's freight boats but are a very inferior set of men and not understood to be either cruel or heroic. If Mr. MacDougall and Colonel Dennis could make soldiers of them or teach them to do their duty creditably as Native troops, these gentlemen would deserve the congratulations of their friends.

RED RIVER, January 8, 1870.
Throughout the earlier part of the week, the Council of the Insurgents was busily occupied into the cases of individual Political Prisoners. The result

of their deliberations was the liberation of nearly twenty of the captives. It is said that many members of the Insurgent Council have for some time past advocated the expediency of setting free all the less important prisoners, but that others have opposed the measure, which has been so keenly debated as to have threatened a rupture among the French Party. Some, if not all, of those liberated were compelled to leave the country, being allowed only a few hours time to make the necessary preparations for their journey. The more obnoxious Prisoners will certainly be detained for a period the termination of which must be fixed by events regarding which I have not the means to speculate.

On the morning of the 6th inst., Mr. Snow, the Surveyor, left the Settlement for Canada. Although virtually under surveillance, Mr. Snow was fortunate enough to have been permitted to remain at large during the last month. Along with him Messrs. Arthur Hamilton and Stewart Mulkins who have been kept since the date of the general capture in close confinement, were permitted to return to Canada. I cannot let this opportunity escape of saying that Mr. Snow carries with him the sympathies of a great many who regret the unfortunate auspices under which he commenced his career at Red River, and deeply regret the miseries and annoyances against which he has had to contend. Probably a sense of this weighed with the insurgent leaders who expressed it by the leniency they have latterly shown him.

On the same morning of Mr. Snow's departure, Col. De Salaberry arrived from Pembina and went to reside at St. Boniface. It is generally understood that the delay which has taken place in the arrival of this gentleman was caused by the length of time necessary to make arrangements regarding the terms on which he was to be permitted to enter the Settlement. No intelligence has reached me regarding his proceedings since his arrival.

Yesterday, appeared the first number of a newspaper to be published in this Settlement, called the "New Nation." It is conducted by an American citizen, named H.M. Robinson, and is the organ of the "Half-breed Republic."[2] I regret to say it advocates "Annexation," and professes to do so on principle. I shall probably have a good deal more to say on this paper, in connection with the general subject of our local Press, in a future letter, than I can at present put into what space is left me. With regard to this subject of "Annexation," I must, however, remark I hope, in the interests more especially of the half-breeds, that the date at which it will take effect is still at an infinite distance of time. Red River Colony has been nursed by the United States. Without their assistance we would yet have only two mails annually instead of the same number weekly. The Great Republic has also brought civilization, railroads, trade and population to our doors. The Red River settlers may well therefore desire close commercial and social relations of the most friendly nature to be continued between them and their mighty neighbour. Politically, however, they ought to prefer British connection.

Canada claims her share in the trade of her sister Territory of Winnipeg. If there be any vitality at all in the tie which binds each to the mother country her claim must be allowed to be just and most reasonable and good. But the price at which the territory of Winnipeg is to become one with the Provinces of Canada is a railroad from Ottawa to Fort Garry. It is a "military, a political and commercial necessity," as I think was said about the "Union Pacific," while it was still in embryo.

I beg to conclude by saying that, as I see the fact of my having adopted no specific signature to my letters seems likely to end in committing me, through mistake, to the opinions of brother correspondents, from which in reality I might dissent, I shall adopt for distinction's sake in any future communications to your Journal the signature

RED RIVER.

EDITOR'S NOTE

[Regarding the murder at St. Andrew's, according to Begg's journal, "A man named Thos. Johnson was found yesterday near his own door frozen. At first it seemed as if he had frozen to death—but on closer examination it turned out that he had been shot." On 21 December a coroner's inquest decided that Ryder Larson, who had already fled the country, had shot Johnson. Morton, ed., *Begg's Journal*, 232-34.]

# ALEXANDER BEGG

## 11 JANUARY 1870

[This exceedingly chatty letter from Alexander Begg provides us with a good bit of detail found nowhere else, including the meeting at the house of James McKay with the Sioux Indians, and the establishment of *The New Nation*. Printed in the Toronto *Globe*, 14 February 1870.]

LETTER NO. V.
(To the Editor of the Globe)

RED RIVER SETTLEMENT
January 11th, 1870

SOCIAL CUSTOMS AT RED RIVER

SIR,—

Christmas and New Year's Day are past, and we have entered upon another voyage of Time—1871 being our destination. Our holiday festivities this season in Red River were not as they used to be. Few felt inclined to indulge in gaiety when the prospects for the future are so uncertain and dark. The beginning of a new year is signal in our Settlement for the commencement of marriages, dances and parties of every description—indeed, we resemble Lower Canada very much in this respect. During summer we are all work and no play, and in winter all play and no work. Meetings for political purposes instead of for dancing and fun are more the rage at this time, although there have been a few exceptions, both amongst the French and English speaking settlers, and I have to chronicle up to the present time about a dozen social parties in Red River, instead of about a hundred or more as would have been the case had we not been in the plight we are at present as a people. As the contents of this letter are not likely to be of a bright and cheerful nature, there can be little harm in my giving you a description of a "social" in this part of the world. It may serve as an oasis in the desert of gloomy tidings I have to serve up in this epistle.

When a marriage takes place amongst the French half-breeds it is celebrated with the greatest of spirit: dancing and fun run rife, and good feeling is abundant amongst those invited to the wedding; old, or any

differences, are laid aside for the time being, and everyone, friends or ene-
mies, meet each other on the most amicable footing.[1] If there should be a
fight among the guests it is a rare occurrence, and one that seldom or ever
results in serious consequences or bad feeling in the future. A drive to the
church where the ceremony is performed—the united couple return in
company with those invited to the home of the bride's parents. A fiddler,
or perhaps two having been engaged, the guests in the neighbourhood
begin to assemble about sundown and dancing commences, led by the
bride and bridegroom. Shouts and laughter are the order of the evening,
and if ever you would wish to see dancing in earnest you would find it on
an occasion such as I am describing. A Red River jig is something that
means business. A gentleman leads a lady to the middle of the floor, and
at the sound of the fiddle they commence dancing to each other as if they
wished to burst through the boards beneath them. Round and round,
backwards and forwards from one end of the room to the other they go,
the man endeavours to outdo himself if possible, and the woman takes care
not to be outdone by him. After they have danced some time, a swain from
amongst the guests steps up and cuts out the one on the floor—he is succeeded by another. The ladies exchange places in the same way, and thus
it goes—the dance being kept up as long as the fiddler is able to ply his
bow. A Red River fiddler, too, is worthy of notice. The tunes he plays are
quick and spirited, and he invariably keeps time with his feet on the floor.
Eating and drinking are part of the entertainment, the latter sometimes
exceeds the bounds of sobriety but not as a a rule. I have known weddings
kept up in this way for three or four days, the guests going home for a little sleep and returning afterwards to keep the thing up. Usually, however,
dances are kept up in this country all night and part of the next day. Anything short of that would be no party at all. During the winter dances are
of nightly occurrence, especially amongst the French; but alas! for fun,
this year these social gatherings are few and far between.

PROGRESS OF EVENTS.

Some time has elapsed since I have sent you a communication, but this
break in my correspondence can easily be explained. Many and grave
rumours of the mails being tampered with at some point between here and
St. Paul's have been prevalent in the Settlement, and coming from so many

quarters it certainly began to look as if there were some truth in the reports. It is not known, however, who or where the guilty parties are. Each has his own idea on the subject, and even Mr. McDougall has been suspected of having a hand in the matter. Poor McDougall is in for everything, but you know the devil is generally painted blacker than he is. Not receiving any returns for the letters to you in the way of acknowledgment for some time I hesitated about sending another, and I have only just now seen a printed copy of mine of the 1st December, and on that account have taken heart once more to write you at this time.[*] In my last I left off on the 17th ult., and will resume the chain of events from that date. There may be items in this letter that will prove stale in their interest to your readers, but as I have endeavoured to keep you posted with events in their proper relation as they have occurred, I will ask you to print this, my letter, as I have written it, although part of it may be somewhat late in the day. I mentioned in my last the inauguration of the Provisional Government. One of the first acts that Government was called upon to exercise its authority over was in the case of Mr. Snow, the Road Superintendent. It appears that some Indians, well armed, went in a body to the man in charge of the works during Mr. Snow's absence and demanded provisions, [obscured on microfilm] stating, at the same time, that if they were not given they would take by force. Fearing lest they would put their threats into execution, the young man gave the savages what they wanted. The goods, &c. belonging to the Canadian Government were then hauled away from the depot and distributed amongst the neighbouring houses. Mr. Riel's attention was called to this outrage by Mr. Snow, and the Secretary of the Provisional Government went out himself with a guard, and it appears settled matters to the satisfaction of all parties concerned, and Mr. Snow was assured that he would not suffer any further molestation.

I stated, also, in my last that a newspaper was about to be started in the interests of the people. An American gentleman, one Major Robinson, took the matter up, and how far he has fulfilled the anticipations of your correspondent will be seen before the end of this letter. It began about this time to be whispered amongst the settlers that the Queen's Proclamation was not really out, and that the document which was given out by the

---

[*] This explanation is not very convincing, but no other reason is known.

Dennis party as being the real thing was nothing more nor less than "bogus" in its character, being, it was believed, only a copy of Mr. McDougall's commission as Governor of the North-West. You can hardly imagine the reaction that took place in the minds of the people when this news became spread abroad. Supporters of Mr. McDougall denounced him; and when you take into consideration the "war" and "peace" proclamations that followed each other afterwards in succession, you can hardly wonder at the people being dumbfounded in earnest. These facts, in the face of Col. Dennis having left so suddenly for parts unknown, created a feeling not easily portrayed amongst the English speaking population. The blunders of Canada's officials were now at their climax, as it will be seen. No one felt the unaccountable turn affairs had taken more than the poor fellows in prison, who (they felt) had been led into a trap, serious enough as it has turned out for some of them. What say you? Even if Mr. McDougall had authority for what he and his officials have done, has their course been such as would tend to reconcile the people of this country to their government?

A GOVERNMENT WANTED.

A fatal occurrence took place about this time, that, unfortunate in itself, did a great deal towards showing the people how helpless they were, as long as they did not unite in some way for the general government of the country, until arrangements could be entered into with Canada or Great Britain. It seems that a party of men met in the house of one Peter Pruden, and that in the course of the evening, there being a good deal of drinking going on, a quarrel ensued which terminated in the shooting of a man named Thos. Johnson.* The body of the murdered man was found the next morning near the house where the deed was committed, frozen stiff; and although an attempt had been made by those interested to conceal the wound, it was discovered, and the murderous act was laid to the charge of one Ryder Larson, who has fled to parts unknown. This is the second murder that has taken place in the country for the past number of years; so that you see we are not a very desperate and wicked people. The fact, however, of the murderer in this case going at large, without any effort being made to take him into custody, goes to show how weak we are at present

---

* Thomas Johnson was a Canadian newcomer to Red River.

as regards protection to life and property. The Provisional Government is formed it is true; and on three or four occasions, has exerted its judicial authority; but, as the whole Settlement has not joined it, the power is not much to here, nor can it extend protection beyond the limits of its own people. The Hudson Bay Company's rule is dead without doubt, having handed over its sovereignty of the land back to the Crown, from whence it claimed that right.[*] Canada, as yet, has no authority over the country. Therefore, we are alone as a people; subjects of Great Britain, but not at present enjoying any material protection from that power.

The feeling in favor of joining the Provisional Government is becoming stronger and more general throughout the Settlement, and in fact it is the only course now open to us for our own protection in the meantime; and that we may be in a proper position, as a united people to affect arrangements with Canada or the Old Country.

It was reported in the Settlement that Mr. McDougall and party were preparing "jumpers," or sleds, commonly used in this country, and sundry surmises were afloat as to the intended movements of our would-be Governor. Some said he proposed going overland by way of Lake Superior, others that he was preparing to come into the Settlement at all hazzards—the last version; and as it turned out the true one was that he was on the eve of starting back the way he came, via St. Paul.

Sure enough the news came that the whole McDougall party, with the exception of Messrs. Provencher and Cameron, had left Pembina *en route* across the plains in the direction of Abercrombie. A sense of relief was felt throughout the whole Settlement at their departure—peace became more certain, for as long as McDougall remained on the frontier we were kept in a constant state of excitement; indeed, he would have done more good had he turned back at first, when he was repulsed, instead of his hanging about the outskirts as he did. And now, Mr. McDougall, adieu! your Governorship here was short lived. On the 1st of December, when under cover of the night, you proclaimed yourself to the dreary prairies as their master, you had the only taste you will ever have in this country of the pleasures and pales of being or aspiring to be a despot.

---

[*] Begg was wrong here. The Hudson's Bay Company retained possession of Red River until it entered Confederation as the province of Manitoba.

I may here state that before Mr. McDougall left Pembina he came to log-
gerheads with Capt. Cameron, who, if report speaks true, turns out to be
pretty much of a gentleman—impulsive, it is true—and although unac-
quainted with the character of the people he had to deal with when he
proposed his famous charge of 400 to take Red River by storm—ridiculous
as we may look upon it—it throws no dishonour on the bold Captain.
Speaking, however, in good earnest from all we have heard, Capt. Cameron
is not looked on here in any other way than that of a perfect gentleman.
Indeed, with the exception of the Governor himself, the whole staff are
viewed by the people generally, as far as report bespeaks them, favourably;
but having come with McDougall they are done for individually and collectively, as far as Red River is concerned.

AMERICAN EXAGGERATIONS.

I see it reported that Messrs. Schultz, Bown and Ross were expected to have
been the first who would have suffered in case of a collision between the
French and those upholding Mr. McDougall; this is all humbug. The first
ones who would have suffered in the affair would have been the poor fellows who were confined in Dr. Schultz' house—Schultz amongst the rest—
but Dr. Bown, as I have previously told you, skedaddled, and has since been
heard from in the interior near Fort Alexander, where he has taken refuge
in one of the forts belonging to the old grandmother, whom he has so often
abused. James Ross never was in any danger of his life. He knows too much
for that, and, in fact, he never was looked on here as likely to be a sacrifice
to the sanguinary intentions of the half-breeds, his own brethren by blood
relation. I may remark here, that the correspondence you have doubtless
seen from a Pembina quarter in the St. Paul papers, especially the *Press*, is
of the highest order of sensation. For instance, the residence of Dr. Schultz,
a lath and plaster house, comfortable in itself, but which could be entirely
demolished by two or three shots from a cannon, is called Fort Schultz;
Louis Riel is called "General," and so forth. I could give you a hundred of
the like; everything is exaggerated in proportion. The war reports from the
New York *Herald* were nothing in comparison to the bombast descriptions
we read of "our troubles" in the St. Paul newspapers.[*]

---

[*] Begg here demonstrates his awareness of the importance of his correspondence in setting the record straight.

THE SEIZURE OF COMPANY'S MONEY.

I reported in a previous letter the seizure of the cash and books belonging to the Government of Assiniboia. I have now to chronicle the taking of the cash on hand in Fort Garry belonging to the Hudson Bay Company, amounting to some thousand and odd pounds sterling. It appears Mr. Riel made a demand in person on Mr. McTavish for a loan of, it is said, £10,000 to the Provisional Government which he (the Governor) refused to grant. On the refusal being given, Mr. Riel proceeded with a guard, in company with Mr. O'Donohue, and politely requested the cashier, Mr. J.H. McTavish, to hand over all the funds he had in his possession on H.B.C. account, which Master John decidedly refused to do, whereupon the guard were ordered to search his person for the keys of the safe. This being done, the keys were found, and the unlucky cashier was requested to show the method of opening the money-box. This was also declined, and some time was consumed in endevouring to find out the secret of opening the safe door. At last, when the patience of Mr. Riel had been nearly exhausted, the lock was turned, and on lifting the lid the contents were displayed. Roll after roll of H.B.C. bills were taken out and counted, and then came gold and silver, and when Mr. McTavish had taken a memorandum of the amount of cash, Mr. Riel and his guard walked off with the safe and its contents, and at the present moment it is lying in the headquarters of the Provisional Government.

Various reasons are assigned for this proceeding—one that the money is merely on account of duties due by the H.B.C. to the old Government of Assinboia—another that it is a lean [sic] taken under the force of circumstances to be repaid at some future day, when arrangements are completed for the future government of the country. It became rumoured about this time that Mr. O'Donohue was on the eve of starting for the States, and that gentleman being suspected of Fenian proclivities, it was immediately supposed by many that his intended mission to Uncle Sam's Dominion was for the purpose of soliciting or obtaining Fenian aid—whether such was his idea or not it has not been carried out as he is still a resident in Red River and a member of the French Council. It was said, indeed, that a portion of the money seized from the H.B.C. was to go towards outfitting O'Donohue for his trip; this however, was nothing but idle rumour. On the 24th of December the greater portion of the French were paid off by Riel, the payment being in goods taken from the stores of the Hudson Bay Company. A guard of from 50 to 100 men are, however, to be kept in Fort Garry during the winter.

Midnight mass was celebrated as usual on the night of the 24th ult., and about twelve o'clock p.m., a salute of eighteen guns was fired from the gates of Fort Garry. I mentioned in my last the illness of President Bruce. He has, however, recovered and is moving about once more; but on account of his poor health he resigned his position as President, and is now acting merely as a Councillor, while Riel reigns in his stead.

ARRIVAL OF THE GRAND VICAR.

Grand Vicar Thibeault arrived here on Christmas Day and was escorted to St. Boniface to the Bishop's palace; Col. De Salaberry for some reason did not accompany him further than Pembina. The Grand Vicar Thibeault preached the next day (Sunday) to the French at La Rivière Sale; he is very much beloved by the people at White Horse Plains, he having resided at that place on and off for over 30 years. The Rev. gentleman would not act in any way in his capacity as Commissioner until De Salaberry should arrive from Pembina. A guard was therefore despatched to bring him in, and in the meantime Dr. Tupper made a hurried visit to Fort Garry, arriving on the evening of the 27th ult., and leaving the next morning. He came merely to obtain the release of some clothing &c. stored in the Settlement belonging to his son in law and daughter, Mr. and Mrs. Cameron. The only one here who had an interview with the member from Nova Scotia was Mr. Riel, but the result of their meeting is unknown, except that Captain Cameron's servant man soon afterwards left here for Pembina, in charge of a number of goods seized—trunks and boxes.[*] On the 27th of December the following notice was sent round to the several hotels and saloon keepers in the town of Winnipeg, much to their dissatisfaction I assure you:—

---

[*] Tupper also spoke to Father Ritchot.

FORT GARRY, 27TH Dec., 1869

"Mr.———, Sir,

> I do hereby respectfully pray you to let nobody have any liquor at
> your place from this date up to the 10th of January next. In so
> doing you will grant the country a great favour, and very likely
> preserve it from great misfortune.

> Very respectfully yours,
> (Signed) LOUIS RIEL,
> Commander at Fort Garry"

The above probably had reference to the fact that rumours were afloat
about this time to the effect that Indians were on their way into the Settlement, and it was not known what might be their intentions.

THE SIOUX.

On the 30th ult, word was brought in by one Pierre Lavellier that a band of
about 50 Sioux Indians, well armed, were on their way from Portage La
Prairie, coming towards Fort Garry—that they had been met about White
Horse Plains, and were there advised to turn back the way they came, as
they were not wanted in the Settlement at present; that they refused to
do this, and insisted on continuing on their journey as far as the town. It
was also rumoured that this was only an advance band of the main body of
Indians in considerable numbers, and that they were all well supplied with
arms and ammunition, at the expense, it was said, of the Canadian Government; even the squaws being armed with knives and guns. This truly
alarming intelligence startled the good people of the town considerably. A
meeting was called, at which it was decided that the Sioux would not be
allowed nearer the town than a mile off, and that if they should insist on
coming beyond that point it would be the signal for a fight. The next
morning the news seemed to be confirmed, and the citizens were hastily
assembled, all well prepared for a brush with the enemy. Scouts were sent
to find out, if possible, the whereabouts of the savages. In the meantime,
the French half-breeds had sent a deputation as far as James McKay's
house, about six miles from Fort Garry, to meet the Sioux and warn them
to come no further, unless they wanted to fight.

Your correspondent had the curiosity to go and see for himself, and drove as far as Mr. McKay's, where the Indians were sure to call in on their way, he being looked upon by them as a great friend and father of theirs. The towns-people in the meantime were on the alert all day and that night in case of a surprise. Mr. McKay assured us, however, that he believed these Indians were only down on a begging expedition, and that they would turn back from his place. There were ten or eleven Red River settlers besides myself in the house awaiting the coming of the Sioux.

A PALAVER.

About five o'clock in the evening an advance guard of three Indians arrived and were invited in—these three tried to conceal the fact that the rest of the bands was now near, but shortly afterwards the Chief and 44 warriors came up. Mr. McKay then cleared out his large dining room, and having asked the Indians into it, we all met in a Council. The Indians squatted on the floor rather densely packed, we being furnished with chairs, ranged ourselves along one side of the room; the Chief sat on a chair at the head of his men. When the pipes were lighted and silence had reigned in the room for some time, one Francis Dauphinais, a French half breed, arose and made the first speech—followed by Jas. McKay, and afterwards by one Pierre Poitras—each of these advised the band to turn back as there was trouble in the Settlement, in which they had no right to interfere. After the usual how! hows! the Chief arose, took off his head dress which he laid at his feet, and spoke pretty much as follows:—

That he and his braves having heard so many tales regarding the difficulties amongst the settlers, had determined on coming down to see for themselves so as to find out the truth—that they did not wish to interfere in the quarrel—nor did they want to harm any one being at peace with the Settlement—referring to a large silver medal with Victoria's head on one side and British coat of arms on the other, he said that he and his band had received protection during the last eight years under that medal, and he wanted to know if there was any fear of his losing that protection. He ended up by saying that he would be pleased to receive their usual New Year's presents. At this time Mr. Riel arrived, having with him about twenty-five pounds of tobacco, which he presented to the Chief, and promised further presents in the morning, the Chief having agreed to return to the Portage the next day. So ended with the Council. We were then favoured with a regular break down Indian dance—the band consisting of a drum and the grunts from five or six Indians—in every possible posture, one time rolling on the floor, another bending nearly double, then jumping and shouting—these savages with their hideous faces, made still more so by the daubs of paint on them, looked like a lot of demons let loose from the lower world. They kept good time to the sound of the drum, and at the end of each dance one of the braves would make a speech. After the dance Mr. McKay brought in a galvanic battery, which the Indians called "medicine." We dosed the whole band, each in turn, one poor fellow, fainting under the shock, which was too much for him. We then shook hands all round, and thus ended this Sioux scare. During all the interview we did not hear a word that would lead us to think that these Indians had been hired to commit an outrage on the Settlement. These Indians are the remnant of the band that massacred so many Americans in Minnesota in 1862, an ugly lot in every meaning of the word, fit at any time to murder their best friends. All that I have been describing took place on the night of the 31st ult; and at twelve o'clock Mr McKay invited us all (Indians excepted) to have a glass of wine and some cake, which we gladly partook of, thus ushering in the New Year, with a lot of howling Indians outside looking at us through the windows. Mr. Riel, in wishing Mr. McKay and family happiness in the future, said that as 1870 had been commenced in good feeling, he hoped it would so continue, and that to the benefit and future welfare of the Settlement. New Year's day was celebrated for two trotting matches and a few social calls. Mr. Riel addressed a meeting of the French at Oak Point in the course of which he said, that he as a loyal British subject desired the welfare of the Settlement, repudiated annexation to the States, and stated that he only wished for the future good of his people.

On the 2nd inst, one of the prisoners named Nimmons[*] escaped; and has fled to parts unknown.

A movement began about this time amongst the English speaking people for the purpose of uniting the Settlement and joining in the Provisional Government. On the evening of the 5th inst. Mr De Salaberry arrived and took up his quarters also at St. Boniface in the Bishop's palace.

---

[*] This was the first escape from Fort Garry.

CANADIAN EXODUS.

On the morning of the 6th, Mr. Snow left the Settlement, bound for Ottawa in company with Messrs. Mulkins and Hamilton, two released prisoners of war—the former is the nephew of Col. Dennis. Like Mr. McDougall I do not suppose we will be favoured again with the presence of Mr. Snow in a public capacity in this Settlement. Mr. Riel told him before he left that he would yet be required to go on with the road and requested him not to leave Red River; however Mr. Snow concluded not to remain and left— peace to his ashes—enough said!

AMERICAN SYMPATHY.

In my letter of the 1st December I had occasion to say that the Americans had kept themselves aloof up to that time in the troubles of the country. I am sorry, however, to be obliged to say that I have now to reverse my judgment. At first they did indeed keep "shady," but for some time back they have evinced an unaccountable interest in the affairs of this people, until at last it has culminated in the motive that actuated that interest is an open and undisguised expression of their opinion, their motto being plainly seen "Annexation to the States." Uncle Sam is a very good sort of fellow in his way, and the settlers in Red River have much cause to feel the greatest of friendship for his children. As far as friendship goes we are certainly bound together, but when a closer tie is spoken of, it becomes another thing. For our rights as a free people we will fight if necessary, but do not for a moment imagine that the generality of our settlers forget their allegiance to our Queen as British subjects. It is true we have, to a certain extent, been ignored, but we are ready to forget all that when matters will be mended and arranged. At present the feeling is a toss up between a Crown Colony and annexation to Canada, but one or the other it is sure to be. The few Americans that are resident here in company with those in Pembina need not think they are going to lead this whole Settlement by the nose; they cannot do it. American newspapers doubtless inflamed by the sensational articles written from Pembina by interested parties are speaking very freely at the present time with regard to Annexation of the North-West to Uncle Sam's domain, but they are wasting their breath and using their ink and paper to no purpose. That the American residents here, combined with those at Pembina, have done their "darndest," to use a vulgar expression, to get up feeling in their favour I will admit; that they have succeeded I deny. The last piece of news that has come to our ears is that a filibustering expedition is on the way to the relief of the Red River settlers—relief from what! The information caused universal indignation, and if the United States will countenance such movement against a friendly people it will be a standing disgrace, and a blot on its character as a nation, not soon to be got over. But, let the filibusters come along from any quarter, we know too well what they mean, and sooner than allow our country to be laid open to bands of lawless men we will sacrifice every-thing to resist them, and they will be taught to know what frontier men can do in the way of opposing their "soft persuasion." I mentioned in the first part of this letter that one, Major Robinson, had taken the newspaper business up, and we were expecting his efforts to result in a sheet devoted to the interests of the people here. Alas! how vain are expectations! At first, it was supposed he would purchase the type and press of the old *Nor'-Wester*, but not being able to find Dr. Bown the proprietor, he had recourse to an arrangement with Caldwell & Co. of the *Pioneer*. The necessary docu-ments being drawn out, the purchase money was paid, and the *Pioneer* newspaper became the property of Robinson & Co., and was converted into *The New Nation*. On the first issue, it was found that, properly enough, it advocated a Union of the whole people; but for what end? Annexation to the States. This is not the general wish of the people; although, of course like you in Canada, we have some here who advocate that doctrine. Major Robinson being himself an American, I can see no great harm in his advo-cating a principle that must be dear to himself and his countrymen, but do not, for one moment, imagine that his paper is the people's paper, or that the sentiments it contains are those of Red River settlers generally. We are actually as badly off in the newspaper line as we were during the *Nor'-Wester's* time—with this difference, the new sheet will not, I am sure, abuse the private character of persons, or corporate companies, as did our windy defunct friend. *The New Nation* will, I feel certain, stick to the text it has adopted, and write up Annexation principle; but this will be done in no bitter spirit. What we want now is another paper to keep him in check, and advocate the true feeling of our settlers as loyal British subjects.

THE PROVISIONAL GOVERNMENT.

The Provisional Government is steadily gaining ground; officers have been elected, and, as I said before, a movement is on foot to unite the whole Settlement, and I shall not be surprised if, in my next, I will have to acquaint you with the thorough union of the people—the object being either to treat with Canada or Great Britain.

Col. De Salaberry and Grand Vicar Thibeault, it appears, are powerless to grant anything the people want; but I will not be surprised if the former gentleman carried back overtures from the people to Canada. In the meantime neither of the Commissioners here have been out amongst the people, as it is the desire of the French Council that they should remain quiet in the matter. Mr. Donald A. Smith is still at Fort Garry, and is likely to remain for some time, as the health of Governor MacTavish is far from improving.* You may call it a pro-Company idea if you will, but it is nevertheless true that the deepest solicitude is felt for the recovery of the old Chief, for he is beloved and respected throughout the land both by rich and poor.

A number of the prisoners, twelve, I believe, succeeded in escaping from the gaol where they were confined on the night of the 9th last.† Five or six have been since retaken, and some of them were found to be badly frozen, one named Hyman especially having his feet badly injured; every attention is being paid to him, I believe. Mr. Mair was amongst those who escaped. He, however, has been able to evade the vigilance of his pursuers.

PERSONAL.

Twelve prisoners have now been released on parole, some of whom have left for Canada, while others are employed at the usual avocations, and it is expected that most of those now confined will be let go shortly, but how soon no one can tell. I have observed that in your remarks on my letters you have termed me pro-Company and anti-Canadian.[2] The former I do not demur at as far as I have endeavoured to do justice where injustice has been done, although I am in no way connected with the Company, nor am I bound to that body by any ties of interest, still I cannot, whether you

---

* William Mactavish (McTavish) was dying of consumption.

† These escapees included Thomas Scott.

believe it or not, help speaking a good word in favour of the old lady. She has been, and is still a good friend to our people and she has been most unjustly dealt by all along in Canadian journals. This I can vouch for as being the sentiment of most of our settlers. With regard to the latter term I must ask you to score that out—I deny being at all anti-Canadian, although I have been rather anti-Canadian—if denouncing the actions of certain persons from Canada makes me Anti—then keep it in, but I will also ask you to attach the same term to yourself, but who is more bitter in showing up what you feel to be the errors of your fellow countryman than you are. It is true I am Red River in feeling and interests, and should Canada endeavour to force a wrong on this country, I would be as ready to resist her as I would be to resist the like on the part of any other nationality or country; but I feel that it will be for the welfare of the country to be annexed to Canada, and I have and will uphold that doctrine throughout, providing of course, that the rights and future prosperity are provided for. I have every reason to be attached to the people of this country, and I am deeply so—you may therefore add to the term pro-Company that of pro-Half-Breed, but do me the justice to show that I have not forgotten the land of my birth, and scratch out the words "Anti-Canadian" as referred to me.

Yours truly,
JUSTITIA
WINNIPEG, Jan. 14, 1870

EDITOR'S NOTE

[According to Begg in his journal, a page of *The New Nation* was discovered inside the fort, having "been used in the performance of a natural duty in which a man must necessarily place one hand behind him—directing it towards the end of his spine—enough said!" Morton, ed., *Begg's Journal*, 253.]

# J.J. HARGRAVE

## 22 JANUARY 1870

[Like "Justitia," J.J. Hargrave devoted much of his correspondence to attempting to counteract what he regarded as the misinformation and false assumptions of both the Canadian newspapers and the Canadian government. In this letter he attempted to explain how dangerous was the American threat, and to correct the prevailing Canadian view that Red River required liberation from the despotic hand of the Hudson's Bay Company. Much of what he says here is repeated with more detail in his 1871 book Red River. Hargrave offers considerable detail on the negotiations between Donald A. Smith and Riel. His most interesting point is to emphasize the dissension within the ranks of the Métis themselves, with a faction clearly forming in opposition to Louis Riel. Printed in the *Montreal Herald and Daily Commercial Gazette*, 12 February 1870.]

RED RIVER SETTLEMENT,
British North America,
January 22nd 1870

The incoming accounts of recent events in this Settlement as pourtrayed [sic] in the Canadian Journals, are fruitful in matters for comment and reflection. The misstatements, though by no means infrequent, are scarcely greater in number than might have been expected when the very unusual character of the events and the amount of false information previously in circulation regarding the country and its people, are considered.

To one personal matter, in which a very strange perversion of the truth has got abroad, I feel bound prominently to allude. In various newspapers I see a report diligently circulated to the effect that Lieutenant Colonel Dennis had found it necessary to escape from the hands of the insurgents, by assuming the disguise of an Indian "Squaw." This incident has been made the basis of a considerable amount of small wit at the expense of the gentleman of whom it has been narrated. I beg to state that there is not one word of truth in the whole story; that it is an idle tale from beginning to end, and that people here are divided in opinion respecting its being a calumny, knowingly originated by some personal enemy of Mr. Dennis, or a false version of the method of escape effected by Dr. Bown, editor of the Nor' Wester newspaper who left the village of Winnipeg disguised in the capot and dress of a half-breed, and was subsequently a good deal in Colonel Dennis' company, while that gentleman was organising a very hopeless attempt at raising a military force in Lower Fort Garry. Colonel Dennis, during the whole time he resided in Red River, acted so as to secure the good will of people of all ways of thinking. He was always accessible, willing to open his mind regarding the probable policy of Canada in her dealing with this country, and anxious to hear the opinions of every body else. It was not his fault that any misunderstanding arose; his tone and policy were most conciliatory; and he was generally liked and respected. When he returned from Pembina with Mr. McDougall's commission as "Conservator of the Peace," he certainly committed outrageous faults. These were not, however, those of the pusillanimous character suggested by the story above alluded to; but having once commenced hostilities, he persevered with determination and rashness which covered him with failure and obloquy.

It is not without regret that one can see, even in Canada, the expression of a wish that the North West Territories should be left to their own resources, as being too remote to be valuable for a long time to Canada or England. I would remark that the strengthening of the ties between this country and England is a work which has already been too long delayed. American influence is already powerful in the Settlement, and its effects have been strongly marked in the series of mischances, which have befallen Governor MacDougall and his staff. It will increase in a very rapid ratio as the wave of population in the States sweeps westward. International complications will arise, with which it is absolutely necessary the Governments should deal directly, without the intervention of a company of merchants.

An idea seems to exist, that, were Canada, disgusted with the conduct of the insurgents, to withdraw from the bargain with the Hudson's Bay Company, the heaviest inconvenience would fall on the present population of the country, who would, according to Canadian journalists, be consigned to the state of political serfdom, from which they have so lately been emancipated. The events of the past few weeks ought to have convinced the most skeptical of the absurdity of such a view. No such thing as political subjection has ever been known in Rupert's Land. The circumstances of the country, and the utter absence of material force to support the authorities against anything approaching to a popular uprising, would effectually hinder systematic abuse of official power. *Tact* to persuade men, has hitherto been the great engine, for driving the State Coach at Red River; and the difficulty of getting certain Canadian incomers to pay their lawful debts to English outfitters, has formed the chief material in the composition of what, for some years past, have been known to the outside world as "Red River politics."[1]

The ideas of Hudson's Bay despotism are very much the creation of a party of Canadians who, for some years past, have dwelt in the Colony, and who have established for themselves such a character of untruthfulness and treachery in money and other matters, as to have rendered them the objects of great dislike and dread. The apparent connection between Governor MacDougall and his Canadian forerunners in office, and these men has created a general feeling, that he is altogether such a one as the latter—a person whose word is not certain guarantee, and whose position, if once attained, will give him the coveted power of placing his foot on the necks of the humble—of doing in fact, what his partizans have for years gloried in falsely describing the Hudson's Bay officials to have done.

So far from desiring a continuation of their term of political position, it is well known here that the Hudson's Bay officers in Rupert's Land ardently long to be freed from the annoyance and responsibilities it involves, and will, with the utmost cheerfulness, resign their political functions, so soon as arrangements can be matured, by which compensation may be given for the withdrawal of the rights which the Company enjoys under the same instrument which renders its duties incumbent upon it.

The serious nature of the physical barriers which intervene between Red River and the nearest Canadian settlements, must now have so impressed itself on the public mind as to have carried practical conviction of the absurdity of the opinions of those who profess that the geographical nature of the country renders the boundary between Canada and the Hudson's Bay Territories generally so indistinct as to leave any doubt respecting the absolute isolation of the latter from the former. Commercially, the separation between Red River and Canada is almost as great as it is geographically. Very few Canadian goods are imported, and the exports consist only of a comparatively small consignment of Buffalo robes. I am certainly happy to be able to say that an improvement in this particular seems to have commenced, and that a few Canadian Houses in Hamilton and Montreal have opened relations with Red River firms. Socially, the state of matters is most deplorable. By a strange fatality the Canadian *as such*, appears cut off from Red River sympathy. So much has been written in various parts of my correspondence to throw light on this most painful subject, that I need not now do more than advert to it.

Between Red River Settlement and Great Britain the practical connection is not very much stronger than between the former place and Canada. The whites and half-breeds regard Britain as their native country, or that of their nearest ancestors, and the Queen as the representative of the power to which they owe an allegiance which will always prevent them enjoying certain practical advantages open to their Yankee neighbours. But the living ties which alone remind them of their citizenship in the proudest empire in the world are the Hudson's Bay Company and the English Church. The former provides them with a very rude form of government and with certain commercial facilities, while the latter possesses a considerable organization and foothold throughout the country, its operations being directed by a bishop nominated and appointed from England.

The commercial transactions between the colony and England, apart from the Hudson's Bay business which is almost entirely with it, are not inconsiderable. English goods are those in most general use here.

The United States, however, offer the only channel of export or import, or of Postal communication between this country and the outside world. Until American Settlements had reached points in the neighbourhood of this place, the only communication with England consisted of an annual goods route by York Factory, and a semi-annual packet for letters. This state of matters still prevails throughout the interior of the Indian country, and to the liberality of the United States Government alone are we yet indebted for our bi-weekly Mail. Our freighting traffic and trade carried on in Minnesota are of course advantageous to American merchants, some of whom conduct a very profitable and somewhat extensive business with Red River people.

In glancing over the foregoing facts it is pretty plain that the natural tendency of events is not such as can be satisfactory to one who values English connection. As things go a vast tract of British ground must very soon become American in every respect except in name and nominal government. Absolute annexation of Rupert's Land can, of course, never take place without the express or implied consent of Great Britain, and any amount of desire therefore, on the part of the residents or settlers must be valueless as bearing in favour of such a change. Nor could it well be otherways, as it is pretty evident that an American wedge driven home between Canada and British Columbia must prove fatal to the great project of confederation of British American Provinces. Not only the mother country, therefore, but all her colonies, within the limits of the proposed confederation are closely and nearly affected in the political fate of Red River.

As they have mutual interests so also have they duties. For reasons already given by me at great length, England ought to have extinguished the Hudson's Bay title. It was a creation of her government and favourably affected her trade. In the development of this country, however, the Province of Winnipeg has a certain claim on the sister Provinces, in whose interest she is and must ever be prevented from drifting towards her natural tendency to the States. Assistance in smoothing the difficulties in the way of carrying out the great Inter Provincial necessity of a Canadian Pacific Railway, is what the older Provinces must prepare themselves to give. It alone will prove the disturbing agency requisite to divert a fair portion of the North West trade into Canadian markets.

Regarding current events I have to report that, since last week, the situation of public affairs has undergone serious modification. Previous to the evening of the 14th inst., Mr. Chief Factor Smith had held several interviews with Louis Riel with the object of ascertaining whether, in the event of his qualifying himself by going through the requisite forms, Riel and party would be disposed to receive him as a Commissioner from the Canadian Government. No assurance of a favourable hearing could be obtained, and as Mr. Thibeault had never been seen in public beyond the precincts of St. Boniface unattended by a priest, and Mr. De Salaberry had been rarely seen at all, it was inferred by the public that the priesthood had determined to quash the attempt at negotiation.

On the Friday evening referred to, however, Mr. Smith was placed under a permanent guard of four half-breeds, two of whom slept across his bedroom door. He was permitted to speak to no one and he was warned any letters he might write would be submitted to Riel's inspection. I may mention that ever since his arrival, Mr. Smith had been detained within the walls of Fort Garry. Early on Saturday morning, Mr. Chief Trader Hardisty, who had accompanied Mr. Smith from Canada, started under guard for Pembina to bring down the commission and papers which had been left at that place. It being understood that Riel had determined to possess himself of the papers before they could be handed to Mr. Smith, two half-breeds named Pierre Leveiller and Charles Nolin, who had until within the last few weeks been members on Riel's "Council," but had recently separated themselves from it, determined to go and meet Mr. Hardisty on his return, and protect him in the possession of the important documents he carried. They were influential men and were accompanied by about fifty followers.

On their way down, Riel met the procession, and attempted to interfere with Leveiller, who threatened to shoot him and caused him to be put under temporary restraint. The Revd. Mr. Richot also tried to interfere, but was roughly ordered to stand aside. The papers were brought to Fort Garry and Riel's guard removed from beside Mr. Smith's person. Nolin and Leveiller, with a considerable guard, remained to protect Mr. Smith from any new outrage and will remain for an indefinite time.

On Wednesday morning, according to previous arrangements, a public meeting of people from all quarters of the colony took place in Fort Garry. Mr. Smith produced and read his commission and papers relative thereto. Louis Riel was nominated interpreter. The Rev. Mr. Thibeault complained that *his* papers had been seized by William O'Donaghue, who refused either to deliver them up or to admit having them in its [sic] possession. Riel denied having them in *his* possession and proposed a motion that they should be produced, which was unanimously carried by a show of hands. The Rev. Mr. Richot said that legally the papers could not be required of Mr. O'Donaghue, but that doubtless the request of the meeting would be respected. Mr. O'Donaghue thereupon delivered them up.

Before the meeting dispersed a settler proposed the release of all the prisoners. On this, Riel's party ran to their armoury and seized their guns. A panic ensued and the meeting dispersed about sun-down.

On Thursday morning it was resumed, and the remainder of the papers were read. The formal preliminaries having thus been completed it was proposed that twenty French and twenty English delegates should be elected and appointed to meet in the court room on Tuesday the 25th instant at noon, for the purpose of taking into consideration the terms offered by Canada. This proposal was received with great enthusiasm.

Speeches were made by Riel, the Rev. Père Lestance and Mr. Richot, and there seemed reason to believe that the parties were agreed regarding the prospect of a speedy solution of present troubles.

I regret to say that as I close this letter, matters seem again to be getting complicated. Charles Nolin and Leveiller had remained with a considerable body of their party in Fort Garry till this morning, when they went away to see about their election to next Tuesday's meeting. Riel immediately threw a large force of his partizans into the house of the gentleman in charge of Fort Garry, whom he abused as one whose name would be handed down to infamy for trying to sow dissension among the French half breeds. He seized the keys of the Fort sale shops, and re-commenced the issue of the Company's goods to his people. The ten men of Leveiller's party who have remained with Mr. Smith are very awkwardly situated, in the midst of the multitude of opponents poured round them by Riel.

RED RIVER.

EDITOR'S NOTE

[Another version of the events that follow is given in Reverend George Young's letter to the *Guardian*, dated 22 January 1870, and reprinted in his book *Manitoba Memories: Leaves from My Life in the Prairie Province 1868-1884* (Toronto: William Briggs, 1897):

> After remaining quiet for some two weeks [Mr. Smith] seems to have deemed it time to be 'up and doing,' and accordingly it is said he intimated to Mr. Riel that he was now under instructions to inform him that when he should have permission to do so, he had certain things to say to him from the Governor of Canada, and also certain documents at Pembina which he would like to present. This information, I doubt not, took our little Napoleon by surprise; but as he keeps his wits generally about him, Riel directed, I understand, a guard to accompany Hardisty and bring in the papers. In the meantime some of the most influential and intelligent and brave of Riel's counsellors and army had become 'enlightened' ('tis not necessary to say how), and a goodly number of this class, we are told, set out to meet the party returning with the papers, and having met them, forthwith demanded the prized documents, and took the guard and all under their charge.

Proceeding towards Fort Garry they met Riel, who, not going about his business as they thought he should, it is said one of his French fellow-religionists placed his revolver to his presidential head, and hinted that he must be careful how he acted or he would send him where he would not care to go. Arriving at the fort, some thirty or forty of the loyal French, with some others, were there to receive and guard the papers, and to insist that the commission of Mr. Smith should be made public, and these messages or proclamations, whatever they were, should be read and made known. After a good deal of parleying, and some sharp hints from the 'seceders,' Riel, I am told, consented, though reluctantly, that a 'mass meeting' should be called, when Mr. Smith should explain his mission and read his papers.]

# J.J. HARGRAVE

## 29 JANUARY 1870

[Joseph Hargrave spends most of this letter arguing for a transcontinental railroad, and only in the concluding paragraphs reports almost incidentally on the proceedings of the Convention of Forty, which was preparing a bill of rights to take to Ottawa. This was his last letter. Printed in the *Montreal Herald and Daily Commercial Gazette*, 25 February 1870.]

RED RIVER SETTLEMENT, British North America,
January 29th 1870.

In a former letter I mentioned that the only reliable agency for creating a diversion of the natural influences which tend to separate Rupert's Land from the older provinces of Canada, is a Canadian Pacific Railway connecting Red River with the Railroad system of the Dominion as at present existing.

Were any argument required to substantiate the necessity of the speedy execution of this scheme, I would advance our present condition as positive proof that if this country is to be governed from Ottawa, she must possess means of constant communication with that place, of a nature to be traversible throughout the year, and passing entirely over British Territory.

With such a means of travel our present difficulties could never have occurred, and a popular uprising, to which the circumstances of the Colony impart a serious character, would have been impossible. Moreover, it is to be hoped that a closer union between the settlement and the old provinces of the Dominion would have established so good an understanding between the people of this place and their Canadian fellow subjects, that the entertainment of cool feelings such as exist in the minds even of our non-insurgent population towards Canadians, would have been out of the question. At present, however, Canada is to Red River a foreign country. Her newspapers, with few exceptions, are little read; her public men are known only by name; her politics and schemes create no living interest; her sympathies are unknown.

With daily and direct communication by rail, how happy would be the change effected! The people of Red River would then feel themselves brought as if by enchantment into intimate relationship with a new neighbour, to whom the political ties, which have hitherto nominally bound them to England, are vital influences exercising a real power over the national life. The uninhabited plains of British North America would be covered with an English population, and become fertile under the experienced efforts of practical farmers. Centres of industry would spring up at many points, where thriving towns with their workshops and markets would form a basis for the enterprize of the manufacturer and the merchant. A feeling of nationality would be created at Red River, and would doubtless be strengthened even in Canada, which, from the position of a thriving, but isolated Province, would become the ferm [germ?] from which the creative [sic] influence of a mighty Empire would expand.

To Great Britain, the growth of an enormous territory extending across the American Continent could scarcely be a benefit. Of all her colonies, the Canadian group is nearest home, and the practical distance will doubtless be diminished more and more as the increase of travel and traffic necessitated the employment of improved and more frequent means of communication. The Hudson's Bay Territories have heretofore been maintained without expense to the Empire and have, on the contrary, been to her a source of profit. The vast regions in question have annually consumed immense quantities of her manufactured goods for which she has imported in return the materials of a large Fur Trade. Her revenue has been increased by direct taxation levied not only on the profits of the Company, strictly so called, but also on those parties actually carrying on the business and resident in Rupert's Land, collectively known as "Partners in the Fur Trade." Surely, if any colony of the Empire ever possessed a claim on the generous assistance of the Mother country, either on account of past usefulness or present need, Rupert's Land and the North West Territories have so done. And with reference to the future, it is to be hoped that, were the country in fair process of development, the trade of the past would sink into insignificance in comparison with that which would spring up.

To the shameful neglect of the Colonial Office, the country owes the troubles which at present disturb it. Now that the mischief has developed itself, it is not impossible that steps may be taken to prevent its further spread. One of the best and cheapest methods by which Great Britain could secure the maintenance of Imperial interests in the North-west, is that of assisting the early construction of a Through Line of Railway. So long ago as to July 1862, we find this subject brought under the attention of the late Duke of Newcastle, then Secretary of State for the Colonies, by six eminent London Capitalists and bankers, with the more immediate view of securing communication with British Columbia and Vancouver's Island.[1] This memorial formed the first link in the long chain of correspondence which ended with Earl Granville's famous proposal to Cartier and Macdougall. During the seven intervening years, the subject had "traversed its slow length along" without being productive of greater result than an increase in bulk of correspondence. Meanwhile, the progress of American settlements, interrupted by the Southern war, and the Sioux Massacre in Minnesota, had been such as to bring them very near the Red River of the North; and consequently, to attract attention to the importance of the position occupied by the British settlements on that stream, at least, in the minds of the inhabitants of Canada and the United States. The original purpose for which Postal and Telegraphic communications across the continent was projected, has consequently given way to a nearer object, and through communications between Canada and British Columbia, though still the ultimate end to be attained, becomes for the present obscured for the immediate necessity of connecting Central British America, with the older Provinces of the Dominion, and developing the agricultural capacities of the former.

The project of a Canadian Pacific Railroad, a bill for which is to be brought before the Dominion Parliament at its next session, will doubtless receive due attention. The idea of commencing the construction of this work at Fort Garry, by a branch line to Pembina, though possibly possible enough under peaceable auspices, will, I suspect, under existing circumstances, be found unadvisable. It is a public necessity that the portion of the line between the Province of Ontario and Red River be completed at the earliest possible time.

The first object to be attained will, I presume, be the purchase of a right of way from the Indians occupying the country, to be traversed by the Line, and this will be the duty of the Government.

The physical nature of the region to the north of Lake Superior appears to be yet surrounded with a good deal of mystery. The propriety of clearing up what uncertainty exists in the matter at the earliest possible date cannot, I think, be considered doubtful. The difficulties to be surmounted must be ascertained by means of an accurate survey; but with regard to the generally inhospitable character of the section in question, I believe there is no controversy. The construction of the portion of the Line East from Red River will involve a heavy sacrifice, for which, probably, the Government will consider it necessary to recompense the Railway Company, at least partially, by large land grants in the fertile regions West from this place, and probably also by other privileges and guarantees. The urgent necessity for constructing the unremunerative sections of the Line first will place the Company under a serious disadvantage, which will, of course, necessitate the granting of more favourable terms than could reasonably have been demanded had it been advisable or possible to commence the work at this place, and penetrate southward and westward before providing for the connection with the Canadian Railroad system now in operation. To this necessary sacrifice the public must, however become reconciled.

The preliminary arrangements necessary to be completed before the actual construction of a railway can be commenced, are therefore of a character which will require some considerable time. But if Canada is to govern the North West Territories, the establishment of a strong garrison at Red River is a duty which cannot be delayed beyond the coming summer. The idea of importing or collecting merchandise in a place where it will be subject to pillage, such as has been perpetrated within the last few months, is one which will not be entertained by merchants who intend to pay for their outfits. Respectable settlers will probably quit the place in great numbers, and remove southwards to Minnesota, while the French party will doubtless split into numerous factions, so soon as the supplies they can find to seize get scarce, and the country drift in a civil war, in the midst of which the pursuit of any settled avocations will become impossible.

The coming year will, in many respects, be full of difficulties. It will be remembered that towards the close of autumn the settlement was again invaded by swarms of locusts, which have deposited their eggs in the ground. In the present state of excitement, to which the minds of the people have been raised, it is doubtful whether, under even the most favourable auspices, any large crop would be laid down. But considering the probability of civil tumult on the arrival of half-breeds and Indians from the plains, and the Canadian immigrants in the spring, combined with the almost certainty that the greater part of the young crops will be snapped up by the locusts, it is unlikely that the farming community will, as a whole, throw away their valuable seed by laying it in the ground.

The approaching famine will tell very heavily on all classes, though, as last season was unusually remunerative, many settlers have enough of grain on hand to last them for two years. The heaviest sufferers will doubtless number many of the present insurgents among their ranks, and, as the charitably disposed people of England and Canada are unlikely to minister with their former promptitude to the necessities of men who have made so equivocal a return for past benefits as our French half-breed people have done, it is only too probable that the latter will within the year, have more reason than they have yet had to plunder their more provident neighbours of their provisions.

Of course the troops which may be sent into the country during Summer will require provisions for their use to be imported by the United States. The same remark will apply to immigrants.

During the whole of the past week Fort Garry has been entirely in the hands of the insurgents, who, as I mentioned in my last letter, had violently wrested the keys of the Company's Sale Shops from the hand of the gentleman in charge of the Fort, and have since entirely excluded the functionaries, whose business it is to attend to the stores, from these places, and issue supplies only to their own people. Louis Riel claims that the entire Fort is *his*; and he has overthrown all its business, and, in fact the business of the whole Settlement. The Company's officers have been expelled from their own Messroom, which is in the possession of the French, and is used every Sunday morning as a chapel where Mass is sung by a Priest from the Roman Catholic establishment at St. Boniface.

On the night of Thursday, the 23rd inst., Dr. John Schultz, who, of all the prisoners was most obnoxious to the French, effected his escape from the room in which he was detained in solitary confinement, by cutting his buffalo robe covering into strips, and lowering himself from the window, half of the sash of which he contrived to remove. Diligent search was made for him without, as yet, being successful in discovering his whereabouts. William Hallett, another of the prisoners, has since Schultz's escape, been confined in irons.

The election of delegates, twenty of whom, chosen from each section of the population, were to meet to consider Canadian terms, were completed before Thursday last, on which day they met in the Court House near Fort

Garry, but in consequence of delays necessitated by the state of the weather, no business was done until the succeeding day.

Mr. Recorder Black, who has been returned as one of the representatives, from St. Andrew's Parish, was elected Chairman of the meeting. Mr. Louis Riel and Mr. James Ross were appointed joint interpreters. There were two complaints as to unfairness which had taken place in the election of delegates, which were referred to the arbitrament of the brother delegates of complainants, each party being declared arbiter in the affairs relative to the election of its own members.

After some days spent in the discussion of preliminaries, it was decided to appoint a committee, consisting of three English and three French members, who should draw up a "Bill of Rights" to be presented for the approval of the whole body of forty, previous to being handed to Commissioner Smith. The names of the English members of this sub-committee are Dr. C.J. Bird, James Ross, Thomas Bunn, and of the French members, Louis Riel, Louis Schmidt, and Charles Nolin.

The results of the deliberations of these gentlemen were to be presented to-day to the full body of delegates. I understand the best feeling has prevailed between the parties, and that at present there appears to be no obstacle in the way of an ultimate solution of the difficulty.

The general opinion is, however, that the hold which the insurgents have gained on Fort Garry will be maintained, and that the *real* question at issue is largely composed of the amount of plunder yet to be obtained from the Company's warehouses, and the length of time it will last.

Meantime Mr. Smith has been very successful in his progress with the mission entrusted to him, and I have no doubt the idea of the Government in sending up Messrs. Thibeault and De Salaberry was a most happy one, and has borne the best of fruits.

RED RIVER P.S. The following articles of the new bill of rights, are said to meet with general assent, though none have yet been adopted.

[there is no item numbered the lst in the newspaper]

2nd. That as long as this country remains a Territory of Canada there shall be no direct taxation except such as shall be imposed by the Local Legislature.

3rd. That during the time this country shall remain in the position of a Territory of Canada, all expenses in connection with the general government of the country, or that have hitherto been borne by the public funds of the Settlement, shall be met by the Dominion of Canada.

4th. That while the burden of the public expenses in this Territory is borne by Canada, the country be governed under a Lieut. Governor from Canada, and a Legislature, three members of whom, being heads of Departments, shall be nominated by the Governor-General of Canada.

5th. That after the expiration of this exceptional period, the country shall be governed, as the Provinces of Ontario and Quebec are now governed—by a Legislature elected by the people, and Ministry responsible to it, under a Lieut.-Governor, appointed by the Governor-General of Canada.

6th. That there shall be no interference by the Dominion Parliament in the local affairs of the Territory, other than is allowed in the Provinces, and that this Territory shall have and enjoy the same privileges, advantages and aids in meeting the public expenses as the Provinces have and enjoy.

7th. That while the North-West remains Territory the Legislature have a right to pass all laws local to the Territory over the veto of the Lieut.-Governor by a two-thirds vote.

8th. A Homestead and Pre-emption law.

9th. That while the North West remains a Territory the sum of ($25,000) twenty-five thousand dollars yearly be appropriated for schools, roads and bridges.

10th. That all public buildings be at the cost of the Dominion Treasury.

11th. That there shall be guaranteed uninterrupted steam communications to Lake Superior within five years, and also the establishment by rail of a connection with the American railway as soon as it reaches the International Line.

EDITOR'S NOTE

[William Hallett engaged in a word-slinging match with Louis Riel the night John Schultz and others escaped from Upper Fort Garry and was thrown in irons. He was bailed out for $450 on 12 February 1870. It was later claimed that he never recovered from his prison experience.]

# ALEXANDER BEGG

1 FEBRUARY 1870

[This letter from Justitia sounds a hopeful note. The two mixed-blood communities are meeting and working together to produce the bill of rights. Printed in the Toronto *Globe*, 19 February 1870.]

THE BILL OF RIGHTS

Red River Settlement, February 1, [1870]

As it may be interesting to you to learn how matters are progressing under the favourable auspices to which I referred in my last, I send you a few lines by this (Tuesday's) mail, so that you may have the latest news on the subject—if my letter does not miscarry.

On Saturday, the 29th ult, the Convention of delegates again met, Friday having been taken up by the Committee of six in preparing the "Bill of Rights."

There are, I believe, 21 clauses in it altogether, but as your correspondent has only been favoured with a cursory glance at them, and as they have to be first adopted by the delegates as a body, or rejected by them, I will only give you those that have passed the ordeal.

On Saturday, therefore, the following four resolutions were adopted by the Convention, being the first four of the list:—

lst. That in view of the present exceptional position of the North-West, duties upon goods imported into the country shall continue as at present (except in the case of spiritous liquors) for three years, and for such further time as may elapse, until there be uninterrupted railroad communication between Red River Settlement and St. Paul, and *also* steam communication between Red River Settlement and Lake Superior;

2nd. That as long as this country remains a territory in the Dominion of Canada, there shall be no direct taxation except such as may be imposed by the Local Legislature, for municipal or other local purposes;

3rd. That during the time this country shall remain in the position of a territory, in the Dominion of Canada, all military, civil, and other public expenses, in connection with the general government of the country, or that have hitherto been borne by the public funds of the Settlement, beyond the receipt of the above-named duties, shall be met by the Dominion of Canada.

4th. That while the burden of public expense in this Territory is borne by Canada, the country be governed under a Lieutenant-Governor from Canada, and a Legislature, three members of whom, being heads of Departments of the Government, shall be nominated by the Governor General of Canada.

On Saturday we were honoured by a visit to the Settlement from a Mr. Gay, who (so he says) hails from Paris, France [Norbert Gay]. He is supposed to be a correspondent of some French newspaper, although great doubt exists as to his true errand.

Shortly after his arrival here he was taken a prisoner, and confined in Fort Garry; but afterwards liberated. He is now doing the handsome at Emerling's Hotel. He is said to be (for I have not met him) a very affable person; but his affability has not gone down, so far. It is reported he advised the French to go and take the Stone Fort; but the reply he received was that if he was very anxious to see it taken to go and do it himself.

On Monday the Convention met again, and remained sitting till a late hour in the evening. They passed the following resolutions in addition to the four given above:—

5th. That after the expiration of this exceptional period, the country shall be governed, as regards its local affairs, as the Provinces of Ontario and Quebec are now governed, by a Legislature by the people, and a Ministry responsible to it, under a Lieutenant-Governor, appointed by the Governor-General of Canada;

6th. That there shall be no interference by the Dominion Parliament in the local affairs of this Territory, other than is allowed in the Provinces, and that this Territory shall have and enjoy, in all respects, the same privileges, advantages and aids in meeting the public expenses of this Territory, as the Provinces have and enjoy;

7th. That while the North-West remains a Territory, the Legislature have a right to pass all laws, local to the Territory, over the veto of the Lieutenant-Governor, by a two-thirds vote;

8th. A Homestead and Pre-emption law;

9th. That while the North-West remains a Territory, the sum of $25,000 yearly be appropriated for schools, roads and bridges;

10th. That all public buildings be at the cost of the Dominion Treasury;

11th. That there shall be guaranteed uninterrupted steam communication to Lake Superior, within five years; and also the establishment by rail of a connection with the American railway as soon as it reaches the International line.

This is as far as I can give you by this mail. While the last clause (the 11th) was being discussed, Mr. [Alfred] Scott, delegate from Winnipeg, wished to have the time allowed for communication with Pembina curtailed to an unreasonable degree. The calculations and figures he gave to the Convention were found to be impracticable, and at last the question was put, "What would be the use of a railway to Pembina before it is connected with another line further east from that point?" A Mr. Cummings rose and said the only use he could see for such a road would be, "to bring Statesmen to Fort Garry." This finished the discussion, and the clause passed as I have given it to you. I have not time by this mail to make any remarks on the "Bill of rights" as far as it has gone, but I hope by next mail to go into the subject fully, when it will have passed the Convention complete.

There is a great deal of work before the delegates yet; ten more clauses have to be gone through with, and then the whole Bill has to be placed before Mr. Smith; and as that gentleman's real powers are not properly known, there may be a necessity for a delegation to Ottawa from this country. In the meantime, however, the people of the Settlement will have to take some steps for their own protection until matters are fully arranged with Canada. So far the greatest hopes prevail of a speedy settlement—the best of good feeling existing amongst all classes. If you, in Canada, find some of the rights claimed unreasonable, wait before passing judgment until you hear the peculiarities of our case, that necessitates the making of such, and consider, as well, that even if Canada pursues a very liberal policy towards the North-West, she will ultimately be the gainer by it, for the reason that the extra inducements offered to emigrants under that liberal policy to settle the country will be the means of rapidly and materially increasing the populated districts of the whole North-West, a matter of vital importance to the Dominion in its acquisition of this Territory. The rapid opening up of this vast country will make the sway of the Dominion worthy of its name; whereas, if the process is slow, the acquisition of this Territory will be a drag on, instead of a benefit to, Canada.

JUSTITIA

# ALEXANDER BEGG

25 FEBRUARY 1870

[For the most part, "Justitia," in the following letter, does review from a
Red River perspective the various items of the bill of rights passed by the
Convention of 40. Presumably much of the discussion that follows reflects
the debate in the Convention. His original letter does not include the text
of the several clauses of the bill of rights, which have been placed here in
brackets. Printed in the Toronto *Globe*, 25 February 1870.]

THE RED RIVER BILL OF RIGHTS
*Our Correspondent at Fort Garry, to whom, under the signature of "Justitia,"
we have been indebted for a series of very interesting letters, sends us a further communication, some of the contents of which, including the Bill of
Rights as finally settled by the Convention, have been anticipated by telegraph.* * But his exposition of the reasons which may be assumed to have dic-
tated the demands comprised in that document, will justify our devoting
space to its insertion. He says:*

Let us review, in a Red River point of view, the articles one by one, so
that you in Canada may have some idea why we urge our Bill of Rights.

Article lst. ["That, in view of the present exceptional position of the
North-West, duties upon goods imported into the country shall continue
as at present (except in the case of spiritous liquors) for three years, and
for such further time as may elapse, until there be uninterrupted railroad
communication between Red River Settlement and St. Paul, and also steam
communication between Red River Settlement and Lake Superior."] The
duties on merchandise is an important item to the people of this country
at the present time. Already we have to pay a heavy toll on the cost of
goods in the way of freight, and until some cheaper method of transportation than we have now is effected, the settlers in Red River cannot afford
to pay any additional cost on the accessories and comforts of life. As we
are, we have to pay higher prices for almost every description of goods at

---

* In the newspaper of 21 February 1870.

our shops than you have to in Canada, what then would we do were we obliged to pay still more in the way of duties. The merchant here does not realize such large profits as one might suppose on comparing prime cost and the price obtained for his wares in Red River. There are many other charges besides freight equally high in proportion. Were their profits cut down still more, there would be no advantage in keeping store at all, and the present price of goods in the Settlement cannot stand a farther advance. Those who outfit for Indian trading have to give their goods on credit to the fur dealers, and it is from six months to two years before they receive any return from the same, and these returns sometimes fall far behind covering the value of the original outfit, besides the loss of interest. Doing business in Red River is therefore not such an extremely paying affair as I have heard some parties describe it to be. With steam communication to and from the East, however, our cost of transportation will be materially decreased; charges that we now have to pay to agents, &c., &c, will disappear altogether; and then, and not until then, will we be able to pay a higher rate of duty on goods.*

Article 2nd. ["As long as this country remains a territory in the Dominion of Canada, there shall be no direct taxation, except such as may be imposed by the local legislature, for municipal or other local purposes."]— In proportion to the taxes imposed on a people, so far are they supposed to enjoy the benefits of this taxation—unless, indeed, it has been caused by the cost of a war. We in Red River, so long as we remain isolated as we are, cannot expect to derive the same advantages, either socially or politically speaking, as you do in Canada. A frontier life, pleasant though it may be in its roughness, is not literally worth as much as one spent in a more civilized part of the country; for that reason, therefore, while we do not enjoy the same advantage as you do in Canada, neither ought we to be taxed in the same proportion as you are. A person living in the country is not taxed as highly as one residing in a city. The same scale can apply to us here, away from the comforts of civilization, and you in the midst of them. We have not been a party to, or participators in, the causes of your taxation, and therefore you ought to pay your own debts; while we, in, as it were, commencing life, should have a fair start; and, as years creep over

---

* As a merchant, Begg knew about such costs first-hand.

the land, and our extra requirements oblige us to go into debt, then let us pay the penalty of that debt in extra taxation.

Article 3rd. ["That, during the time this country shall remain in the position of a territory, in the Dominion of Canada, all military, civil, and other public expenses, in connection with the general government of the country, or that have hitherto been borne by the public funds of the Settlement, beyond the receipt of the above-mentioned duties, shall be met by the Dominion of Canada."]—In opening up this country, heavy expenditure must necessarily follow. There will be for the next number of years an outlay in advance of the population of the Settlement, in preparing the way for emigration, &c. The Dominion will ultimately be the gainer by this. The North West will in time become the source of power and greatness to Canada. While the present settler and incoming emigrant will, to a great extent, be the gainer by this outlay, still it could hardly be expected that they should foot the bills, or pay part of them to pave the way for others. It would be like obliging a man with a small capital to go into some vast undertaking beyond his means; he might commence very well, but failure in the end would surely follow. Canada, in assuming a heavy expenditure in this country, is only making an investment that will surely prove to the advantage of her people in the future. When we enter the Dominion as a Province, with all the advantages of a close connection with the eastern markets, and our country well populated, then we will be in the position to assume the same independent attitude as do the other Provinces.

Article 4th. ["That while the burden of public expense in this territory is borne by Canada, the country be governed under a Lieutenant-Governor from Canada, and a Legislature, three members of whom, being heads of departments of the Government, shall be nominated by the Governor-General of Canada."]—It is but fair, while we are in the position of a Territory, that our Governor should come from Canada; and it is considered that three heads of departments will be sufficient to give Canada a voice in affairs here, while she is subject to the several expenditures mentioned in our Bill of Rights. Other inferior offices can be well filled from amongst the present settlers and those who may come to settle with us in the future. It is deemed proper that the officials of our Territorial Government, with the exception of the three provided for, should be appointed from amongst those who have some interests in the country, and are most likely to be the best judges of the wants and character of the people. The number of representatives in the Council appointed by the people here has been left an open question by the delegates for the reason that at present it is a difficult matter to decide in a short time, and will require a good deal of deliberation to determine as to the proper division of the Settlement into districts. The subject will have to be taken up soon, perhaps by the Convention before the end of the session. Of course any division decided upon will be only temporary, until the land is surveyed into townships or such like.

Article 5th. ["That, after the expiration of this exceptional period, the country shall be governed, as regards its local affairs, as the Provinces of Ontario and Quebec are now governed, by a Legislature by the people, and a Ministry responsible to it, under a Lieutenant-Governor, appointed by the Governor-General of Canada."]—That as soon as the country becomes settled with a sufficient population to warrant our admission into the Union, as a Province, so soon do we expect to enjoy all the advantages of such a change; and at the same time, we will enter the Dominion on an independent footing, and we desire to be in as good standing as any other part of Canada.

Article 6th. ["That there shall be no interference by the Dominion Parliament in the local affairs of this territory, other than is allowed in the provinces, and that this territory shall have and enjoy, in all respects, the same privileges, advantages and aids in meeting the public expenses of this territory, as the provinces have and enjoy."]—In this respect we wish to be in as good a condition as the neighbouring Territories; independent in the management of our own local affairs; yet, while acknowledging ourselves as a Territory of the Dominion, we expect to derive all the advantages of such a connection, in proportion as we stand, as regards our population and relative requirements.

Article 7th ["That, while the North-West remains a territory, the Legislature have a right to pass all laws, local to the territory, over the veto of the Lieutenant-Governor, by a two-thirds vote."]—This is peculiarly a Territorial right; and, although not exactly in unison with the British or Canadian Constitution, still, as we will be the sole Territory possessed by Canada, she can, on this account, make an exception in our favour. Our exceptional position warrants that we should not be at the mercy of any one man and it is reasonable to suppose that a two thirds vote of the people's representatives is in reality the popular voice, and should not be outweighed by any single vote, especially as while in the position of a Territory our Government to a certain degree will be incomplete; and although we may be influenced to an extent by the Governor, still we should not be wholly under his control should he have the prerogative of a veto over the measures proposed by our Council.

Article 8th. ["A homestead and pre-emption law."]—This is almost a necessity in a country like ours, and will do much to foster and encourage emigration, while at the same time it will be a protection to settlers, and will enable them to secure a provision for the future, which to a man coming all this way with a family and, as it were, commencing life anew, is far from unreasonable.

Articles 9th and 10th. [9. "That, while the North-West remains a territory, the sum of $25,000 a year be appropriated for schools, roads and bridges." 10. "That all the public buildings be at the expense of the Dominion Treasury."]—Come under the head of my remarks on No. 3, and I may add that Canada has already voted a million and a half dollars towards developing this country. There can, therefore, be no great harm in our pointing out the way in which she can best expend that sum. She must remember also that her own emigrants will derive a large amount of benefit from her expenditure; and I would suggest that it would be better that she did not squander her money quite so lavishly as she has done in the case of the Fort Garry section of the Thunder Bay Road and in some other ways that we deem extravagant.

Article 11th. ["That there shall be guaranteed uninterrupted steam communication to Lake Superior, within five years; and also the establishment, by rail, of a connection with the American railway as soon as it reaches the international line."]—As the Americans stoutly assert that in a couple or three years they will have Railway to Pembina, there is every reason to suppose in that time the Dominion Parliament will find it necessary to take such steps as will give us a Railway from the boundary line to Fort Garry. At the same time while it is evident that Canada must have steam communication with this country through British soil, and the sooner the better; yet it will be a great advantage to her Territory and her interests in that territory that there should be direct all rail connection with the east, and the only way at present known to be practicable for some years is via Pembina, to which point the proposed American Railway is projected.

Article 12th. ["That the military force required in this country be composed of natives of the country during four years."]—This resolution was lost after a good deal of discussion, and was finally lost by a vote of 23 to 15. Had it been carried it would certainly have acted against the natives of the country, for in a year or two the task of keeping order over strangers and foreigners who will most undoubtedly flow into the Settlement would be greater than could be borne by the people of the country, and besides there are a large number of the natives who are adverse to take up arms, either for pleasure or duty. British troops would, on the other hand, be a direct benefit to us in more ways than one; but I would strongly advise that Canadian volunteers, if they could be induced to come, should not be sent here. They will prove unpopular, and instead of keeping down trouble, they would make it.[1] There will be sufficient means of raising a volunteer force from amongst the settlers, both from those who are here already and those who are likely to come to live amongst us. This, with a British regiment, would be sufficient for all the wants of the country for some time to come at least.

Articles 13th and 14th. [13. "That the English and French languages be common in the Legislature and Courts, and that all public documents and Acts of the Legislature be published in both languages." 14. "That the Judge of the Supreme Court speak the French and English languages."]— These two are especially necessary in this country, and are likely to continue so in the future, as we are inclined to think there will be a good emigration from Lower Canada. Many of our French half-breeds have connections in the Province of Quebec, and this fact will lead many of their friends and relations from that quarter to come to the Settlement to settle. In this respect, we will resemble the Lower more than the Upper Province.

Article 15th. ["That treaties be concluded between the Dominion and the several Indian tribes of the country, as soon as possible."]—This is also a necessity, which, it appears from the Government despatches to Messrs. McDougall and Smith, the Dominion Parliament are perfectly aware of. The Local Legislature here will be able to afford Canada much information on this subject, which she will do well to take advantage of. The most dangerous Indians in the North-West are the Crows and Blackfoot, and these two tribes will have to be settled with at once, as well as the more friendly tribes by sending judicious agents to treat with them; and by taking the strongest measures to prevent these men from defrauding the Indians after the treaties are completed much future trouble will be avoided. The chief cause of the American difficulties with their Indians has been the fraudulent transactions of their agents with the tribes. An Indian, as long as he has confidence, will never suspect until that confidence is broken, and then it is impossible to have it renewed. The Hudson Bay Company have never had difficulty with the savages of the North-West, although Mr. Chas. Mair once tried to prove to the contrary. At the trading-posts, in the interior, they have to deal with different tribes, and it often occurs that these are hostile to each other, and it generally happens each year that bands of this description meet and there are many records of savage fights outside the walls of the Forts between the Indians themselves; but never against the officers of the Company.

Article 16th. ["That, until the population of the country entitle us to more, we have three representatives in the Canadian Parliament; one in the Senate, and two in the Legislative Assembly."]—This will probably appear formidable to the Dominion Parliament, and I am of opinion we are asking more than we have a right to. Still it is not a matter of vital importance; and although our population at present is small, let the future prospects of our country be considered and it may be that it would prove advantageous on all sides to have a large representation at Ottawa from here; it would, at all events, be the means of agitating measures for the development of the North-West more than if no one was present in the Council of the Dominion to present the proper state of matters here. One thing is certain, there must be an equal representation in the Dominion Parliament of French and English, if any at all.

Article 17th. ["That all the properties, rights and privileges, as hitherto enjoyed by us, be respected, and that the recognition and arrangement of local customs, usages and privileges be made under the control of the Local Legislature."]—In the letter of December 7th, from Hon. Joseph Howe, as Secretary of State, to Hon. Wm. McDougall at Pembina, it appears that the Council at Ottawa has already agreed to this article; and it is but an act of justice to the people that the privileges to which they have been so long accustomed, should not be taken from them.

Article 18th. ["That the Local Legislature of this territory have full control of all the lands inside a circumference having Upper Fort Garry as a centre, and that the radius of this circumference be the number of miles that the American line is distant from Fort Garry."]—This article, in the original, merely had reference to the hay privilege granted by the H.B.C. to each settler when he became an owner of land; but afterwards the amendment, which was carried; was more general in its meaning and took in a radius of over sixty miles around Fort Garry. This is chiefly to prevent speculators from cutting up the present Settlement and also to ensure that when a railway is built to Fort Garry from any point, the farms and lands now the property of settlers should not be cut up or damaged unless through the concurrence or mediation of the Local Legislature. The General Government might disregard the claims of settlers, and seriously interfere with their interests when placing the line of railway, while the Local Legislature will be better able to deal with such matters and to arrange about hay privileges and so forth, than would be the General Government.

Article 19th ["That every man in the country (except uncivilized and unsettled Indians) who has attained the age of 21 years, and every British subject, a stranger to this country who has resided three years in this country, and is a householder, shall have a right to vote at the election of a member to serve in the Legislature of the country, and in the Dominion Parliament; and every foreign subject, other than a British subject, who has resided the same length of time in the country, and is a householder, shall have the same right to vote, on condition of his taking the oath of allegiance, it being understood that this article be subject to amendment exclusively by the Local Legislature."]—On reading this article you will perceive that my ideas of annexation have all along been right, and that no such feeling was nor is at the bottom of the present movement. British we are, and Canadians we mean to be, and every alien wishing to be a voter with us must first swear allegiance to the Crown. The three years' residence of all new-comers, before they are entitled to a vote, is meant as a security to the people already here from being over-ruled by those to come, and make the blending of strangers with the natives of the country a gradual, and thus more lasting, bond of union.

Article 20th. ["That the North-West Territory shall never be held liable for any portion of the £300,000 paid to the Hudson's Bay Company, or for any portion of the public debt of Canada, as it stands at the time of our entering the Confederation; and if, thereafter, we be called upon to assume our share of said public debt, we consent only, on condition that we first be allowed the amount for which we shall be held liable."]—We wish to be secure, as a people, from any liability as regards the £300,000 paid to the Hudson's Bay Company, as we were never a party to the bargain; and when we enter Confederation we wish to be put on the same footing in proportion as were the Maritime Provinces when they became part of the Dominion; if it was right in their case, why should it not be in ours?

Thus ends the Bill of Rights, as it has passed the Convention of Delegates. That body met again this morning (Saturday) discussing a motion of Mr. Riel's to overthrow all the negotiations between the Imperial and Canadian Governments and the Hudson Bay Company. Cool!! Thus, as it were, depriving the Honourable Company of any part of the £300,000 or the grant of land given them, and transferring the whole to the people of the country. It is needless to say, however, that the motion was lost. I wonder what those who have said that the Company were at the bottom of all these troubles will say when they hear this, and mark the friendly resolution of Mr. Riel *in favour of* the H.B.C.

On Monday at one o'clock the delegates will meet again, and Mr. Donald A. Smith's views will be taken on the List of Rights. It is not known what action he is empowered to take in the matter, although some declare he can do a great deal more towards settling affairs than is generally imagined.

Col. De Salaberry in the meantime has delayed his departure from amongst us till next week, to see if he can bring with him any despatches of importance to the Council at Ottawa. Should it require that a delegation, either in the person of De Salaberry or some other party or parties, then will come the question of self government until word is received from Ottawa. There are strong hopes that this can be arranged without any trouble on the part of Riel, he having stated that he would resign his present position as President as soon as there should be a union of the people. It is likely he will remain, however, with a small force in Fort Garry to act as a constabulary for the public peace and safety.

There are others, however, who think that Riel will give some trouble before he gives up the reins of power, which, undoubtedly he must to satisfy the popular votes. Riel is apparently *down* on the H.B.C. for some reason, and has given way to many expressions of dislike towards Governor McTavish especially. Things, however, look so hopeful at present in other respects that we must look at matters in as cheerful a light as possible, although, through all this atmosphere of brightness, there is a small cloud looming up in the distance which, I think, will blow over.[*]

The only other news I have to give you is, that the prisoners are not yet released, and some of them, I am sorry to say, are beginning to feel the effects of their close confinement. Poor fellows, I trust that their miserable position will soon be altered for freedom, and that they will suffer no evil consequences from their imprisonment. Walter Hyman, the young man who had his feet frozen in his attempted escape from Fort Garry, is improving, and will not lose his toes as was at one time feared. Mr. Charles Mair has turned up at Portage la Prairie, where he owns some property, and where he is at present living with his wife, at the house of Rev. Henry George Episcopal Minister. Dr. Bown is at a place called Eagle's Nest, in the interior, where he is resting in the arms of that grandmother he has so often abused.

On the night of the 3rd [] instant we experienced the coldest weather of the season, the thermometer having reached 30 below zero. The memory of that night has thrown such a chill over my literary efforts that I am obliged to close this somewhat lengthy epistle by subscribing myself,

Yours warmly,
JUSTITIA

---

[*] This reference is probably to the rumours of an impending movement of armed men from Portage la Prairie.

# ALEXANDER BEGG

## 9 FEBRUARY 1870

[This letter from Alexander Begg deals briefly with events in the Convention and activities behind the scenes in the settlement. Printed in the Toronto *Globe*, 26 February 1870.]


(To the Editor of the Globe)

RED RIVER SETTLEMENT,
February 9th 1870

SIR.—

Since my last, stirring events have taken place. When Riel was defeated in his motion to nullify the negotiations between the Imperial Government and the Hudson Bay Company, he stated openly that he would take some other measures to gain his end. On Sunday, the first news we heard was that a guard had been placed over Gov. McTavish, and that Dr. Cowan, chief trader in Fort Garry, was confined in the same room with Hallett. This produced some considerable excitement, and soon afterwards it was increased on hearing that Mr. Bannatyne, Postmaster had also been arrested and confined as a prisoner in the Fort. It is not known exactly what Mr. Bannatyne has done to cause his arrest, other than, in company with Mr. H. McDermott, he went to see whether Gov. McTavish, who is very ill in bed, was suffering from the presence of the guard in his sick room or at the door of his house.* A report was about that Riel meant to arrest one of the French Delegates, Chas. Nolin; the friends of the latter, therefore, collected to protect him, and one of Riel's men had a narrow escape from being shot dead by one of the Nolins.[1] Mr. Smith visited the Convention yesterday, and assured the Delegates that Canada would grant most of the Rights claimed, and perhaps all. It was therefore proposed that a delegation from the

---

* According to Begg's journal, Bannatyne was arrested on 6 February. McDermott was soon released. See Morton, ed., *Begg's Journal*, 297-98.

people of this country proceed to Ottawa to confer with the Council there on the subject, and bring back proper assurances from the Parliament to guarantee the Rights. The delegation to Canada will, I hear, consist of two or four members, and probably Riel himself will be one of them. The Convention is sitting again to-day, to consider who the delegates are to be, and also to provide some means for the restoration of peace during the time that elapses between now and the return of the delegates from Canada. I hope to be able to acquaint you by next mail that three delegates have left, in company with Col. De Salaberry. The latter gentleman has guaranteed the payment of the delegates' expenses to and from Canada, on behalf of the Canadian government.

Yours truly,
JUSTITIA.

EDITOR'S NOTE

[Begg does not mention that a delegation from the Convention on 9 February visited Governor McTavish and asked him about forming a provisional government. McTavish advised the delegation to form any sort of government that would keep law and order, but he refused to delegate his authority. The *New Nation*, 18 February 1870. See also *Preliminary Investigation and Trial of Ambroise D. Lépine for the Murder of Thomas Scott* (Montreal: Burland-Desbarats, 1874), 74.]

# ALEXANDER BEGG

18 FEBRUARY 1870

[Printed in the Toronto *Globe*, 12 March 1870.]

Letter No. II

RED RIVER SETTLEMENT, Feb. 18.

SIR—

The events of the past few days only go to strengthen the statement contained in my last—that the union of the French and English did not come from the heart—as it now appears that a greater gulf than ever exists between the two sides.* It appears to me that, under the circumstances, it is a pity that the actions of the English delegates have not been confirmed by their people with the prospect of a speedy settlement of our difficulties in view—but of this, I will speak further in the course of my letter. That I may be understood with regard to my remarks on the subject of troops, I will now endeavour to be more explicit in my meaning. I have all along contended that the sending of soldiers to this country to quell the troubles, and coerce the people into measures distasteful to them, would have been unwise and not likely to produce satisfactory results. I am in a better position to judge of this than you can be in Canada and than parties who have only resided here a short time and who may have party interest at stake. When, however, the Canadian Government have concluded peaceful negotiations with the people of this country and are in a position to annex the North-West to the Dominion, to the satisfaction of the settlements and all concerns (which I hope will be soon done) then, I should say would be the time to send regular troops here. The differences that have arisen among the several classes of people here will not be likely to die out soon, and it will be almost necessary that a force should be sent to enable the Local Legislature of the country to more effectually enforce their laws and

---

* A letter must be missing here, since the previous printed letter from Begg does not make this point.

strengthen their Government. At the same time, the presence of troops would tend to keep down party disturbances that are very likely to arise in the future. I do not mean by this that our settlers will be found generally unruly; on the contrary, I feel certain that they will be law-abiding as they have ever been—but it must be apparent [illegible] have done without a great deal of party and private ill-feeling having been engendered amongst the whole people, both in this country as well as in Canada, and this in itself will make it very difficult for the new Government to unite and work harmoniously with the several classes already in the Settlement and those likely to come amongst us. It is perfect nonsense for people to speak of sending troops in here to rule us with a high hand—to treat us as the Northern do the Southern States. Such a thing cannot be done success-fully, I assure you. But strengthen the hands of the Local Legislature here, so that that body will not be obliged to call on one part of the settlers to force another, and in time the wounds existing will gradually heal, and the people of the country will unite in time in bonds of amity under a happy and peaceful Government. And now to the course of events to date, which, no doubt, will appear to you as they have to us startling in the extreme, and which, indeed, have once more spread a gloom over the whole Settle-ment. A party of French went down on Friday, the 11th inst, to the house of Wm. Dease to arrest him. When they reached the place, they found and captured six or eight men amongst whom were Sabine (of Schultz notori-ety, a Canadian long resident in the country) and an English half-breed named Wm. Gaddes. Wm. Dease himself escaped through a window at the back of the house, and has not been heard from since.

On Saturday [12 February 1870] 14 of the prisoners in Fort Garry were released on giving their parole that they would keep the peace and abide by the laws of the country. Wm. Hallett had to give security to the amount of 450 pounds, and Wm. Drever for 400 pounds sterling, before they [] released, a young man named Davis, succeeded in eluding the vigilance of the guards and escaped without giving the oath. During Monday, a party of French in charge of Wm. O'Donohue, were busy carrying away the goods and chattels belonging to Doctor Schultz into Fort Garry. Dr. Cowan, at the same time, was ordered to leave his house in the Fort, and Riel began immediately to furnish it with Schultz's furniture, for the purpose of con-verting it into a Government-House.

The mail bags on Monday came in empty, the carrier not having been

able to reach Pembina. Word was brought at the same time of six men having been frozen to death near Fort Abercrombie. On Thursday morning,
about 4 o'clock, a body of from 80 to 100 men passed through the town in
carioles and sleighs on their way towards the Stone Fort; while in the town
they surrounded the house of one Henry Contee, a relation of Riel's, and
demanded whether he (Riel) was there at the time.[1] Riel had been in the
habit of sometimes sleeping at Contee's house; but on this occasion he
happened not to be there, and, consequently, escaped capture. The party
was commanded by Captain Boulton, belonging to the staff of Col. Dennis.
These were the same men from Portage La Prairie, who were reported to
have turned back from Headingly on their return home. Rumour had it
that they were provided with ladders to scale the walls, and were well
armed and that they had gone down to raise the Settlement against the
French at Fort Garry. The fact of these men passing through the town at
night was known to those in the Fort, and Riel, it is said, had hard work to
prevent a sally out upon them.

The reports regarding the object of their mission did much towards
unsettling things, and probably prevented the immediate release of the
balance of the prisoners. Word came up soon after that the men of St.
Andrew and lower down the Settlement were rising, and that general discontent was felt towards the delegates of the late Convention for agreeing
to Riel's Provisional Government. The avowed object of the rising, however,
was to obtain the release of the whole of the prisoners. Riel at once began
to collect his men, and preparations were made to receive the threatened
attack. The force of the English was said to be between 600 and 700 men,
and that of the French about 500. At this stage, a young lady, lately from
Canada,[*] called on Mr. A.G. Bannatyne and asked him if he would go with
her to the Fort, to try and get the prisoners released, so as to prevent
bloodshed if possible.

Mr. B. immediately consented to accompany the lady, and together they
visited Riel, and made known their mission.[†] He said he was just about

---

[*] Victoria McVicar (c. 1842-1899) was visiting Red River from Fort William
over the winter of 1869-70.

[†] Begg doubtless had the details of the negotiations that follow from
Bannatyne.

giving the prisoners another chance, although they had already twice refused to take the oath. The young lady and Mr. Bannatyne asked to be allowed to see the prisoners which was granted—when they urged upon them to take the oath for their own sakes as well as the sakes of their friends outside. They then went back to Riel, and soon afterwards the prisoners were brought one by one before him. The three first who were told to swear and sign hesitated upon the ground whether all their fellow prisoners were to have the same chance. Mr. Bannatyne spoke, and urged them—putting the pen in their hands he begged of them to sign, which at last they in turn did. The last one was Dr. Lynch. When he read the nature of the oath he said, "I can sign that," and put his name down immediately.

Riel refused to take the oath from Mr. Farquharson, saying that he had already broken his word twice while in prison, and ordered the guard to push him out of the Fort.

Walter [Walton] F. Hyman, who had his feet frozen in endeavouring to escape some time ago, and who had not yet recovered the use of his limbs, had to be taken from the Fort in a sleigh. I am happy to say, however, that he is doing well, and is expected to be soon able to walk about. Some of the prisoners look as if they had suffered a good deal from their close confinement, while others do not appear altered in appearance the least. They all say that the guards, as a general rule, were as kind as they could be under the circumstances, while in some cases they met with great roughness and incivility. When all the prisoners were gone, Riel turned round to the young lady and Mr. Bannatyne and said, "I knew there is something else behind this. Schultz will try and attack the Fort; but let him come; I hope he will." Both the young lady and Mr. Bannatyne declared the only object of the rising among the English to be the release of the prisoners, and that they would now all return to their homes. "Well, well," said Riel, "this is the last thing I will grant the other side."

Mr. James Ross and Maurice Lowman soon afterwards visited the Fort, to endeavour to obtain an amnesty for those prisoners who had escaped. This of course, would include Dr. Schultz (to whom Riel has a particular dislike). Riel was not in the humour to receive those gentlemen, and plainly told Mr. Ross if he would ask that again he would have him at once.

Word was sent to Major Boulton who was in command of the whole English party, that the prisoners were released, and a feeling of relief was felt by every one that the calamity of an encounter between the English and

French had been averted. Indeed in the morning of the next day people were congratulating themselves on the favourable turn affairs had taken, when information was brought in that changed the whole aspect of affairs, and put us in a worse plight than ever. It appears that the English party took some prisoners on suspicion of their being spies from the French side, amongst whom was one Variseau, a desperate character.[*] By some means this man happened to escape, and took with him a gun belonging to one of his guards; as soon, however, as his absence was discovered he was pursued. As Variseau ran along the river he and a young man named Sutherland, the son of one of our most respected Scotch settlers, and thinking, no doubt, that he would stop him, as the pursuers called out for him to do so, or as some say, in order to get his horse, he levelled his gun and shot the young man, first through the hand and then through the body. Sutherland dropped from his horse to the ground, and Variseau fled on to the woods, followed by three men in pursuit, who soon afterwards overtook him, and in securing him gave him some ugly gashes in the head. When he was brought into the camp it was with difficulty that some of the men present were prevented from lynching him on the spot. Young Sutherland in the meantime was carried into the house of the Rev. John Black, where he lay in a critical state. Mr. William Fraser immediately went and saw Riel but received no satisfaction from the visit, especially as while he was in the Fort a messenger named Norquay arrived with a letter from Rev. John Black, I believe, stating that the English speaking people down the settlement would not recognize the proposed Provisional Government. Riel tore up the Letter in bits and detained Norquay a prisoner for a few hours, releasing him, however, at the expiration of that time.

The excitement in town now became very great. Shops were shut, women and children were removed to places of safety. A party of about fifty men, headed by O'Donoghue, made a raid on all the firearms and ammunition that could be found in town, thus securing quite a quantity of both. Crowds of French collected from all parts into the Fort, and every preparation was made in case of an attack from the English party. All looked forward to a commencement of hostilities that night, and no one doubted if raids [] did take place that the town would be reduced to ashes.

---

[*] Begg has him elsewhere—correctly—as Norbert Parisien.

Amongst the English were a party of Indians (Swampies) from the lower Settlement, headed by Henry Prince, their Chief. These had torches prepared to set fire to buildings. The English had also three or four cannon on sleds, one of which was an eighteen-pounder, rifled. The force of those under Major Boulton amounted, some said, to between 800 and 1,000 men. The number of French was not known, but it must have been considerable. They had, however, [illegible on film because of fold on paper] taken over to defend the Roman Catholic Cathedral, and a guard of over 100 men was placed to protect the convents and other buildings around the church at St. Boniface. The sisters left the convent with all the children under their charge. Horses were pressed into the service by the French wherever they could find them, and the English raided on the neighbouring farm houses for supplies of every description. Everything was in the course of a few hours on a war footing. At one time there were hopes entertained for the recovery of young Sutherland, but they were not realized, as he died during the night.

It is said that Riel sent word to the English party that they were at liberty to form any government they wished, but if they wished to fight they could come, and he would be prepared for them, but he did not intend attacking them. A council was held, composed of some of the principal men amongst the English, which resulted in their resolving to disperse, as they had got what they had come for—the release of the prisoners. It was determined, at the same time, that Variseau should be taken to the Stone Fort and kept there a prisoner till better times. In accordance with this determination, the English separated for their respective parishes.

A great deal of sympathy is felt for Mr. John Sutherland, the father of the young man killed by Variseau.

Ever since our troubles have commenced he has exerted himself in the cause of peace, and at the same time to benefit his country. In his endeavours he has on several occasions had to bear with the taunts of his neighbours that he was a sympathiser with Riel, and so forth. So has it been with many others who have striven to promote unity amongst the people, and if possible prevent bloodshed. There are those in this Settlement so narrow in their own minds that they are careless of how matters go as long as they do not interfere with them personally, forgetting that the weal or woe of the country will ultimately affect their immediate interests either for the better or the worse.

Mr. John Sutherland, unlike this [?], has viewed the state of affairs in a more liberal sense—perfectly sensible of the blunders commited somewhere in the proposed change of Government for his country he considered what he thought to be wrong, at the same time he has been throughout loyal to his Queen and loyal to his own people; but being Christian enough to look with unbiased eyes on the French party, he has suffered reproach the most undeserving. And now this man of peace, who in spite of all reproach, commands the deepest respect of his people, is the first one to suffer from a hostile act. His son, his pride, is taken from him as it were at a moment's notice; yet in the midst of his affliction the first request he made was that the act should be forgotten, and that it was his earnest desire that his son's death should not be made the means of plunging the whole Settlement into war and desolation.

On Thursday morning, the 17th inst., we had lulled ourselves into the belief that the danger of war was past, when once more we were roused from our fancied security by an unfor[e]seen occurrence.

Capt. Boulton, in returning to the Portage instead of passing the town at night, or by some roundabout way, struck out from about the Scotch church with a party of forty-eight, including himself, and took the plains in a direction to connect with the roads leading up the Assiniboine. Some of the party were in carioles, and others on horseback; but on account of the snow drifts they were unable to proceed faster than a walk. As soon as they came in sight, from Fort Garry a party of about fifty French darted out on horseback in pursuit, cheered by their comrades on the walls as they left. The movements of the two bands could be easily viewed from the houses in town, and the residents, fully expecting to see a fight, thronged every available spot suitable for sight-seeing.

Nearer and nearer the two parties approached each other. The French plunging their horses through the deep snow at a hard gallop. At times when the horses would stick, the men would jump off, cane their animals, and then leap on again, hardly stopping their speed in doing so, thus showing them to be as expert horsemen, as our plains Indians. The Portage men now came to a halt, and awaited the coming of the French. Everyone on the lookout now expected to see a flash, and hear a report, the signal for the commencement of hostilities, but none came. At last, the French and English seemed to mix up in one body. A considerable halt then occurred, when the whole party moved off in the direction of the Fort.

"They are taken prisoners" were the words passed from mouth to mouth amongst those on the lookout, and such indeed turned out to be the case. Their arms were taken from them, and as they neared Fort Garry the holsters of many of the prisoners were found to be empty, looking as if they had thrown away their pistols. Two men were therefore detailed to go and search for them. While they were hunting about they came across a man hidden amongst some bushes, who turned out to be a Portage man or one of that party. He had secreted himself before the capture took place, and would have escaped if the two men had not been sent to search for the missing arms. I have not learned the name of him who was thus taken prisoner.

The captors and captives as they marched towards Fort Garry, resembled a funeral procession more than anything else. Crowds were on the walls and battlements of the fort, and a number of people from the town went up to see their arrival. Some of the prisoners would not give up their arms without a good deal of resistance, but all were disarmed before they went inside the walls.

Thus ended another bloodless encounter. The following are the names of those taken and now confined as prisoners in the hands of Riel and his party:

Capt. Boulton, John McLean, Robert McBain, Wilder Bartlett, James McBain, Dan. Sissons, A. Murray, Wm. Farmer, Laurence Smith, Charles McDonald, John Switzer, H. Williams, Alex McPherson, W. G. Bird, Alex McLean, Jas Paquin, Geo Sandison, Wm. Paquin, J. Dillsworth, Wm. Dillsworth, R. Adams, J. Paquin, M. McLeod, Archibald McDonald, James Jack [or Jock], Thomas Scott, James Sanderson, George Wylds, D. Taylor, A. Taylor, George Newcomb, H. Taylor, J.B. Morrison, Wm. Salter, Magnus Brown, N. Morrison, Wm. Sutherland, Robert Dennison, Jos. Smith, Chas. Millan, Thomas Butler, John Taylor, John McKay, Alex. Parker, Sergeant Powers, John Ivy, G. Parker. One name I have not got, probably the man who hid himself.

When will complications cease—only two days have elapsed since the release of the late prisoners, when another batch almost as numerous as the former are captured. While I regret their imprisonment in more ways than one, I cannot justify their actions in leaving their houses before the late Convention had finished its labours, this was breaking faith with their own delegates as well as the French, and only tending to excite and inflame the minds of the people to the detriment of a peaceful settlement of our difficulties. In the face of Riel's guaranteeing the release of the late prisoners, and with the prospect of a speedy arrangement with the Dominion held out by the commissioners from Canada, those who came down, and by their presence in a body armed and vowing vengeance on those in Fort Garry, they fanned the flame of discontent amongst the English, until it burst out in a manner that will now sow seeds of discord in the future amongst our settlers that will take years to eradicate.

Oh! for a Solomon amongst us!

I did not feel that the actions of the English delegates would meet with a hearty response from their people, for the simple reason, that they are—like a house divided within itself—uncertain, coy, and hard to please; while, on the other hand, the French are as a unit on matters that concern them as a people; but I did think that good sense would lead them to back up their representatives in the only course left them to pursue under the circumstances for obtaining a speedy settlement of our troubles, and a bright prospect ahead.

What will war and destruction of life and property amongst ourselves do for us? Will letting loose our prejudices and passions now help us or our families in the future? A moment's reasoning and thought will teach us that such a course is unwise and mad-like. The French feel themselves repelled by their English neighbours, and the English, on the other hand, consider that they are being ridden over rough shod by the French. How easy, then, with these feelings existing between two divisions of a small settlement like ours, is it to fan a flame, that will result in what, in our sober and calm moments, we cannot but view with horror. A people far removed from the outside world exterminating each other to give place to strangers in the future, who will reap any advantages—the work of years—that may be left after the carnage is over. Would troops sent in here to aid one party against the other do any good? would the wiping out of one class of settlers benefit the other? or would such a course assist the formation of a happy government in this country for years to come? Oh! no, believe me it would not. Let Canada, now that she has the chance settle peacefully and satisfactorily with this country, and then let her send troops to sustain that peace, and, if possible, prevent any ill effects happening from the present ill feeling that has been engendered within a few months amongst our settlers.

How are we placed now? We are yet without any sort of protection in the way of Government, and likely to remain so for some time. We are a rabble, in truth. The French stick to their Provisional Government, and appear to be the strongest party. A gulf is between the two sides of the Settlement. The French are sending their delegates to Canada, [] [Mr. Scott, and Mr. Richot]. Mr. Scott, a young man of about twenty-five years of age, of little experience in such matters, goes to represent no party at all, unless it is a few of the town people in Winnipeg, chiefly Americans.* Judge Black has declined the position of delegate; therefore the English are not represented in the matter.† These two delegates, accompanied by Mr. D.A. Smith, and Col. De Salaberry, leave next Monday for Ottawa.

And now I would advise the Canadian Parliament to take up the matter as if the late difficulties mentioned in this letter had never taken place. It is quite certain the Bill of Rights, as agreed upon by the late Convention, represents the feelings, to a great extent, of the whole Settlement; and although one portion is not represented,‡ any proper action taken by the Canadian Government, based on the Bill of Rights, will more than proba-bly, meet the views of all parties here.

My letter has reached a greater length than I expected, so that I will bring it to a close.

Yours truly,
JUSTITA.

EDITOR'S NOTE

[The beginning of the movement opposing the Convention's acquies-cence in Riel's Provisional Government was described more fully by "Red River," writing on 19 February from St. Andrews to the Montreal *Witness* and reprinted in the Toronto *Globe*:

Last Sabbath two men from the Portage came down here telling the people that they had 200 men ready; that Dease had posses-sion of the Stinking River barricades; that Nolan was at Oak Point;

---

* This is Alfred Scott, an American.
† Black subsequently agreed to serve.
‡ Presumably the Canadian Party.

Leviny at White Horse Plains, all keeping back the French from joining Riel (the three above named are loyal French) while they, with the help of the Indian settlement and St Andrew's, would take the Fort, liberate the prisoners, and establish a Government with Mr. Donald Smith at its head. Our people had no notion of such a move at the time, but being all favourably disposed mustered on Tuesday morning at the Rapids church, and then marched up to Mr. Black's church in the Scotch settlement, where the Portage men and the Scotch were to join them. They got there in the evening, but found that less than 100 were from the Portage, the Scotch would not move at all, no provisions prepared for them, no loyal French to join them, and Riel's men gathering from all parts. On Wednesday morning all our people had arrived, and there were more than in the church and school-house about 100 Portage men, chiefly Canadians, 200 men from St. Andrew's and Mapleton, the parish below, and between 200 and 300 Indians from the Indian settlement and Lake of the Woods, the latter all painted and feathered in high style, and armed with guns and war-clubs.

"Red River" in the *Witness* also describes in detail the circumstances leading up to the release of the prisoners taken by Riel.

A council . . . was then called, composed of men from the various parishes. Capt Boulton, Schultz, Rev. Mr. Black, and the Bishop [Machray] were there also. They drew up a list of demands on Riel, to be sent up by a messenger, who was to be followed by the whole force; and if he did not agree to these demands, the Fort was then to be attacked. These were, that all prisoners be liberated at once, and a guarantee given that neither escaped prisoners nor any others be taken in future; that all confiscated property be stored; safety for Schultz's life be promised, and that we form a Government of our own, allowing him to carry on his without any interference, but letting it be understood we countenanced him in no shape or manner. Also, freedom of all highways for us through the country. The messenger was sent, but no movement was made forward. In about two hours we heard that he was kept a prisoner. Many were then for marching at once, but no order was given. Meanwhile many were going home, having nothing to eat, and being wearied waiting so long and nothing done.

Another letter dated 19 February, and printed in the Toronto *Globe* on 30 March 1870, adds:

> The people rose entirely, one may say, and joined together at the Scotch Church. The numbers were estimated at from 500 to 700 men, almost all armed with some sort of weapons. They sent a message to Riel at Fort Garry, demanding the release of the prisoners, and stating that they did not wish to have anything to do with his Government. The prisoners were released; but even before this in consequence of there being no arrangement whatever being made for provisions the people had begun to disperse, many of them having had nothing to eat for 24 hours—the cold during the time was great, varying from 10 to 35 degrees below zero. Mr. Riel sent back word that the prisoners should be released, and they were, but at the same time the French poured into the Fort from all sides, many coming from St. Josephs, in the U.S. Territory. On news arriving that the prisoners had been released most of the people started home, and the gathering melted away faster than it rose. One great reason of the rising was, that Mr. Riel declared in Convention that Dr. Schultz was an outlaw, and any one might shoot him that liked, and that all his goods were forfeited, also that W. Dease, who had been loyal, should lose his place in the new Government. Great dissatisfaction was also expressed at Mr. Donohoe being appointed to the Treasury, a man with no stake in the country whatever, and suspected of being a Fenian.

According to "Red River," writing on 19 February:

> In the morning they had taken two spies of Riel's, and not being well guarded, one escaped and being pursued had snatched a gun out of a cutter near and shot one of the Scotch who was riding towards him on a horse, and who, he supposed was about to seize him. One of the men, after a chase, came up to him, when the spy broke his gun over the horse's head; the rider then struck him on the head with his tomahawk, when he was at once surrounded and led off bound. The Scotchmen died the same night. The French prisoner was brought down here, and I suppose, will be tried when he recovers.

When the prisoners had been released, the English dispersed. A party of forty-eight, led by Captain Boulton, in passing the Stone Fort, encountered a party of fifty men sent by Riel. "Red River" has it:

> After we went home, some of the Portage men came down this way, but the body went on to near the town, sending a message to Riel that they were going home, but would hurt nothing. He promised not to interfere with them; but when they were on the road he sent a party after them, and took them prisoners, nearly fifty in all.

# ALEXANDER BEGG

26 FEBRUARY 1870

[This was Justitia's last letter to the *Globe*. Why he ended his correspondence is not known, and there seems no particularly cogent reason for the termination. Alexander Begg certainly continued keeping a detailed journal of the rebellion for many more months beyond 26 February, on the basis of which he produced his book *The Creation of Manitoba: A History of the Red River Troubles in 1871*. Nothing written in this letter ought to have persuaded the *Globe* against publishing further correspondence from Justitia, and Begg gives no hints in his journal. Indeed, beyond opening the journal with Justitia's letter number one, Begg makes no mention whatever of the Justitia correspondence in his journal. Printed in the Toronto *Globe*, 19 March 1870.]

LETTER NO. XII

(To the Editor of the Globe)
RED RIVER SETTLEMENT
February 26th, 1870.

MAJOR BOUTON SENTENCED[*]

SIR,—

Captain Boulton has had a narrow escape with his life.[1] It seems that four of the prisoners lately captured were tried by court martial and condemned to be shot the next night. Mr. and Mrs. John Sutherland, father and mother of the lad killed by Varieau [Parisien], on hearing of this went up to Fort Garry and pleaded with Riel for the sake of the boy they had lost to spare the lives of the prisoners. Riel, Mr. Sutherland says, was deeply affected, and told both him and his wife, that it was far from his wish to shed blood. The crime of raising Indians, however, he said, was one against

---

[*] The discrepancy in Boulton's rank probably reflects the fact that the subheads were added in Toronto.

humanity, and deserving of nothing short of death. He finally pardoned three of the condemned men; but Boulton, he declared, would be shot that night. Archdeacon McLean, on hearing of his sentence, visited Boulton and promised to remain with him to the last. A deep gloom settled on every one at the thought of the approaching execution. Several parties interceded, but seemingly with no success.

## BOULTON REPRIEVED

At last, Riel and the French Council on being importuned, held a meeting which did not break up until near midnight, and resulted in Boulton's life being spared. On Saturday night people in the vicinity of Fort Garry retired to their beds but few went to sleep—the thought of a fellow creature being sent to eternity at such short notice was horrible in itself, and I have no doubt many an anxious prayer was uttered on behalf of the unfortunate man. Sunday morning, however, revealed the fact that the man still lived, and was likely to do so.

## THE BOULTON SCHULTZ EXPEDITION

The expedition in which Capt. Boulton took part was altogether a mad enterprise, and uncalled for at the time; but I hope it is the last one originating from the Dennis party. The Portage people, from whence the captured men chiefly started, condemn the expedition; and those in St. Andrews and lower down the Settlement, who in the middle of the excitement joined it, now that they look upon it in a sober light, scout the whole proceeding.

In my last I unwittingly did a great injustice to a brave man; I mean Capt. Boulton. It now appears that he was not in favour of the movement from the Portage, but could not in honour withdraw from it. That, further, it was through his means and advice that the people gathered around the Kildonan school house were kept from going to extremes, and were finally induced to return to their homes. He was also strongly against the party for the Portage starting as they did on their return home, and urged their taking some other route. Hence it is perfectly plain that Capt. Boulton has been the victim of circumstances, and was not, as I stated in my last, the leader of the movement. That Boulton is a brave man, and deserving of the highest praise for his conduct during the late unhappy events, is now the opinion of everyone who knows the circumstances. While he was under sentence of death his bearing was calm and resigned, as became the character of a true soldier. His only feeling was for his friends in Canada what they might suffer on account of his sad fate. Since his escape from death, he has earned hosts of friends in the Settlement by his noble conduct. His French guards deem it no greater pleasure than to go into his room and shake hands with him. ["]You don't hate us, do you?["] they continually ask. All express the greatest admiration and friendship for him, from Riel downwards. He is provided with every comfort that can be obtained under the circumstances, and I feel safe in saying that a great length of time is not likely to elapse before he will be once more restored to freedom.

## THE SUPPRESSION OF THE "NEW NATION"

The *New Nation* came out on Saturday, the 19th inst, but Riel, on looking over its pages declared it to be unworthy to be read abroad, and immediately sent a guard to stop its publication and distribution. Major Robinson, the editor, was taken to Fort Garry and kept there a prisoner till one o'clock on Sunday morning. If you have received the newspaper in question you will have observed that its Annexation views have moderated considerably since its first number.[2] I have contended all along, and I do so now, that a union with the United States is the last thing thought of or wished for amongst our settlers in Red River. And once we become a part of the Dominion you will find none more loyal nor staunch than we will prove to be.

## UNION OF PARTIES

At last we have a prospect of a union of the people, which bids fair to be a lasting one, since it is a spontaneous movement on the part of the English settlers—by the latter I include the Scotch. After the late capture of prisoners, and seeing no other way open to secure the peace and safety of the Settlement, the parishes of St. Clements, St. Andrew, St. Paul, St. John and Kildonan resolved on joining the Provisional Government, and backing up the acts of their delegates. The settlers up the Assiniboine are following in the foot steps of those down the Red River; it only remains for the Portage people to come in, which I have no doubt they [] soon do.

On the head of this resolution on the part of the English people to join the Provisional Government, Mr. Donald G. Smith, in company with Mr. H. McDermott, one of our most respectable settlers, went down towards the Stone Fort to reassure those living in that direction, and to do what he could in the way of bringing about harmony and peace. This visit of Mr. Smith was well timed and will do much to strengthen the resolution of the people to unite.

## HUNTING FOR SCHULTZ

On Sunday morning about 1 o'clock, a company of about 50 horsemen went down the Settlement in search of Dr. Schultz, as far as the house of one Mr. John Tait, where they found Mrs. Schultz, but not the doctor. The answers of Mr. Tait to their inquiries regarding the missing man not being considered satisfactory, they took him prisoner to Fort Garry, where he was detained till the next evening. On Monday night Riel himself headed another band, and went as far as the Stone Fort which they ransacked in every corner, but did not find him whom they were after. These two expeditions after one man, and that, too, through a district where only a few days ago the people were up in arms to attack them, shows the earnestness evinced by the French for the capture of Schultz. The latter gentleman, it is said, was at the bottom of the late armed riots down the settlement, and so bitter were the French half-breeds against him, that they were continually crying out for his capture, and no doubt Riel, to satisfy them and himself, too, organized the two expeditions just mentioned.

## BISHOP TACHÉ

Bishop Taché is expected to arrive in the Settlement at any moment, and horses have been sent off in charge of a few men to bring him in. It is expected his presence will do much good amongst us, and tend to keep down excitement; in fact we would not be astonished to find that he has full powers to arrange the existing difficulties; but a day or two will tell. Last Thursday's mail did not get through, and on that account I fancy the roads must be very bad. Another man has been frozen on the plains. If the weather has been so severe, and the roads bad, Bishop Taché may be delayed some time longer in his journey.

THE HUDSON'S BAY COMPANY

We see by late Canadian papers [newspaper reports] that the Imperial Government has decided not to allow any compensation to the Hudson Bay Company for losses sustained by that body during our late troubles. We can hardly credit this—the fact of its being so would show a great injustice done to the Company. It has been admitted by those high in authority that while we were under the rule of the Hudson Bay Company we were still considered in the light of a Colony by the Home Government. This being the case it is well that we should look back some length of time on certain circumstances that occurred having a bearing on this question of compensation for loss. While the Duke of Newcastle was Colonial Secretary during the years 1862 and 1863 I believe, and just after the Sioux massacre, a couple of petitions embracing the signatures of the entire Settlement were sent to the Colonial office, setting forth the isolated and dangerous position of the settlers and praying for troops to be sent for their protection.[3] The Duke of Newcastle, who was an inveterate enemy of the Hudson Bay Company, turned a deaf ear to their petitions, and the whole settlement, while claiming the protection of British subjects, might have been slaughtered for all the Imperial Government seemed to care. Many petitions followed these two, all praying for the same thing, troops, yet no heed was taken of them. Now who had the Company to apply to in such a case but the Government from whom it received its charter, and at the same time the Hudson Bay Company offered to pay a part if not the whole of the expenses of the troops asked for while in the country. If troops had been in this country during the last number of years the rule of the Hudson Bay Company would not have been set at defiance as it has been on several occasions, by evil-minded persons. Had troops been here, our present troubles would never have reached the extent they did. The question now is, had the Company a right to demand troops for their promotion and that of the people under their charge, while owing allegiance to Britain? Has any Colony, under such circumstances, more particularly that of danger, the right to demand troops from the Mother Country, more especially when she is not expected to foot the bills? One would reasonably suppose that the Imperial Government, for its own honour, if nothing else, would be bound to defend her Colonies in the time of need. How would Great Britain have liked it if the Hudson Bay Company, failing in getting troops from England, had applied to the United States for the same? Another view to be taken of it—where lay the fault of the mistakes made in the transfer of the country to Canada? The Hudson Bay Company never pretended to tell the people; but the Imperial Government apparently did. Who was the cause of our troubles from first to last? They commenced with the Colonial Office at home—where the Imperial Government next thing to told the Hudson Bay Company to sell or lose the whole thing. Then the Canadian Government, following on the footsteps of the Imperial, committed a series of blunders in respect to the people of Red River. Had their policy been different, the Hudson Bay Company would have suffered no loss; Canada would not have been called hard names, and the Imperial Government would have got the verdict of having done a good thing.

Riel has been very ill from a threatened attack of brain fever, brought on by want of rest and excitement as well as overwork, but he is now recovering.[*]

Yours truly,
JUSTITIA.

---

[*] Not much more is known about this illness experienced by Riel.

# APPENDIX:

**Ashdown, James Henry** (1844-1924): Born in London, he came to Red River in 1868 and established his first hardware store in 1869. He was one of the Canadian party at John Schultz's house that surrendered on 7 December 1869.

**Bannatyne, Andrew Graham** (1829-1889): Born in the Orkney Islands, he joined the Hudson's Bay Company at an early age. He quit the company and in 1868 had joined Alexander Begg in a partnership running a store and post office (of which he was Postmaster) in Winnipeg.

**Bird, Curtis James** (1838-1876): Born in Bird's Hill, he was educated at St. John's College and Guy's Hospital, London. Returning to Red River he served as coroner of the settlement from 1861, and was a delegate to the November 1869 council from St. Paul's and to the Convention of Forty in 1870.

**Black, John** (1818-1882): Born in Scotland, he was educated at Knox College, Toronto, and came to Red River in 1851 as pastor of the newly established Presbyterian Church at Frog Plain.

**Black, John** (1817-1879): Born in Scotland, he came to Red River in 1839. He later went to Australia and returned to the settlement in 1861 to become recorder and president of the General Quarterly Court of Assiniboia. He wanted to resign as recorder in 1868 but agreed to stay on until he was replaced, and so was still in office when the uprising began. He became chairman of the Convention of Forty and was a delegate of the provisional government to negotiate terms with the Canadian government.

**Boulton, Charles Arkoll** (1842-1899): Born in Upper Canada, he was a member of John Dennis's survey party, and reluctantly led the Portage party in Feburary 1870. After his capture on 17 February, he was threatened with execution by Louis Riel.

**Bown, Walter** (1828-1903): Born in England and raised in Upper Canada, he came to Red River as a dentist in 1863 and became editor of the *Nor'-Wester* in 1868.

**Bruce, John** (b. 1831): A resident of St. Norbert, he was a carpenter before being elected president of the Métis National Committee in October 1869. He resigned in Riel's favour in December 1869 and retreated from prominence.

**Bunn, Thomas** (1830-1875): Born in Red River, he was a mixed blood who lived in Mapleton. He served on the Council of Assiniboia from January 1868, and continued under the provisional government. He attended the November 1869 Council as delegate from St. Clement's and was also a delegate to the Convention of Forty.

**Cameron, Donald R.** (1834-1921): Born in England, he was an officer in the Royal Artillery and the son-in-law of Charles Tupper. He was seconded to the imperial government to become a member of William McDougall's council and was apparently intended to organize a paramilitary police force in the west.

**Coldwell, William** (1834-1907): Born in London, England, he came to Red River from Canada in 1859 with William Buckingham to found the *Nor'-Wester*. He was an excellent shorthand reporter and recorded the 1870 Convention of Forty.

**Corbett, Griffith Owen** (c. 1823-1909): Born in England, he came to Rupert's Land in 1851 and founded Holy Trinity Church in Headingley in 1854. A contentious man who became leader of the anglophone mixed bloods in Red River, he was tried and convicted of five counts of procuring an abortion upon his pregnant serving girl in 1863. In the course of this affair he was several times released from prison by a mob.

**Cowan, William** (1818-1902): Born in Scotland, he was a trader for the Hudson's Bay Company and chief officer of Upper Fort Garry after 1867.

**Dauphinais, François (Francis)** (b. 1815): He was a delegate to the November 1869 council from St. François-Xavier, and was later vice-president of the provincial government.

**Dease, William** (1827-1913): He was a Pointe Coupée farmer who was a member of the Council of Assinboia and a principal Métis opponent of Louis Riel. Suspected of being a spy, he was imprisoned by Riel in February of 1870.

**Dennis, John Stoughton** (1820-1885): Born in Upper Canada, he was educated at Victoria College, Cobourg, and was a classmate of William McDougall. He became a surveyor and in 1869 was sent to Red River to survey lots for the Canadian government. He hobnobbed with John Christian Schultz (also a Victoria alumnus), and one of his survey teams was obstructed by the Métis in October 1869. He subsequently was commissioned by McDougall (on the assumption of his supposed authority) to raise a volunteer force against the Métis, although he soon left the settlement.

**Drever, William (Jr.)** (b. 1844): Born in Red River, he was a mixed-blood scout and petty merchant who was regarded by Riel as a spy who had helped prisoners escape from Upper Fort Garry.

**Eccles, John:** A Winnipeg clerk, he was one of those who surrendered in the Schultz house in December 1869. Legend has it that, when he subsequently escaped from Upper Fort Garry, he hid from Riel's men at his mother-in-law's house in Kildonan, where he was secreted under a voluminous skirt.

**Emmerling, George:** A Winnipeg hotel owner of German extraction, he came to Red River from the United States in the early 1860s and was known as "Dutch George." He left Winnipeg in May 1871, selling out to R.A. Davis.

**Farmer, William:** A member of A.C. Webb's survey party in 1869, he was one of the Portage party captured on 17 February 1870. He later gave the information that led to the arrest of Ambroise Lépine in 1873.

**Farquaharson, James** (1820-1874): Born in Glasgow, he came to Red River in 1864 from the West Indies, working as a house painter. John Schultz's father-in-law, he was briefly detained by Riel in February 1870.

**Fonseca, William Gomez da** (1823-1905): A Winnipeg merchant born in the West Indies, he came to Red River from Minnesota in 1860. He was also a carter and freighter. Arrested by Riel on 13 December 1869, he was released two days later on surrender of his American citizenship papers. He was suspected of carrying messages for William McDougall.

**Fortney (Fortinay), George** (1846-1925): Born in Upper Canada, he was one of those fined with Thomas Scott for assault on John Snow at Oak Point in November 1869. He also surrendered at Schultz's house in December of that year. He later became a Red River steamboat captain.

**Gaddie (Gaddee, Gaddy, Geddee), William** (b. 1815): A mixed blood, he was part of the Portage party and was captured by Riel as a spy in February 1870. Riel suspected him of acting as a courier for Schultz. He was supposed to be executed by the Métis, and was actually put up against the wall, but was allowed to escape.

**Gay, Norbert:** A Frenchman who arrived mysteriously in Red River in January 1870, he claimed to be a corresondent of a Paris newspaper. Rumours were he was a spy, but for whom? He became a loyal Riel supporter, and tried to instil European cavalry tactics into Riel's horsemen in the spring of 1870.

**George, Henry** (1832-1881): Born in England, he was the rector of St. Mary's Church, Portage la Prairie, from 1865 to 1881.

**Goulait (Goulet), Roger** (1834-1902): He was collector of customs for the Hudson's Bay Company and a member of the Council of Assiniboia; his papers were seized by Riel on 24 November 1869.

**Granville, Earl:** See Leveson-Gower.

**Gunn, Donald** (1797-1878): Born in Scotland, he came to Red River in 1813 with the Hudson's Bay Company, formally settling there (at St. Andrews) in 1823. He was a delegate to the November 1869 council from St.Andrews, and was a delegate to the 1870 Convention of Forty.

**Gunn, George:** A Poplar Point merchant, he was a Scots mixed blood who served as a delegate to the November 1869 council (from Ste. Anne's parish) and the 1870 Convention of Forty. He was elected to the new provisional government on 28 February 1870.

**Hallett, William** (1824-ca.1873): He was described by Charles Mair as a leader of the "English Plains Hunt." He helped free James Stewart from jail in 1863. He was employed as a guide by Charles Dennis, and was subsequently imprisoned by Riel. While incarcerated, he srgued with Riel on the night of the escape of John Schultz, and ended up in irons.

**Hardisty, Richard** (1832-1889): A chief trader with the HBC, Hardisty was Donald Smith's brother-in-law and accompanied him to the settlement in 1869. He was later appointed a senator from Manitoba.

**Howe, Joseph** (1804-1873): Born in Nova Scotia of Loyalist parentage, he had led the Reform party in Nova Scotia and served for many years as provincial premier. He had opposed Confederation in 1866, was elected to Parliament as an anti-confederationist in 1867, and had been won over to the government, becoming secretary of state. In October 1869 he unofficially visited Red River, and subsequently had to defend himself against charges that he had fomented the rebellion.

**Hyman, Walter (Walton):** In 1869 he came to Red River from Canada and set up at Stinking River as a tanner. Some said he was a spy for John Schultz. He was one of those surrendering at Schultz's house in December 1869, and had his feet frozen in an abortive escape in January 1870.

**Johnson, Francis (Frank)** (1817-1894): Born in England, he was called to the bar in Lower Canada. In 1854 he was appointed recorder of Rupert's Land by the Hudson's Bay Company, chiefly because of his bilingualism. He served to 1858, and came back to Manitoba in 1870 as recorder for one year.

**Johnson, Thomas** (d. 1869): He was a murder victim in Red River in December 1869.

**Kennedy, William** (1814-1890): Born at Cumberland House, the son of a chief factor and a Cree wife, he was educated in Scotland. After some years with the HBC he resigned over its liquor policy, and subsequently served as commander of Lady Franklin's second private expedition to find her husband. He did not find Franklin, but brought the party home without loss of life. He led a second expedition in 1853. Kennedy subsequently took the lead in attempting to establish transportation connections between Canada and Red River, and advocated union with Canada. In 1860 he settled at the Maples, in St. Andrews. At one meeting there in October 1869 he opposed welcoming William McDougall because of suspicions of his characer.

**Kline (Klyne), George** (b. 1828): He was a Métis Roman Catholic who was imprisoned by Riel in 1869 and then became a French delegate to the 1870 Convention of Forty. He voted against Riel and in support of the HBC at that meeting.

**Larson, Rider** (b. 1850): Born in England, he married Caroline Pruden of Red River. A coroner's inquest blamed him in November 1869 for the shooting death of Thomas Johnson, and he reportedly fled the country.

**Lépine, Ambroise** (1840-1923): Born in St. Vital, he was captain of the party that sent William McDougall back across the border in early November. He was a French delegate to the 1870 Convention of Forty from St. Boniface. He presided at the court that condemned Thomas Scott, and refused to spare him. In 1873 he was tried for Scott's murder, found guilty, and sentenced to death. The sentence was subsequently commuted, although Lépine refused to take up the offer of amnesty by going into exile for five years.

**Lestanc, Joseph-Jean-Marie** (1830-1912): Born in France, he was an Oblate father who came to the Northwest in 1855 and to St. Norbert in 1857. He was placed in charge of the diocese in Bishop Taché absence in 1867-70. Probably less sympathetic to the Métis than other clerics, he was once described by Donald A. Smith as very ignorant of Canada.

**Leveson-Gower, George Granville, 2nd Earl Granville** (1815-1891): He was appointed secretary of state for the colonies in the first Gladstone administration in Britain in December 1868, and held that office through the Red River troubles.

**Lynch, James Spencer:** Born near London, Canada, he graduated in medicine from the University of Toronto and moved to Red River in 1868. He was one of those captured at Schultz's house in December 1869 and among the last to be released.

**Macdonald, John A.** (1815-1891): He was prime minister of Canada in 1869-70. When trouble emerged in Red River, he postponed the formal date of the transfer to Canada. During the negotiations with the delegates from Red River over the admission of the settlement into Confederation, he was ill with gallstones, but was well known to be opposed to any general amnesty to the insurgents, particularly in view of the death of Thomas Scott.

**Macdonald, John Sandfield** (1812-1872): He was premier of Ontario in 1868 when his government promised $5000 for famine relief for Red River.

**Machray, Robert** (1831-1904): Born in Aberdeen, he studied at King's College, Aberdeen, and Sidney Sussex College, Cambridge. He was appointed bishop of Rupert's Land in 1865. He opposed the Métis resistance in 1869 and advocated the use of force to suppress it until it was clear that the insurgents had all the power, at which point he counselled the anglophone hotheads to lay down their arms.

**MacPherson, Alexander:** A St. Andrews shoemaker, he entertained a meeting in Winnipeg in late 1869 with his account of his experiences with the Republic of Manitobah. He was a member of the Portage party captured 17 February 1870.

**Mair, Charles** (1838-1927): Born in Perth, Upper Canada, he was educated at Queen's University with John Schultz. He helped organize Canada First in 1868 and came to Red River that same year to work on the road. He was in Schultz's house in December 1869, but escaped, then headed east with Donald A. Smith.

**Mair, Elizabeth (Eliza) Louis McKenney** (1849-1905): Born in Ontario, she married Charles Mair in 1869. She was in the Schultz house in December and was imprisoned with her husband in Upper Fort Garry.

**Malmros, Oscar** (1826-1909): Born in Denmark, he settled in St. Paul, Minnesota, in 1853 and was appointed American consul in Winnipeg in July 1869, arriving on 13 August 1869. He reported on the insurgency to his government until his departure in March 1870.

**McDermot, Andrew** (1790-1881): Born in Ireland, he came to Red River with a Sligo party recruited by Lord Selkirk in 1812. After retirement from the Hudson's Bay Company he opened a store and speculated in real estate. He supported free trade and stayed out of the disturbances of 1869-70.

**McDougall, William** (1822-1905): Born near York (Toronto), he was educated at Victoria College, Cobourg, and became a leader of the Clear Grit party that joined John A. Macdonald's Tories in the "Great Coalition" to produce Confederation. Rumours continually circulated about his part in an aboriginal rebellion on Manitoulin Island in 1862-63. He stayed in the coalition after Confederation, and advocated the incorporation of Rupert's Land into the Dominion. His colleagues in the cabinet were pleased to be rid of him when he was appointed as lieutenant-governor designate of the North-West Territories. He refused to consider the possibility of self-rule for Red River until it had a Canadian population. He actually entered Red River territory only briefly, and spent his time in the West at Pembina. He made the supreme blunder when he declared his authority over Red River on the assumption that its transfer to Canada had gone through, and he returned to Canada angry, embittered, and humiliated.

**McKay, James** (1825-1879): A mixed blood born at Edmonton House, he was educated in and settled in Red River. His house at Deer Lodge was let to William McDougall in 1869. He became a councillor in the provisional government.

**McKenney, Henry** (1826-1886): Born in Amherstburg, Upper Canada, he built the first house and store in Winnipeg in 1862, and was an advocate of American annexation, perhaps because of his hostility to his half-brother, John Schultz, with whom he carried on a running battle. He was a delegate from Winnipeg to the Council of 1869, but left for Pembina in 1870.

**McLean, Alex:** He arrived with his family in Portage in 1862 and was acquitted—in a highly publicized court trial—of the manslaughter of a Métis in August of 1868. He was subsequently a member of the Portage party captured 17 February 1870.

**McLean, John** (1828-1886): Born in Banffshire, he was educated at King's College, Aberdeen. He came to Canada in 1858 and, as an old friend of

Bishop Machray, was invited to Red River in 1866 to become rector of St. John's Cathedral and archdeadon of Assiniboia. He also became warden of St. John's College. McLean was active in administering to the spiritual needs of Riel's prisoners, including Charles Boulton and Thomas Scott.

**McTavish (Mactavish), John H.** (b. 1837): Born in Upper Canada, he was the Hudson's Bay Company accountant at Upper Fort Garry and was suspected of being a Riel sympathizer. He surrendered the company's books and records to Riel late in 1869.

**McTavish (Mactavish), William** (1815-1870): Born in Edinburgh, he came to Canada in 1833 and moved to Red River in 1857 to be in charge of Upper Fort Garry. He married the mixed-blood daughter of Henry McDermot in a Catholic ceremony that caused much restiveness in the settlement. In 1869-70 he was governor of both Rupert's Land and Assiniboia, but dying of consumption, which limited his energy and activity in dealing with the insurrection. He was known to be unhappy about Canadian policy toward Red River. He left the settlement on 17 May 1870.

**McVicar ("Vickie"), Victoria** (c. 1842-1899): Related to various residents of Red River, her father was an HBC trader. She came to Red River from Fort William over the winter of 1869-70. She was active in visiting the prisoners in Uppper Fort Garry, and with A.G.B. Bannatyne she helped plead for the release of the prisoners. She returned to Fort William where she became a successful real estate speculator.

**Meade, Roland P.** (b. 1838): Born in Upper Canada, he was editor of the *Nor'-Wester* in 1869 and was captured at Schultz's house in December 1869.

**Mulkin (Mulkins), Stewart:** A nephew of Colonel Dennis, he was captured at Schultz's house in December 1869. Soon released, he was back in Canada in early April giving interviews to the local press on his experiences.

**Mulligan, James** (b. 1814): Born in Ireland, he came to Red River as one of the Chelsea Pensioners in 1848. He had only one arm, and served for years as a Winnipeg constable. He was one of those who surrendered in Schultz's house in December 1869.

**Murray, Alexander:** Two Alexander Murrays resided in Red River in 1869-70. One, born in 1840, was an Upper Canadian member of the Portage party captured 17 February 1870. The other, born in 1839, was a Red River mixed blood from St. James, who was part of the contingent arrested at Schultz's house in December 1870.

**Nault, André** (1829-1924): His was the hay concession two miles from the Forks where Louir Riel and eighteen Métis first stopped the survey crews by stepping on the chains on 11 October 1869. He was subsequently part of the tribunal that condemned Thomas Scott and was captain of the guard at the execution. He was eventually tried for the murder of Scott in 1874 and released after a hung jury.

**Newcastle, Duke of (Henry Pelham Fiennes Pelham, Fifth Duke)** (1814-1864): He served as British colonial secretary 1852-1854 and again in 1859-1864.

**Nolin, Charles** (1837-1907): Born in St. Boniface, he was educated by Bishop Provencher and was a member of a prominent Métis family that was opposed to Riel and supportive of the transfer to Canada. Nolin was a delegate to the November 1869 council and was elected to the 1870 Convention of Forty from Oak Point. He clashed frequently with Riel in the convention, ultimately voting against Riel on the issues of provincial status and repudiation of the Hudson's Bay Company. He was described in 1870 as a "Loyal Halfbreed," part of a group that included Brélands and Hamelins. In later years Nolin tried to assume leadership of the Métis while Riel was in exile. Removing to Saskatchewan in 1878, he was an early supporter of inviting Riel to lead the protest movement against Canada, but broke with Riel again when matters turned violent. He was a principal Crown witness at Riel's trial for treason.

**Norquay, John** (1841-1889): Born in St. Andrews, he was educated at St. John's Collegiate School and then moved to High Bluff. A huge man, he weighed about 135 kilograms. He was at Kildonan in February of 1870, and served as a messenger between the forces assembled there and Riel. He was later elected a member of the provisional council by parishioners of St. Margaret's parish. After confederation he became the leader of the moderate English-speaking mixed bloods in the provincial assembly, and in 1878 he became premier of Manitoba, the first mixed blood to lead the province.

**O'Donnell, John** (1844-1912): Born in Stratford, Canada, he came to Red River with his wife late in 1869 to practise medicine, arriving just in time for the couple to be part of the party surrendering in Schultz's house. He later served as a doctor in Winnipeg, and issued the warrant for the arrest of Ambroise Lépine in 1873.

**O'Donoghue, William Bernard** (1843-1878): Born in Ireland, he came to Red River in 1878 via New York and Michigan to teach mathematics at St. Boniface College and study for the priesthood. A fervent Fenian, he joined Riel and the Métis in 1869 and was a delegate to the November council and the Convention of Forty. He led the armed force that captured the Portage party on 17 February 1870. He increasingly saw Riel as too moderate and too British, and in 1871 he joined the Fenians, drawing up a constitution for Red River and naming himself as president. He led a small force of thirty-five men across the border in 1871, but was captured and returned to Minnesota, dying of tuberculosis.

**O'Lone (Bob), Hugh** (d. 1872): An American, he was proprietor of the Red Saloon and served as a delegate from Winnipeg to the November 1869 council. He was later killed in a barroom brawl.

**Parisien, Norbert:** Most sources agree that he was a young man, often described as "mentally defective." Probably from St. Norbert, Riel called him a Schultz supporter. But he was captured by the Portage party as a spy. He escaped from confinement and shot Hugh John Sutherland,who subsequently died. Chased by a crowd of men at Kildonan, he was roughed up and died of his injuries on 4 March (the day Thomas Scott was executed). The Métis frequently tried to argue that his death should be set against that of Scott in some kind of balance of violence during the resistance.

**Power (Powers), Michael** (b. 1813): Born in Ireland, he was a Chelsea Pension who had come to Red River in 1848 with the rank of sergeant from the Regiment of Dragoon Guards. As a member of the Portage party, he had argued for returning to Portage in a band via the main road, which took them by Upper Fort Garry, where the group (and Powers) were captured.

**Prince, Henry** (b. 1819): He was a son of Penguis and chief of the Saulteaux. In his own tongue he was known as Pa-bat-or-kok-or-sis. He insisted that Lord Selkirk had only leased rather than purchased First Nations land for the settlement. As a delegate from St. Peter's to the November 1869 council, he complained about not being allowed to speak in his own tongue. The Salteaux subsequently opposed Riel and the provisional government, and served as guides and scouts for Colonel Wolseley in 1870.

**Pritchard, Samuel** (1828-1915): Born in Red River, he was curate of St. Paul's Church, Middlechurch, 1866-1870.

**Provencher, Joseph Albert Norbert** (1843-1887): Born in Canada, he was a journalist who was appointed secretary to William McDougall because his uncle had been bishop of Red River. He returned to Manitoba in 1871 and later served as commissioner of Indian Affairs. He helped found the University of Manitoba.

**Racette, George** (b. 1819): A mixed blood born in Red River, he traded on the plains and was known as "Shaman" or "Shawman" (in French "Chamane") and was reputedly attempting to raise the Sioux against the provisional government.

**Ramsey, Alexander** (1815-1903): Born in Pennsylvania, he was appointed territorial governor of Minnesota in 1849 and served to 1854. He was elected governor of the state of Minnesota in 1859, serving until 1863. He then served as Senator, 1863-1872. He was a fervent exponent of the annexation of Red River to the United States.

**Richards, A. N.** (1823-1897): He accompanied William McDougall to Red River as attorney-general in waiting. He had served as solicitor-general of Canada for a month in 1863-64, and was said to be not very knowledgeable of the law. Later in 1871 he immigrated to British Columbia and was appointed lieutenant-governor of the province in 1876.

**Riel, Louis** (1844-1885): He was described by Oscar Malmros as "a young man of about 25 or 26 years old, ambitious, quick of perception though not profound, of indomitable energy, daring, excessively suspicious of others, and of a pleasing and rather dignified address." He led the Métis in their resistance to Canada in 1869-70.

**Ritchot, Noel-Joseph** (1825-1909): Born in Lower Canada, he came to Red River in 1862 and became priest at the Métis parish of St. Norbert. He helped organize resistance in the autumn of 1869, and was on 11 February 1870 named a delegate to the Canadian government to negotiate Red River's entry into Confederation. Sir Stafford Northcote described him as "a fine looking vigorous man, apparently about 40, with a great black beard. He does not speak English, but makes up for it by speaking French with a marvellous rapidity." He and his fellow delegates negotiated the Manitoba Act, but were unable to obtain written promises of a general amnesty.

**Robinson, Henry** (1845-1907): An American, he was editor of the *New Nation* from January 1870 until he was fired by Riel in March of that year, apparently for his advocacy of American annexation.

**Ross, James** (1835-1871): A mixed blood—his mother was an Indian "princess"—born in Red River, he was educated at St. John's College and the University of Toronto. He returned to Red River in 1858 and became one of the proprietors of the *Nor'-Wester*. He left Red River after he opposed a government effort to bring troops to the settlement and advocated an end to Hudson's Bay Company rule. He returned on the eve of the resistance to establish a new newspaper and became leader of the anglophone mixed bloods in the settlement. Ross served as a delegate to the Council in November 1869 and the Convention of Forty. He was a member of the Rights Committee and was appointed chief justice in Riel's provisional government. He already was drinking heavily. Ross was tall and slender, with black hair and a widow's peak. His face was aristocratic and he was extremely handsome. He usually sported a full black beard and moustache, and he had bushy eyebrows and piercing eyes.

**Salaberry, Charles de** (1820-1880): Born in Quebec, he had served in the Hind expedition to Red River in 1857 and was in 1869 appointed a Canadian emissary to Red River, but without any authority. His assurances that the Canadian government would pay the expenses of delegates to Ottawa were a useful contribution, however.

**Schultz, Agnes-Campbell Farquharson** (1840-1929): Born in British Guiana, she came to Red River with her father James Farquharson in 1864 and married John Schultz in the Catholic Church in 1867. She helped her husband escape from jail in 1868 and was imprisoned with him at Upper Fort Garry in 1869/70.

**Schultz, John Christian** (1840-1896): Born in Amherstburg, Canada, he claimed to have graduated from Queen's University. There is no record of this graduation, nor of a medical degree. But soon after his arrival in Red River in 1861 he advertised as a "Physician and Surgeon." He became proprietor of the *Nor'-Wester* newspaper and the leader of the pro-Canadian party in the settlement. Jailed for resisting a sheriff, he escaped with the help of a party headed by his wife. He was described as a "genial, powerfully built man, over six feet, red, sandy compexion." Louis Riel saw Schultz as his principal enemy, and became obsessed with recapturing him after he had escaped from imprisonment at Upper Fort Garry early in 1870.

**Scott, Thomas** (c. 1842-1870): Born in Ireland, he was one of the workmen who threatened John Snow with physical violence at Oak Point in October 1869. He was subsequently one of those who surrendered at John Schultz's house. He escaped from Upper Fort Garry on 9 January 1870, and made his way to Portage la Prairie, where he helped encourage the march to Kildonan by a party of Portage and Headingley men in February 1870. He was captured 17 February 1870 and was tried by a Métis tribunal for insubordination and rebellion against the provisional government. He was condemned to death, and was executed on 4 March 1870, becoming the martyr of the resistance.

**Shaman:** See George Racette.

**Smith, Donald A.** (1820-1914): Born in Scotland, he joined the Hudson's Bay Company in 1838, serving mainly in the east before his appointment as chief commissioner of the company in Canada in 1870. Smith was appointed by the Canadian government as a special commissioner to Red River in December 1869. He travelled to the colony and spent three months there under house arrest at Upper Fort Garry. He managed to convince the anglophone mixed bloods to meet with the French in the Convention of Forty, and took back to Canada a Bill of Rights that represented the conditions under which the people of Red River had agreed to join Canada.

**Snow, John Allan** (1824-1888): Born in Hull, Lower Canada, he trained as a surveyor and was chosen in 1868 to head the Canadian road-building team that was to construct a road from Lake of the Woods to Upper Fort Garry. He ran into much criticism and opposition to his activities in Red River, from residents and his own workmen.

**Spence, Thomas** (1832-1900): Born in Scotland, he came to Canada in 1852 and to Red River in 1867. That same year he organized a provisional government over the territory around Portage la Prairie that he called the "Republic of Manitobah." This territory was beyond the limits of the Red River Settlement, but its organization was declared illegal by the imperial authorities and the plan was given up. Spence was arrested briefly by Riel on 25 January 1870. He was a delegate to the Convention of Forty.

**Stewart, James** (b. 1827): An Orkneyman, he was a resident of St. James and worked in Dr. Schultz's store. He headed the party that freed G.O. Corbett in 1863. He was himself imprisoned and was in turn freed by a group led by William Hallett and John Bourke. He was one of those who surrendered in Schultz's house in December 1869.

**Stutsman, Enos** (1826-1874): Of German ancestry, he was born in Indiana with no legs; he used crutches throughout his life. Despite his handicap he became a legislative leader in the Dakota Territory after he moved there in 1858. In 1868 he defended Alex McLean on a murder charge in the Assiniboia court. In 1869 he was promoting American annexation of Red River and was often consulted by Louis Riel and the Métis leadership in the autumn of that year.

**Sutherland, Hugh John** (1843-1870): A Kildonan farmer, he was shot by Norbert Parisien on the morning of 16 February 1870. He begged before he died that Parisien not be punished.

**Sutherland, John Senior** (b. 1821): The father of Hugh John Sutherland, he was a supporter of the Métis who was an English delegate to the Convention of Forty from Kildonan.

**Taché, Alexandre-Antonin** (1823-1894): Born in Rivière du Loup, he entered the Oblate order in 1844 and was sent to Red River in 1845, becoming bishop of St. Boniface in 1853. Taché was in Rome for the

Vatican Council in 1869-70, and many thought his absence had allowed the Métis to contemplate rebellion. Returning to Red River in March of 1870 with instructions from the Canadian government, he promised a general amnesty to those involved in the uprising that did not occur.

**Tait, Robert** (1830-1921): Born in Scotland, he was a St. James farmer. He was a delegate to the November 1869 council and to the Convention of Forty.

**Thibeault, Jean-Baptiste** (1810-1874): Born in Lower Canada, he served as a western missionary for many years. He was in Quebec in 1869 when he was asked to return to Red River as a special envoy of the Canadian government, but without any power. He arrived in Red River on Christmas Day 1869, and was immediately placed out of the way in the bishop's palace by the provisional government. He played little role in the events of 1870, but may have helped Riel assert his authority over wavering supporters early in the year.

**Tupper, Charles** (1821-1915): Born in Nova Scotia, he was the premier of that province who brought it into Confederation. His visit to Red River in 1869 is one of the many curiosities of the period. His daughter had recently married Captain Donald Cameron and was expecting a child. Tupper always maintained that he travelled to Red River in the middle of winter in order to convince her to return to Canada rather than winter on the prairies. While in Winnipeg he talked with Riel and Father Ritchot, but he insisted that his visit was private and unofficial.

**Young, George** (1821-1910): Born in Upper Canada, he headed west in 1868 as a Methodist missionary. During the resistance he supported the Canadian party. He ministered to the spiritual needs of Thomas Scott. He later served as one of Scott's principal hagiographers.

**Young, George, Jr.:** Little is known of Young, the son of the Methodist missionary. He was in Upper Fort Garry late in 1869, and managed to avoid captivity after the surrender of the party in the Schultz house, although he was a member of that group.

# ENDNOTES

INTRODUCTION

1. Alexander Ross, *The Red River Settlement* (London: Smith, Elder, 1856).

2. See my *Trials & Tribulations: The Red River Settlement and the Emergence of Manitoba 1811-1870* (Winnipeg: Great Plains Publications, 2003).

3. Gerhard Ens, *Homeland to Hinterland: The Changing Worlds of the Red River Metis in the Nineteenth Century* (Toronto: University of Toronto Press, 1996).

4. See J.M. Bumsted and Wendy Owen, "The Victorian Family in Canada in Historical Perspective: The Ross Family of Red River and the Jarvis Family of Prince Edward Island," in *Manitoba History* 13 (Spring 1987): 12-18.

5. *The Nor'-Wester*, 14 March 1860.

6. The first historical account of the institute, and of other early intellectual endeavours, was by Mrs. George Bryce in "Early Red River Culture," *Transactions HSSM*, 57 (1901).

7. William Smith, in his biographical sketch of James Ross in the *Dictionary of Canadian Biography*, X, attributed the sixteen letters on Red River history published in 1861 to James Ross, rewriting his father's material. Leonard Remis, the biographer of James Ross, is less certain, although he admits that "certain stylistic characteristics . . . suggest that James Ross wrote the series." But Remis also suggests the Reverend John Black, Frank Larned Hunt, and William Coldwell as potential authors. See Remis, "James Ross 1835-1871: The Life and Times of an English-Speaking Halfbreed in the Old Red River Settlement," unpublished MA thesis, University of Manitoba, 1981. In letter 16, however, the writer of these letters disagreed with the *Nor'Wester*—in which James Ross at the time was a partner—over the issue of an elected council. The writer advocated the continuation of the present appointive system, on the grounds that it could more easily represent all the interests of the settlement's population. If the writer were not Ross—or any of the other Remis nominees—it was probably an Anglican clergyman who had arrived in Red River around 1850, for the letters after that date cease relying heavily on Alexander Ross and take on an eyewitness quality.

8. Ross's work appeared in London in 1856 as *The Red River Settlement*. Gunn's was published in book form in 1880, its later sections co-edited by Charles R. Tuttle.

9. Bruce Braden Peel, *Early Printing in the Red River Settlement 1859-1870 and Its Effect on the Riel Rebellion* (Winnipeg: Peguis, 1974), 19-35.

10. Sean Sullivan, "*Canadian Illustrated News* and the Red River Rebellion," National Library of Canada Web site, http://www.nlc-bnc.ca/cic/hl-204-3.html.

11. Other French papers that occasionally covered Red River included: *Le Minerve*, *Le Journal de Québec*, *Le Canadien* (Quebec), *Le Pays* (Montreal), *La Gazette de Sorel*, *Le Courrier de Canada* (Quebec), *L'opinion publique* (Montreal), and *La Gazette des familles canadiennes* (Quebec).

12. Toronto *Globe*, 28 January 1870.

13. See, for example, the letters reprinted in "When the Metis Rebelled," *The Beaver* (June 1941): 14-18.

14. Doug Owram, *Promise of Eden: The Canadian Expansionist Movement and the Idea of the West, 1856-1900* (Toronto: University of Toronto Press, 1980).

15. Toronto *Globe*, 28 January 1870.

16. For gossip and rumour in Upper Canada, see Lynne Marks, "Railing, Tattling, and General Rumour: Gossip, Gender, and Church Regulation in Upper Canada," *Canadian Historical Review* 81 (2000): 380-402. The footnotes to this article provide a good entree into the current literature on the subject, which is fairly extensive, especially in the United States.

17. "Justitia," letter to the Toronto *Globe*, 31 December 1869.

18. This dichotomy is the one employed by Douglas Owram in "The Myth of Louis Riel," *Canadian Historical Review* LXIII, 3 (1982): 315-31.

19. See, for example, Joseph Edward Collins, *The Story of Louis Riel, the Rebel Chief* (Toronto: Rose Publishing, 1885), and Wilbur F. Bryant, *The Blood of Abel* (Hastings, NE: Published for the Author by the *Gazette Journal*, 1887).

20. Major Charles Arkoll Boulton, *I Fought Riel: A Military Memoir*, ed. Heather Robertson (1885; reprint, Toronto: Lorrimer, 1985). George Young, *Manitoba Memories: Leaves from my Life in the Prairie Provinces, 1868-1884* (Toronto: William Briggs, 1897); John Harrison O'Donnell, *Manitoba as I Saw It: From 1869 to Date: With Flashlights on the First Riel Rebellion* (Toronto: Musson, 1909).

21. Donald Creighton, *John A. Macdonald: The Old Chieftain* (Toronto: Macmillan, 1955).

22. Canada, Parliament, *Correspondence and Papers Connected with the Recent Occurrences in the NorthWest Territories* (Ottawa, 1870); William McDougall, *The Red River Rebellion: Eight Letters to Joseph Howe, Secretary of State for the Provinces* (Toronto: Hunter, Rose, 1870); Canada, Parliament, House of Commons, *Report of the Select Committee on the Causes of the Difficulties in the North-West Territory in 1869-70* (Ottawa, 1874).

23. Lewis Herbert Thomas, *The Struggle for Responsible Government in the North-West Territories* 1870-97, 2nd ed. (Toronto: University of Toronto Press, 1978).

24. Auguste Henri de Trémaudan, *Histoire de la nation métisse dans l'Ouest canadien* (Montreal: A. Lévesque, 1936); George F.G. Stanley, *The Birth of Western Canada: A History of the Riel Rebellions* (London: Longmans, Green and Co., 1936).

25. W.L. Morton, ed., *Alexander Begg's Red River Journal and Other Papers Relative to the Red River Resistance of 1869-1870* (Toronto: Champlain Society, 1956).

26. Ibid., 3.

27. Ibid., xxi.

28. W.L. Morton, ed., *Manitoba: The Birth of a Province* (Altona: Manitoba Record Society, 1965).

29. The quotations are from Morton's introduction to *London Correspondence Inward from Eden Colvile 1849-1852* (edited by E.E. Rich and published as volume XIX of the Hudson's Bay Record Society, London, 1956), lxxxix.

30. Submitted at Queen's University in 1973.

31. Brown, Jennifer S.H., *Strangers in Blood: Fur Trade Company Families in Indian Country* (Vancouver: University of British Columbia Press, 1980). The articles include: "A Demographic Transition in the Fur Trade Country: Family Sizes and Fertility of Company Officers and Country Wives 1750-1850," *Western Canadian Journal of Anthropology* 6, 1 (1976): 61-71; "Changing Views of Fur Trade Marriage and Domesticity: James Hargrave, His Colleagues, and "the Sex," *Western Canadian Journal of Anthropology* 6, 3 (1976): 92-105; "Ultimate Respectability: Fur Trade Children in the Civilized World," *The Beaver* (Winter 1977): 4-10, and (Spring 1978): 48-55; "Linguistic Solitudes in the Fur Trade: Some Changing Social Categories and their Implications," in Carol Judd and Arthur Ray, eds., *Old Trails and New Directions: Papers of the Third North American Fur Trade Conference* (Toronto: University of Toronto Press, 1980), 147-59.

32. Sylvia Van Kirk, *Many Tender Ties: Women in Fur-trade Society in Western Canada, 1670-1870* (Winnipeg: Watson & Dwyer, 1980).

33. Brian Gallagher, "The Whig Interpretation of the History of Red River," unpublished MA thesis, University of British Columbia, 1986. Gallagher subsequently published his arguments as "A Re-examination of Race, Class and Society in Red River," *Native Studies Review* 4, 1-2 (1988): 25-66.

34. Gerhard Ens, *Homeland to Hinterland: The Changing Worlds of the Red River Métis in the Nineteenth Century* (Toronto: University of Toronto Press, 1996).

35. Printed from 11 October 1869 to 25 February 1870.

36. Hargrave's early upbringing may be followed in the letters of his mother, edited by M.A. MacLeod as *Letters of Letitia Hargrave* (Toronto: Champlain Society, 1947). I am indebted to an unpublished manuscript by Leslie Castling for many insights into Hargrave and his work.

37. Morton, *Begg's Journal*, 415n.

38. *Canadian Monthly and National Review* 1 (May 1872): 479-80.

39. For further discussion of these points, see Patricia Spacks, *Gossip* (New York, 1985).

40. William Ross to James Ross, 9 February 1856, PAM, Ross Family Papers, MG2 C14, p. 162.

41. Printed 11 October 1869. W.L. Morton, in his edition of the Alexander Begg diary, wrote that Hargrave's letters began in the *Herald* on 21 October 1869, a date repeated in the *Dictionary of Canadian Biography*, vol. 11, 409. See Morton, *Begg's Journal*, 415n. This date, which saw the publication of the letter originally dated 25 September 1869, misses the letter of 18 September published in the newspaper on 11 October.

42. Letter of 18 December, 1869, printed in *Montreal Herald and Daily Commercial Gazette*, 7 January 1870.

43. Printed in *Montreal Herald and Daily Commercial Gazette*, 17 February 1870.

44. "When the Metis Rebelled," *The Beaver* (June 1941): 14-15.

45. Printed 25 February 1870.

46. "When the Metis Rebelled," 15-16.

47. Isaac Cowie, *The Company of Adventurers: A Narrative of Seven Years in the Service of the Hudson's Bay Company* (Toronto: William Briggs, 1912), 153.

48. *Manitoba Free Press*, 10 March 1894.

49. For the "moribund" characterization, see Frits Pannekoek, *A Snug Little Flock: The Social Origins of the Riel Resistance in 1869-70* (Winnipeg: Watson & Dwyer, 1991), 215.

50. I use the term "participant historian" and develop its meaning in William Toye, ed., *The Oxford Companion to Canadian Literature* (Toronto: Oxford University Press, 1984), 351-52.

51. Morton, *Begg's Journal*, xiv.

52. Ibid., 10 December 1869.

53. "Justitia letter," 17 December 1869, printed 6 January 1870.

54. Alexander Begg, *The Creation of Manitoba* (Toronto: A.H. Hovey, 1871), 182-83.

55. According to Hargrave, in his letter dated 11 December,

> Yesterday a large body of the French collected in Fort Garry, and
> went through the ceremony of Raising the National Flag on the Fort
> flagstaff. Speeches were made by Riel and others, and the brass band
> of the scholars at the Roman Catholic school at St. Boniface played a
> series of airs, after each of which a volley of musketry was fired, the
> Company's Field Pieces, which were stationed at intervals outside the
> Fort gates, being also discharged at various periods of the perform-
> ance. The device on the banner consists of three fleur de lys on a
> white ground with a shamrock underneath. The insurgents subse-
> quently marched to the American consulate in Winnipeg, which they
> saluted with music, cheers, and volleys of musketry. This is said to
> have been done as a compliment to the only foreign power having a
> resident representative there.

Hargrave's more careful description of the flag, with *three fleur de lys*
over a single shamrock, makes it appear somewhat less menacing
than Begg's account of the two emblems "combined."

56. Begg, *The Creation of Manitoba*, 304.

57. It seems possible that Riel went to Saskatchewan in 1884 to recover the
sense of accomplishment he had experienced in the early days of 1869-70.

58. *News-Letter*, 4 October 1870.

59. Begg, *Seventeen Years in the Canadian North-West: A Paper Read on April 8
1884 at the Royal Colonial Institute* (London: Spottiswoode, 1884), 4.

60. George T. Denison, *The Struggle for Imperial Unity: Recollections and Experiences* (Toronto: Macmillan, 1909), 14-21.


J.J. HARGRAVE, 18 SEPTEMBER 1869

1. For the English-speaking mixed bloods, see Pannekoek, *A Snug Little Flock*.

2. For the First Nations community in Red River, consult T.C.B. Boon, "St.
Peter's Dynevor: The Original Indian Settlement of Western Canada,"
*Trans HSSM*, 39 (1954), 16-32.

3. See J.S. Clouston, "Orkney and the HBC," *The Beaver* (1936-37).

4. For the transport system of Red River, see my *Trials & Tribulations*, 147-52.

5. For the Canadian post office efforts, see Ibid., 133-34.

6. The cart and steamboat business in Red River is described in detail by J.J.
Hargrave in his *Red River* (Montreal: J. Dovell, 1871).

7. For the Sioux War and its effect on Red River, consult A.G. Gluek, Jr., "The Sioux Uprising: A Problem in International Relations," *Minnesota History*, 34 (Winter 1955): 317-24.

8. For the famine of 1868, see my "The Red River Famine of 1868," in *Thomas Scott's Body and Other Essays on Early Manitoba History* (Winnipeg: University of Manitoba Press, 2000), 149-62.

9. In general, consult Alvin C. Gluek, Jr., *Minnesota and the Manifest Destiny of the Canadian North-West: A Study in Canadian-American Relations* (Toronto: University of Toronto Press, 1965).

J.J. HARGRAVE, 25 SEPTEMBER 1869

1. For experimental farms in Red River, consult Grant MacEwan, *Cornerstone Colony: Selkirk's Contribution to the Canadian West* (Saskatoon: Western Producer Prairie Books, 1977), passim.

2. For Red River disasters, see my "Early Flooding in Red River, 1776-1861" and my "The Red River Famine of 1868," in *Thomas Scott's Body*, 77-90, 149-62.

3. See my "Early Flooding in Red River."

4. Ibid.

5. See my "Red River Famine of 1868."

6. For the western grasshopper (*Orthoptera: Acrididae*) and Rocky Mountain locust (*Melanoplus spretus*), see my "Red River Famine of 1868," 150-52.

7. The Howe visit is described in greater detail in J. Murray Beck, Joseph Howe; *Volume II: The Briton Becomes Canadian 1848-1873* (Kingston and Montreal: McGill-Queen's University Press, 1983), 259-63. We still do not fully understand what Howe was doing in Red River.

J.J. HARGRAVE, 2 OCTOBER 1869

1. This is a creative explanation for the company's tactics of the mid-1840s. Another is in my "The Colonial Office, Aboriginal Policy, and Red River, 1847-1849," in *Thomas Scott's Body*, 91-115.

2. For the steamboat *Pioneer* and its successors, see my *Trials & Tribulations*, 124-137, and Fred Bill, "Early Steamboating on the Red River," *North Dakota Historical Quarterly* 9, 2 (1942): 77-91.

J.J. HARGRAVE, 9 OCTOBER 1869

1. For more on the Carleton Trail, see Hargrave's *Red River*.

2. The reference is to the Gold Rush party led by Thomas McMicking in 1862. See Richard Thomas Wright, *Overlanders* (Saskatoon: Western Producer Prairie Books, 1985).

3. For the early telegraph projections, consult Elaine Mitchell, "Edward Watkin and the Buying-Out of the HBC," *Canadian Historical Review* 34, 3 (1953).

### J.J. HARGRAVE, 16 OCTOBER 1869

1. For more on the origins of the Council of Assiniboia, see my *Trials & Tribulations*, 70-73.

2. For more on the beginning of resistance, see my *The Red River Rebellion of 1869-70* (Winnipeg: Watson & Dwyer, 1994), 54 ff.

### J.J. HARGRAVE, 30 OCTOBER 1869

1. For the Church Missionary Society, see Pannekoek, *A Snug Little Flock*, and T.C.B. Boon, *The Anglican Church from the Bay to the Rockies* (Toronto: Ryerson Press, 1962).

2. For the Presbyterians, see my *Trials and Tribulations*, especially 115-23.

3. For the Roman Catholic Church in Red River, consult Father A.G. Morice, *History of the Catholic Church in Western Canada from Lake Superior to the Pacific (1659-1895)* (Toronto: Musson Book Company, Ltd., 1910).

4. For the Grey Nuns, see Dennis King, *The Grey Nuns and the Red River Settlement* (Agincourt, ON: Book Society of Canada, 1980); and Estelle Mitchell, *The Grey Nuns of Montréal at the Red River 1844-1984* (n.p., 1987).

5. The Oblates are treated in Robert Choquette, *The Oblate Assault on the Canadian Northwest* (Ottawa: University of Ottawa Press, 1995).

6. See Paul Régnier, *A History of St. Boniface College* (MEd. thesis, University of Manitoba, 1965).

7. For St. John's College and its predecessors, consult Thomas Bredin, "The Red River Academy," *The Beaver* (Winter 1974); and William Fraser, *St. John's College, Winnipeg 1866-1966: A History of the First Hundred Years of the College* (Winnipeg: Wallingford Press, 1966), especially 1-28.

8. For the council meeting, see my *Red River Rebellion*, 57-59.

J.J. HARGRAVE, 13 NOVEMBER 1869

1. For a detailed discussion of the political role of the HBC, see John S. Galbraith, *The Hudson's Bay Company as an Imperial Factor 1821-69* (Toronto: University of Toronto Press, 1957).

2. For an elaboration of this argument, see Hargrave's *Red River*, esp. 260ff.

3. For the Upper Fort Garry occupation, see my *Red River Rebellion*, 64-67.

J.J. HARGRAVE, 20 [27] NOVEMBER 1869

1. See Robert Coutts, *Road to the Rapids: Nineteenth-Century Church and Society at St. Andrew's Parish, Red River* (Calgary: University of Calgary Press, 2000).

ALEXANDER BEGG, 1 DECEMBER 1869

1. Louis Riel's own notes on these meetings are reprinted in Morton, ed., *Begg's Journal*, 420-28.

J.J. HARGRAVE, 4 DECEMBER 1869

1. For the Republic of Manitobah, see Hartwell Bowsfield, "The Republic of Manitoba," *Manitoba Pageant* 7, 1 (1961), and the entry on Thomas Spence by Bruce Peel in *Dictionary of Canadian Biography* xii (Toronto: University of Toronto Press, 1990), 982-84.

2. Supposedly written by the Métis bard, Pierre Falcon (1783-1876). It was reprinted by Begg in his *The Creation of Manitoba* (Toronto: A.H. Hovey, 1871), 137-39.

ALEXANDER BEGG, 9 DECEMBER 1869

1. This proclamation, dated 9 December 1869, is printed in Morton, ed., *Begg's Journal*, 221-23.

ALEXANDER BEGG, 17 DECEMBER 1869

1. Begg provides a list of the prisoners in his journal; see Morton, ed., *Begg's Journal*, 217.

J.J. HARGRAVE, 18 DECEMBER 1869

1. See list in Morton, ed., *Begg's Journal*, 217.

J.J. HARGRAVE, 25 DECEMBER 1869

1. For the visit of Charles Tupper to Red River, see my *Red River Rebellion*, 111-14.

2. Henry M. Robinson (1845-1907) later wrote *The Great Fur Land or Sketches of Life in the Hudson's Bay Territory* (New York: Putnam's, 1879).


ALEXANDER BEGG, 11 JANUARY 1870

1. For another account of a Red River wedding, see Robinson's *The Great Fur Land*, 315-26.

2. Toronto *Globe*, 23 December 1869.


J.J. HARGRAVE, 22 JANUARY 1870

1. For more detail, see J.J. Hargrave's *Red River*, especially 423-49.


J.J. HARGRAVE, 29 JANUARY 1870

1. See Elaine Mitchell, "Edward Watkin and the Buying-Out of the HBC," *Canadian Historical Review* 34, 3 (1953).


ALEXANDER BEGG, 25 FEBRUARY 1870

1. As the volunteers who came with Wolseley demonstrated, Begg was quite accurate. See Neil Edgar Allan Ronaghan, "The Archibald Administration in Manitoba, 1870-1872," unpublished PhD dissertation, University of Manitoba, 1987.


ALEXANDER BEGG, 9 FEBRUARY 1869

1. Further details about the Nolins are in Morton, ed., *Begg's Journal*, 300.


ALEXANDER BEGG, 18 FEBRUARY 1870

1. For more details on this party from Portage la Prairie, see my *Red River Rebellion*, 147-158, and Charles Boulton's *Reminiscences of the North-West Rebellion* (Toronto: Grip Printing and Publishing Co., 1886).

ALEXANDER BEGG, 26 FEBRUARY 1870

1. For Boulton's own account of this incident, see Boulton, *Reminiscences*.

2. The issue of 19 February was not the last. According to Begg's journal on 24 February, "The New Nation came out to-day in a different style from the issue that was seized—it had an extra as well."

3. For this petition see J.J. Hargrave's *Red River*, 280.

Full bibliographic data is posted on the Web site of University of Manitoba Press, at www. umanitoba.ca/uofmpress.